MURDER AND MASCULINITY

MURDER and MASCULINITY

Violent Fictions of Twentieth-Century Latin America

Rebecca E. Biron

VANDERBILT UNIVERSITY PRESS

NASHVILLE

First Edition 2000

04 03 02 01 00 5 4 3 2 1

Library of Congress Cataloging-in-Publication Data

Biron, Rebecca E., 1964-
Murder and masculinity : violent fictions of twentieth century Latin America / Rebecca E. Biron. — 1st ed.
p. cm.
Includes bibliographical references (p.) and index.

ISBN 0-8265-1342-5 (alk. paper)
ISBN 0-8265-1347-6 (pbk. : alk. paper)
1. Latin American fiction—20th century—History and criticism. 2. Politics and literature—Latin America. 3. Violence in literature. 4. Masculinity in literature. I. Title.
PQ7082.N7 B48 2000
863—dc21 99-6497

Published by Vanderbilt University Press
Printed in the United States of America

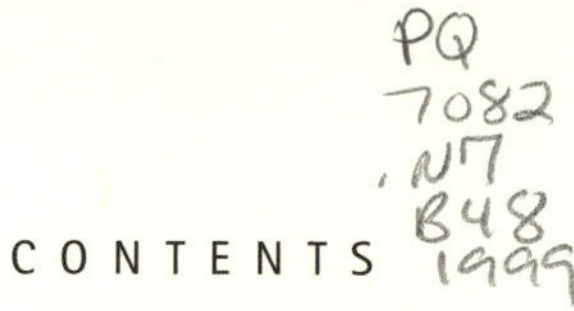

CONTENTS

ACKNOWLEDGMENTS

For their unwavering support, my deepest thanks go to my mother, Beth D. Biron, and to my late father, Doug Biron. Rosalva Bermúdez-Ballín gave me the courage to write about masculinity. Michelle Warren has given me confidence. For generous advice and encouragement during the different stages of this project, I am grateful also to Carlos Alonso, Leslie Bow, Amanda Brooks, Debra Castillo, Jane Connolly, Jacqueline DeCarlo, María Duarte, Thomas E. Lewis, Christina Mehrtens, Adriana Méndez-Rodenas, Craig Nelson, Kathleen Newman, Mary Nunnally, Herman Rapaport, Maarten van Delden, and George Yúdice. A 1998 Max Orovitz grant from the University of Miami allowed me to devote my full attention to completing research for the chapter on Arenas. Finally, I thank the *Latin American Literary Review* for permission to use material from "Armonía Somers's 'El despojo': Masculine Subjectivity and the Problem of Individuation" (42, Spring 1994).

CHAPTER ONE

Murder and Masculinity

An Introduction

Matar debe ser un instante
terrible; tal vez tenga su grandeza.

Elena Garro, *El árbol*

The manly act par excellence is
to murder the mother.

Günter Grass, *The Flounder*

Consensus in Latin American cultural studies holds that modern nation-building projects in the region recognize themselves through analogy with the benevolent patriarchal nuclear family. National portraits insist on the importance of happy, healthy, productive, and patriotic women as well as men, yet national literary treasures often reflect government rhetoric in coding active citizenship as male. The tendency to claim egalitarianism while operating within a fundamentally masculinist framework is not limited to Latin America, of course, and addressing it in regional terms risks reinforcing facile stereotypes about machismo and the supposedly unique form it takes in the Spanish and Portuguese-speaking regions[1] of the Americas. In no way does my study of violent fictions mean to suggest that the association of masculinity with domination troubles this region any more or less than it does other large geographical areas in the world. Rather, I seek to point out some of the particularities of literary discourse on masculinity in Latin America—both the tradition of imagining male domination in certain ways and the emerging tradition of creative resistances to those images. Only by acknowledging the sexist history of national and regional identity-formation can readers of some of Latin America's most innovative and experimental twentieth-century narratives appreciate their explicit interrogation of the philosophical, psychological, and political dimensions of masculinity itself.

Doris Sommer's influential 1991 study of what she calls Latin America's nineteenth-century foundational fictions identifies an erotics of politics that links literary production and nation building in Latin America during the 1800s. Some of the most widely read novels of the period envision the postindependence domestication of civil society to be like idealized heterosexual love and marriage, a hierarchy in which men legitimate their authority by winning the affections and loyalties of women.[2] This connection between love stories and the role of national leaders presumes a correlation between the hero of the romance and male citizens in general. When the new national focus turned from the wars of independence and toward cooperative social organization and productivity, the image of the authoritative yet loving husband became the appropriate model for male roles. Representations of men and women set to the work of legitimating white male *criollo* rule through romantic love in opposition to the former imposed and unwelcome colonial rule: "Without a proper genealogy to root them in the Land, the creoles had at least to establish conjugal and then paternity rights, making a *generative* rather than a *genealogical* claim. They had to win America's heart and body so that the fathers could found her and reproduce themselves as cultivated men" (Sommer, 15). The romantic visions of good husbands for new nations, of marriages between complementary noble souls under benevolent male leadership, looked forward. They imagined a harmonious unity of different social sectors. This kind of unity requires men, and especially male authors, to become the creators of nations as well as fathers to themselves. Winning America's heart and body requires that the ideal heart and body be produced at the same time that they are pursued. Thus, women's productivity and reproductivity are subsumed under a rubric of men who give birth to the new. In this allegorical relationship between nation and heterosexual love, the romantic hero's desire defines and circumscribes the nation/land as well as the female lover. That dynamic pertains to works ranging from Argentina's essayistic *Facundo* (Sarmiento 1845), in which Sarmiento defines, explains, and promises to recover the "natural" soul of the nation, to Colombia's romantic novel *María* (Isaacs 1867), in which the protagonist-narrator establishes his own class and multicultural identity through writing the perfect woman to be the object of his sentimentalist love.

A century later, partly in reaction to those forward-looking romances whose plots in fact often betray the harmonious and productive future of which their narrators dream, "Boom" texts turn a rueful eye on failed or struggling national projects in Latin America. Melding nostalgia, hope, and cynicism, novels such as Gabriel García Márquez's *Cien años de soledad* (*One Hundred Years of Solitude* 1967), Carlos Fuentes's *La muerte de Artemio Cruz* (*The Death of Artemio Cruz* 1962), or Mario Vargas Llosa's *La ciudad y los perros* (*The Time of the Hero* 1962) obsessively revisit a variety of foundational fictions. They draw from indigenous lore as well as from the grand stories of historical periodization—the Conquest, the Colonial Period, Independence, and Revolution—taking them all in some sense to represent the failure of romance. Whereas the nineteenth-century romances place men in metonymic relation to the state and women in metaphoric relation to the land or the people that the state names and governs, the Boom produces narratives of the impossibility of idyllic unions in a region with conflictive, diverse populations and histories. It offers stories in which the old "rhetorical relationship between heterosexual passion and hegemonic states" (Sommer, 31) becomes an allegory of failure.

Attending to the discursive construction of Latin American identity, García Márquez, Julio Cortázar, Fuentes, José Donoso, and Vargas Llosa circle back in the 1960s and 1970s to reconsider foundational myths *as myths*. They deconstruct the pedagogical and didactic rhetoric of romance to explore the large themes of transculturation, economic dependence, political violence, collective shame, and the difficulty of hope. They treat such grand regional concerns through a focus on alienation, comparative cultures, and attention to the inadequacy of any one narrator, myth, or dominant fiction to account for collective Latin American experience. Insofar as they all focus on male authorship and aesthetic originality as the most authentic expression of these complex Latin American issues, however, they perpetuate the old narratives' tendency to privilege men's imaginative or literary *creation* of the New World over their participation in it.

While the nineteenth-century foundational novels organize and project ideal national identities into the future as part of a didactic political agenda, the Boom deconstructs the difference between fictions and histories in order to locate the national within the space of creative textuality. That is to say, the pedagogical function of the Boom may be understood as more synchronic than diachronic. It offers a series of novels that reenact the quest for an original identity, located as much in the immediate act of writing as in the collective histories of the region. While the romances establish models for ideal future behavior on the part of citizens, Boom texts celebrate the deep complexity of the present as a vibrant archive of metaphors in which male authors, or author-identified characters, strive to locate an ineffable cultural history and identity.

Gerald Martin (1989) aptly captures the shared elements of Cortázar's *Rayuela* (*Hopscotch* 1963), García Márquez's *Cien años de soledad,* Fuentes's *La región más transparente* (*Where the Air Is Clear* 1958) and *La muerte de Artemio Cruz,* as well as Vargas Llosa's *La casa verde* (*The Green House* 1966):

> Each of their key novels was about a quest or quests; each was about the nature of Latin American identity; each also provided a metaphor or metaphors for the course of Latin American history—since the creation, the conquest, Independence, the birth of the author, etc.; each was linguistically exploratory and structurally mythological—labyrinthine, preoccupied with consciousness, obsessed with the woman both as muse and materiality: in short, they were Joycean, Ulyssean works, products of patriarchal idealism inspired by and dedicated (though only rarely addressed) to Penelope, the Other, the world of matter, the female, the people, the nation, Mother America. (241)

Sharing this element of "patriarchal idealism" in order to express, explore, or continually seek collective, regional identity, these texts perpetuate a male-centered gesture reminiscent of, though certainly not identical with, the nineteenth-century romances that Sommer studies. In their experimentation with discursive and mythic origins, these novels tend to construct a foundational masculinism that relies on a cult of authorial originality. In *Hopscotch,* for example, the male protagonist Oliveira claims to "describe and define and desire" the rivers in which his lover La Maga unconsciously swims. In *Cien años de soledad,* the ancient Melquíades has always already known the history of the Buendías (men and women alike) and envelops readers' experience of that family's experience in an all-consuming text. Fuentes's Artemio Cruz charts Mexican modernity through his relationships to a series of women and through divisions in his own masculine subjectivity. The Green House of Vargas Llosa's title refers both to the Amazon jungle and to a brothel, explicitly associating wild land with female sexuality from within masculine fantasy.

Insofar as these Boom authors, all male, write of the search for origins as a goal for male protagonists, patrilinear families, or male protagonist-narrators, they link the dilemma of founding an autochthonous and autonomous definition of Latin America to available definitions of masculinity. And those definitions are neither autochthonous nor autonomous. Variously associated with heroism in war, benevolent or authoritarian husbandry, fatherhood, violent destruction, archival organization, or literary productivity, masculinity serves as the problematic, if seldom questioned, core of models of Latin American identity.

However diligently they might try to produce new narratives to express regional identity, Boom authors cannot escape the writing that founds America as the female other to a male authoring consciousness. Even though their range of linguistic, structural, and mythological experimentation continues to amaze readers, Boom authors are nevertheless caught in endless returns to the textual space of regional origins. They are trapped between two conflicting types of foundational texts. One thinks of the Buendía family of *Cien años de soledad,* acting out a predetermined script they hoped to escape, or Artemio Cruz's deathbed reflection on the national betrayal of the ideals of the Mexican Revolution. While such narratives deconstruct tired projections of national identities based on received literary forms (the national romances of the nineteenth century or the *novelas de la tierra*), they also pursue foundational status for themselves as the inventions of radically new and uniquely American narrative forms (the so-called new novel of the late twentieth century). In more general terms, the "repeated attempt to discover or found the newness of the New World" (González Echevarría, 4) in Latin American narratives of the 1950s, 1960s and early 1970s confirms that the problem of regional identity is a complex question of postcolonial political autonomy, legitimate leadership, and cultural or authorial originality.

Sommer sees in comments by García Márquez, Fuentes, Vargas Llosa, and Cortázar a suspicious dismissal of the national romances produced a century before their own international success in the 1960s (Sommer, 1). She argues that the Boom writers' denial of the attraction and power of earlier romances constitutes "a symptom of unresolved dependence," evidence of an "entire tradition of resistances. The paradox borders on a typical irony of writing (in) America, where successive generations may deny literary resemblances to the point that denial itself constitutes a resemblance" (4). This denial of the continued resonance of national romances indicates a desire for literary self-generation that results from a particularly Latin American anxiety of influence.[3] However, I am suggesting that the source of those Boom authors' denial runs even deeper than that. It stems from an ongoing fascination with and anxiety over masculinity as the guarantor of regional independence and autonomy, legitimate leadership, and self-generation for citizens as well as for Latin American literature.

There is a different strain in contemporary Latin American fiction that rejects the promise of foundational fictions altogether and thereby also rejects the association of masculinity with self-generation. Like the Boom novels, the texts I analyze here disallow the naïve didacticism of romance, but they also resist the seductive cult of originality that motivates much positive reception of the Boom. Published during and after the Boom period, these narratives refuse to seek Latin American origins or originality through unexamined masculinist perspectives. In fact, they pointedly interrogate the most extreme forms such perspectives might take. They forcefully critique the intersections between masculinity, violence, and the strategic construction of collective political identities. Foregoing reflection on or projection of love relationships as figures of national identity, they focus directly on the question which logically precedes any allegorical relationship between men's conquests in love or literature and the consolidation of regional identity. They explore what constitutes the masculine subject who is expected to enter into overtly dominant, custodial, or authorial relationships with women and into identificatory relationships with the state.

Although their authors are not typically grouped together in the same literary movements or ideological camps, this key set of narratives orients an old theme in Latin American letters toward a different goal: rather than writing male characters in metonymic relation to governments or nations themselves, these texts develop characters whose deliberate search for a more ethical, psychologically sound definition of masculinity imagines new roles for male citizens in the context of postcolonial politics. Underscoring the differences rather than the similarities between male subjectivity and governance or legal authority, these narratives investigate the psychological and social costs of the unquestioned promotion of masculinist ideals at the expense of both male and female individuals. They explore the cliché of proving virility through violence, offering an array of methods to overcome it. They posit that philosophical reflection, psycho analytic awareness, sociopolitical reorganization, and aesthetic catharsis are all necessary components in the struggle against symbolic and physical sexist violence.

Drawing from Freudian and Lacanian psychoanalytic principles, feminist cultural criticism, and the imaginative and transgressive possibilities of magical realism, these texts literalize the metaphors Sommer locates in the treatment of women in nineteenth-century romance narratives. Rather than eliminating feminine agency through the seemingly benevolent structures of courtship, marriage, and loving husbandry, these more-recent narratives explore the actual erasure of women and its implications for prevailing images of masculinity. They also take to literal extremes the "tradition of resistances" evidenced in Boom authors' early denial of their role as inheritors of a Latin American literary tradition. Instead of depicting the quest for regional identity as primarily an original literary endeavor to be undertaken by bold male authors, these texts probe the desire for masculine self-birth which that denial reveals. Each text in this group stages the murder of a female character by a male character as a crime not of passion, but rather of crisis in the construction of viable gender relations. These fictional accounts of murder allow authors and readers to examine more directly the conceptual frames within which certain masculinities repudiate femininity. By representing and reflecting on the effects *for men* of the most extreme form of that repudiation, these texts reconsider masculinity's dangers, strengths, and promises.

Taking seriously our collective investment in violence against women, the most powerful of these stories permit, indeed often invite, readers to enjoy a fantasy of acquiescence to sexist social constructs regarding masculine identity and increased political strength based on masculine ideals. They also, however, present—sometimes graphically—the inarguably negative effects of murder for both the targets of attack and the attackers. Thus, while appealing to our enjoyment of violent fictions, they demand a reconsideration of the ethics of identity claims based on unconsciously reproduced sexist models for individuation, action, and individual or collective political liberation. Although their representations of men murdering women might be interpreted as little more than *machista* misogyny, I argue that they are ultimately, in fact, salutary narratives. Rejecting the contradictions of foundational writing, which scripts men and women into limited roles in the service of national identities or into procreative models, these works express the need for healed masculinities as integral to the achievement of more fluid, resilient cultural identity and a less reactive or defensive political autonomy in Latin America.

Each of the texts included in this book highlights a specific stage in what I argue is a shared narrative project. They explore what happens to notions of masculinity when their most negative and violent elements come to the fore. Taking masculinity to its most reactive extremes, these narratives reconsider men's imagined relationship to women and to the social order in general by having male characters act out the promise of phallic privilege. That promise entails, in part, an assurance that even though few men meet the normative definitions of masculinity in a given cultural and historical context, they may nonetheless partake of the power associated with hegemonic masculinity.[4]

As R. W. Connell argues in *Masculinities* (1995, 84), individual men take that promise literally and attack or harass women when there is a breakdown of the correspondence between their experience, the cultural ideal of masculinity, and its expression in institutional power centers, such as the top levels of business, the military, and the government: "Violence is part of a system of domination, but is at the same time a measure of its imperfection. A thoroughly legitimate hierarchy would have less need to intimidate. The scale of contemporary violence points to crisis tendencies (to problematize a term from Jürgen Habermas) in the modern gender order" (84). The Latin American narratives of besieged or threatened masculinity that I analyze here display those crisis tendencies. The protagonists blatantly exercise male authority by killing women. In doing so, however, they break the law. Exercising absolute power over women by killing them challenges the imaginary equation of masculinity with legal, or legitimate, authority. Male murderers of women embody the struggle between two forces that contemporary definitions of masculinity impose on individual men: on the one hand an assurance of social superiority over women, and on the other hand an obligation to submit to institutional masculinist authority. When successful manliness is associated with power over women, and successful male citizenship is associated with obeying laws designed in collective male interest, then the criminal male who kills women simultaneously celebrates and undermines hegemonic masculinity.

I have chosen texts that explore this struggle from different angles after the murder takes place. They consider how the male protagonists recover a psychologically adequate sense of masculinity after having understood the contradictions inherent in hegemonic masculinity. Although my readings follow the chronology of publication from text to text (with the exception of Borges) and move from shorter to longer narrative forms, I have in fact organized the chapters according to a thematic progression regarding masculinity in crisis. In chapters 2 and 3 I focus on the promise of male privilege as presented in two short stories, and on how the authors subvert their characters' plans to solidify that privilege through the murder of women. Jorge Luis Borges's "La intrusa" (originally published in 1966, Argentina; "The Intruder") establishes the pleasures and the risks of homosocial male bonding over a woman's dead body. Armonía Somers's "El despojo" (originally published in 1953, Uruguay; "Plunder") highlights the class differences which threaten such male bonds when those ties are predicated upon an unconscious denial of maternal power. Chapter 4 moves beyond a critique of masculinist violence to focus on the secular possibilities of male atonement for crimes against women. Clarice Lispector's *A maçã no escuro* (Brazil, 1964; "The Apple in the Dark") translates into a cynical Brazilian context Dostoevsky's religious solution to threatened masculinity in *Crime and Punishment* (1866). Lispector delivers an ironically Althusserian response to hypermasculinity by fusing religious with civic modes of confession and repentance. Chapters 5 and 6 examine Manuel Puig's *The Buenos Aires Affair* (Argentina, 1973) and Reinaldo Arenas's *El asalto* (Miami, U.S., 1991; "The Assault"). These later novels shift focus away from the case studies of individuals betrayed by impossible myths of masculinity. They employ parody and tragicomic exaggeration of the dominant fictions of gender in order to expose the destructive logic (especially for men) of sexism, both imagined and practiced. Without providing any structures of atonement, both Puig and Arenas offer apparently happy endings to their extraordinarily violent novels, forcing readers to face the contradictions between our enjoyment of violent fictions and our moral condemnation of violent acts. These texts undermine the power that misogynist fictions of masculinity wield over individuals, but they do so only ambivalently. They play with the meeting of multiple fictions, risking and encouraging readers' imaginative transgression of social taboo as well as of generic and disciplinary boundaries.

Like their male protagonists who experiment with the psychological and legal extremes of gender division, all of the texts in my study risk nonconformity to the laws of genre in their quest for liberation from violent social and literary conventions. Although penned by some of the most-acclaimed Latin American authors, these particular texts are not their most widely read pieces. Borges is perhaps best known for *Ficciones* (1944) and *El aleph* (1948); Armonía Somers for *La mujer desnuda* (1966) or *Sólo los elefantes encuentran mandrágora* (1988); Lispector for *Laços de família* (1960), *A paixão segundo G.H.* (1964), and *A hora da estrela* (1977); Puig for *La traición de Rita Hayworth* (1968), *Boquitas pintadas* (1969), or *El beso de la mujer araña* (1976); and Arenas for *El mundo alucinante* (1982) and *Celestino antes del alba* (1967). Notwithstanding the critical success of those works, I examine texts by these authors which focus directly on murder and masculinity per se. They are emotionally challenging, philosophically ambiguous, and sometimes graphically violent. Indeed, because they radically question notions of legitimate and illegitimate masculinities, as well as men's role in literary expressions of national identity, they are some of the most difficult works to place within current debates on nation and on Latin American literary aesthetics in general.

These noncanonical works critique the viability of foundational fictions by homing in on the deepest fissures in images of Latin American collective identity, whether those images correspond to changing government rhetoric, to the nineteenth-century romances or to the more cynical Boom novels' quest for originality. Those fissures emerge most clearly, according to the works I analyze here, in polarized fictions of masculinity and femininity. They show violent gender division to be more fundamental to the edifice of identity than are families, nations, or regions.

Examining texts that stage the murder of women by men, texts sometimes considered second-tier works in each writer's oeuvre, I discover that they combine in surprising ways elements of detective stories, crime narratives, psychological case studies, and magical or grotesque realism. They thus offer fruitful metafictional commentary on a network of discourses that confuses images of masculinity, national identity, and political autonomy in postcolonial Latin America. In order to establish the shared characteristics which allow me to group these texts by male and female, straight and gay authors representing different literary generations, countries of origin, aesthetic sensibilities, and political investments, I have divided my introductory comments into three sections. The first focuses on gender and masculine subjectivities, the second on literary genre, and the third on Latin American murder stories that challenge the integrity of both gender and literary genre in their exploration of fictions of masculinity.

Masculinity

What is masculinity? Who has it, who wants it, and how do we recognize and value it? When understood as a biological condition synonymous with genetic maleness (Badinter 1995, 26) or as "a discourse, . . . a psychic economy, a history, an ideology, an identity, . . . a value system, [or] an aesthetic even" (Middleton 1992, 152), masculinity is something individuals or entire cultures have. Having it somehow explains what one does. When masculinity is defined as a set of prescribed social roles or as a power structure,[5] it always functions as an ambiguous standard against which to measure people and their actions. The degree to which one does or does not measure up accounts for one's social status. If males possess masculinity inherently, through having a penis or through overdetermined hormonal and psychological structures, then the fact that they must also earn it through prescribed behaviors and rituals of initiation poses a serious contradiction. Is it a birthright, or is it an elusive sign of status that men are obligated to obtain in order to bear meaning in the social order?

A parallel incongruity obtains in cultural representations and valorization of masculinity. We celebrate public displays of masculinity—such as authoritativeness, defensiveness, aggressiveness, physical strength, self-assurance, or self-reliance—as heroic and natural in nation formation, military achievement, sport, or business; yet we often deem the very same displays criminally transgressive and unnatural if performed by men who are marginalized ethnically, politically, economically, or sexually. Masculinity for men functions as both an unquestioned ontological guarantor of gendered identity and an unstable, ever-shifting demand for credible performances of that identity. In both guises it signifies social position first in relation to women and second in the stratified system of relations among men.

Late-twentieth-century gender theory relies on research and debates developed in international feminist thought and sociology, as well as in poststructuralist psychology and literary criticism, to focus on the constructed nature of masculinities. As in feminist approaches to theorizing gender, the most comprehensive studies of masculinity tend to divide the topic into two general theoretical approaches. Some attend more to individual life experiences and the explanations of their effects on gender offered by object-relations theory; others rely more on the analysis of gender as an effect of language and social representation.[6] Both approaches, however, focus on the connections between masculine rationality and oppressive forms of masculine sexuality and violence, seeking therapeutic answers to troubled masculinity for individual men or a revolution in the dichotomous signifying system which perpetuates oppressive gender relations more broadly.

One of the most commonsense, transcultural distinctions between masculinity and femininity is that the first represents independence and the second dependence. Ironically, however, every major investigation of gender, no matter what the primary discipline of inquiry, underlines masculinity's dependence on a reaction against femininity for its own definition. Connell (1995), for example, opens his study with a discussion of Karen Horney's "The Dread of Woman" (1932), which established the link between the classical psychoanalytic understanding of masculinity as a reaction formation and the sociological insight that it is also tied to the general economic and political subordination of women. The reactive element appears most strongly in psychic structures as an exaggerated rejection of femininity, represented by the mother. In this version of development, all children reject their own desire for complete identification with mothers in order to enter the symbolic order, but boys accede to masculinity by also rejecting any traces of femininity in themselves. Their sense of individuality is not just about separation from a neutral other, but also about separation from a *feminine* other. Therefore, masculinity is always in part a negative goal: "I am masculine to the degree that I am not feminine."

Masculinity is never simply an identity to be sought and defined in positive terms; one of its essential elements is outright rejection of traces of femininity in the self. Discussing Virginia Woolf's *To the Lighthouse* (1927), for example, Pierre Bourdieu (1990, 23) addresses the metaphor of violence attendant upon masculine reaction against femininity, "the metaphor of the knife or the blade that situates the male role in the area of the cut, of violence, of murder, that is, in the area of a cultural order constructed against the original fusion with the maternal nature." Bourdieu leaps quickly past resisting fusion with the maternal, which is necessary for all subjects to attain a sense of self, to the space of the cut, which situates the male role in particular. The rapid progression to violence and murder as an obvious metaphor for specifically male separation from mothers is striking, indicating a prevailing association with masculinity and violence against women, if only in figurative terms.[7]

While the psychological impulse to be masculine results from that negative defense of self, masculinity's positive content is established in dominant social representations of gender differences and is reinforced through the pedagogical and disciplining functions of idealized identification among men. Mantras like "real men don't cry," "real men don't talk about their feelings," "real men make natural soldiers" (implying that essential markers of femininity are tears, emotional talk, and the need to be defended) claim to reflect self-evident truths, but they are deployed precisely when reality contradicts them. Their normative power depends on individual men who perceive "real men" to embody those ideals of manhood, and themselves to be but aspirants to the status of the real. The relationship between the real and the ideal is inverted in order to discipline individual men into certain kinds of masculinity that will maintain their clear difference from women.

In order to think about masculinity as simultaneously a factor in establishing power positions, a constructed category of difference and hierarchy, and a desired quality, trait, or state of being, it is important to employ at least a threefold model of its structure, "distinguishing relations of a) power, b) production, and c) . . . cathexis (emotional attachment)" (Connell 1995, 73–74). This model overcomes the limits of a simplistic division between object relations theory and Lacanian-inspired poststructuralist approaches, which see gendering either as primarily the result of family organization or as primarily an effect of signification as if the two were not always mutually implicated. It also successfully avoids essentializing masculinity as only a category that cynically protects and disguises male supremacy (the extreme feminist view) or as only one that contains all the most valued human characteristics (the extreme masculinist view).

Combining a psychoanalytic construct with an account of social expectation and desire in her study of masculine subjectivity, Kaja Silverman (1992) delineates masculinity's fragility and its privilege in Althusserian terms:[8]

> The Law of Language dictates universal castration, whereas our Law of Kinship Structure equates the father with the Law, and hence exempts him from it. Our dominant fiction effects an imaginary resolution of this contradiction by radically reconceiving what it means to be castrated. . . . Our dominant fiction calls upon the male subject to see himself, and the female subject to recognize and desire him, only through the mediation of images of an unimpaired masculinity. It urges both the male and the female subject, that is, to deny all knowledge of male castration by believing in the commensurability of penis and phallus, actual and symbolic father. (42)

When masculinity is a positive principle of identification among men and the relationship between being male and having masculinity seems natural and nonconflictive, then the dualistic, male/female system of differentiation required by the symbolic order is not experienced as arbitrary or imposed. The degree to which biological maleness allows all men to see themselves as masculine determines the success of the promise that phallic privilege unites them across class, ethnic, or national boundaries. When that relationship is strained, however, and individuals must struggle to identify with the master signifier of the masculine, its equation "Man=Good=Me" becomes fragile and suspect.

Identity depends on the integrity and status of master signifiers like those of gender ("man," "woman"), nationality or ethnicity ("Peruvian," "Jewish"), and character ("honest," "intelligent"). We secure our claim to a master signifier in one of two ways (Bracher 1997):

> we must either be directly recognized by the Symbolic Other in the form of authority figures, institutions, or peers as embodying the master signifier (as in statements like "You're the man!"), or we must receive indirect and tacit recognition from the Symbolic Other in the form of a system of secondary signifiers that we can perform and that are implicated in or attributed to our master signifier. Anything that reduces either the status of a master signifier or our claim to the signifier will result in a weaker sense of identity. (Bracher, 5)[9]

Bracher observes that forms of prejudice—such as racism, sexism, homophobia, and nationalism—have two primary elements: the subject's projection of id impulses that are unacceptable to the ego onto an other, whom the subject then attacks; and social conditions which enable the projection onto certain others. Projection becomes the obvious outlet for relatively strong id impulses coupled with a relatively severe superego and/or a weak ego. That imbalance, too powerful to be contained in suppression, repression, or direct expression of id impulses, forces them into a disguised form of expression. Whereas secondary signifiers (job status, property, local positions of authority, for example) might offer avenues for displacement or sublimation of those impulses in less harmful outlets, active prejudice results when there is an inadequate system of secondary signifiers at hand and when prevailing cultural representations or social hierarchies offer to the subject a seemingly suitable object of projection.

A stronger sense of masculinity requires that the master signifier of manliness have integrity. Individual men must believe in its legitimacy, feel recognized by it and included in it. Ideally, they will feel themselves to embody it without an uncomfortable feeling of imposture. At the very least, they must have available a system of secondary signifiers which would ensure their performance of it. When those conditions are absent and individual men lose their sense of connection to the master signifier of masculine subjectivity, the underlying opposition of masculinity to femininity comes to the fore and threatens the illusion of integrity and unassailability which supports most societies' myths of masculinity.

This illusion of integrity depends upon the Lacanian concept of *méconnaissance*, a misrecognition which allows the subject to deny unwanted features of the self—to fail to recognize them—by projecting them onto the other.[10] Male misrecognition circumscribes the very category of femininity in the sense that the castration which signifies sexual difference for Freud is not located in or on the female body, but rather "emblazoned across it by the male subject through projection." In other words, male subjects deposit their lack at the site of female subjectivity, defining that site in the process (Silverman, 46). Male *méconnaissance* involves projection of undesirable aspects of the self onto the feminine other, and it also entails a repudiation of those aspects now seen in the other.

All egos require a certain amount of projection in order to remain intact. However, when the male subject addressed by the discourses of law, duty, and morality is constituted through masculinist projections that denigrate women, a rhetoric of violence emerges.[11] This hidden form of violence serves to stabilize gendered subject positions within legal and ethical discourses, but the rhetoric of violence finds literal expression when men murder women. Masculine murder of feminine figures exposes the conflict inherent in the relation of the masculine subject to the institutions that define him as consistent and free, institutions whose purpose is to organize and uphold viable social formations.

When such a crime results from motives proper to the relatively rational, self-aware subject, rather than from some motive like insanity, physical self-defense, accident, or state-sponsored violence, then the ego's imperatives merge with the death drive and available fictions of male privilege. Freud's understanding of the death drive as that which grounds life, but which nonetheless must be resisted, is parallel to the function of femininity for the masculine subject in such a case. In striving to overcome death, the ego reveals death to be not outside of, but rather within life itself.[12] Thus, like death, femininity is not a diametrical opposite to the masculine ego; rather, it inhabits all masculinity as an "otherness, as its own disruption" (Felman 1981: 41). The murder of Woman provides a desired exorcism of femininity's lack both from within the masculine subject (to make him less threatened in his masculine consistency) and from its embodiment in women who act as other subjects upon him. Such an exorcism can never succeed, though, because even attempting it exposes the imaginary nature of the masculine subject's independence and autonomy.

If men's misogynist violence stems from a breakdown in hegemonic masculinity, then the solution to ending it would seem to be greater stability in the signifiers of masculinity. The international boom in the publication of new books on men and movements among the middle class such as the Promise Keepers in the United States or men's cultural groups forming in capital cities throughout the Americas certainly supports that notion. The feminist argument against this solution, however, attends to the dangers of deepening sexual division, precisely the reactive tendency in discourse, governmental structures, and business practices which fuels men's domination over women. In the face of recent debate over the agency of individuals and their status as subjected to the law of language (Frank 1989), the question becomes how resignification of masculinity might overcome the limited access some men have to positive identifications with other men without reinforcing the subject/object dichotomy that Silverman argues is supported by the false equation of penis and phallus.

I examine literary texts that exploit fantasy's constitutive role in subject formation (Žižek 1989). We learn how to desire through fantasy, which inserts us into certain desiring positions that reciprocally give us identities. "[F]antasy . . . involve[s] the insertion of the subject into a particular syntax or tableau" (Silverman 1992, 6), and those scenes are to a large degree pre-scripted by available versions of gender, class, and race relations which form our identities. Therefore, where we find violent, misogynistic fantasies of masculinity, we also find violent social relations between actual men and women.[13] The texts I study focus on precisely that point. They include characters who act out violent fictions of masculinity, and yet their narrative structure provides readers with alternative responses to misogynistic fantasies of masculine identity-formation. Operating beyond—or beneath—other literary products taken to be most representative of Latin American cultural and political history, these works directly advocate profound and nonreductive reflection on the intersection of gender roles, sexual division in psychology, and gendered hierarchies in the social order. As crime stories they transgress norms of social behavior and literary genre. Posing murderous male characters in conflict with the social structures meant to bolster masculinity's authority—the state, morality, the patriarchal family—, they allow readers to identify with both murderers and their victims, the most distanced poles in dominant versions of masculinity and femininity.

My examination of the Latin American works included here is not primarily interested in advocating for more positive literary representations of men or women. Rather, I mean to read them as interdisciplinary (philosophical, psychological, political, and of course literary) meditations on the relationship between dominant fictions of masculinity and individual men. These texts do not offer simple or concrete solutions to the social problem of male violence against women. They do not propose programs for reform in governmental policy or clinical psychological practice. They resonate more with a European-United States bourgeois existentialism than with identity issues of indigenous or otherwise marginalized Latin American social groups. Because of their aesthetic experimentation and theoretical references or risks, they attract a middle- to upper-class, Western-educated readership. Still, like the canonical nation-building and Boom texts of Latin America, they interrogate basic elements in the region's politics and literature. They contribute to solving the social problems attendant upon limited notions of masculinity by illuminating multiple facets of the ethical question: Does/can/should masculine subjectivity have a different constitution?

Crime and Detective Fiction

Powerful narratives of murder horrify us with their display of cruelty and violence, yet they also seduce us into identifying with characters who control life or death situations. A crime story full of blood and mayhem exploits readers' fear of falling victim to criminal attack, but it also affirms rage through the imaginative freeing of our repressed transgressive urges. Where our loyalties lie—when on the side of law and order and when on the side of impulse and violence—depends not only on the generic rules each narrative obeys, but also on the subject positions we occupy as readers. Crime narratives unsettle the very phrase "law and order" when they attend to the unruly violence inherent in any imposition of law, be it the psychoanalytic symbolic, kinship systems, democratic rule making, or despotic decree. They also upset readers' experiences of our own positions in the social order by seducing us into identification with outlaws. When a criminal functions as both protagonist and antagonist in one story and when readers sympathize with both victims and their murderers, the social contract begins to feel less stable. Crime narratives revel (rebel) in the ambivalence they produce for individuals contemplating the possibilities and limits of community.

Murder is aesthetically dynamic because of the ambiguity inherent in representing it. It is condemned as unlawful on the one hand; on the other hand, though, it is glorified when personalized and made symbolic of risk and change.[14] Murder fixes the boundaries between the active and the passive, the victor and the victim, but its most riveting effect is to "[establish] the ambiguity of the lawful and the unlawful" by deconstructing those very boundaries within the subjectivity of the murderer. A murderer exemplifies the extreme of human liberty in wielding absolute power over his victim, but in the act of killing another human being, he transgresses a basic taboo and is immediately defined, or constrained, by the designation of criminal. Precisely at the moment that he most completely disregards the law in favor of his own freedom, he is the most circumscribed by that law. He exists as a murderer insofar as the legal system as well as the symbolic order have recognized him to be a transgressor; therefore his self-determining, liberating gesture only binds him more tightly to the social order he may have desired to escape.

Discussing the dual effect of murder stories, Joel Black (1991) distinguishes psychological crime dramas from detective fiction and suspense thrillers according to the point of view established in the text. Whereas detective fiction diverts attention away from the criminal onto clever plot construction and the "sleuth's deductive brilliance" and whereas suspense thrillers create reader identification with the "helpless victim's terror," psychological dramas focus interest primarily on the murderer's point of view. Black does not analyze this class of crime fiction in depth, but he does group together such "psychological dramas of Shakespeare and Dostoyevsky where murder is presented from the killer's point of view, and where the primary interest lies, according to Auden, in 'the observation, by the innocent many, of the guilty one'" (64). These psychological tales, focalized through the murderer, his motivations, and the psychosocial effects of his actions, afford readers the position of scientist/analyst, observing the criminal from a safe and innocent objectivity. At the same time, however, they rely on reader identification with the murderer as he undergoes a variety of transformations in the course of the narrative. Black discusses this double effect of crime narrative in Foucaultian terms, claiming that contrary to the notion that people enjoy narratives of crime only as a form of thrill seeking, they also enjoy receiving knowledge about the human condition, their own condition, of subjectedness: "how men have been able to rise against power, traverse the law, and expose themselves to death through death" (28).

The desire to know the experience of individuals who "expose themselves to death through death" indicates that such individuals fulfill a wish for the many who observe them. By breaking laws and offering themselves as examples of bravery and existential freedom, these characters model the ideal of the autonomous, self-defined subject of actions. The distinction between detective fiction and crime fiction as I use the terms here does not diminish that element of wish fulfillment for either reading experience. In fact, the mere inclusion of murder in a story celebrates the ambiguity that Foucault identifies. Crime fiction is more relevant to critical consideration of masculinities, however, because it more thoroughly blurs the boundaries between legality and illegality, criminal and victim, men and women.

Ingenious puzzles, the pleasure of discovery, and reader identification with the detective figure constitute the essential elements of classical detective fiction (Symons 1974 and Hilfer 1990). Character psychology often takes a second seat to the cognitive problem to be solved. Crime fiction, on the other hand, deviates from that focus to become "the source of rather more tortuous satisfactions than those of the detective novel" (Hilfer, 1). It foregrounds character over problem solving, engaging not in the discovery of criminal facts so much as the explanation of their psychological causes and effects. Whereas detection stories tend to be conservative, providing a pleasurable fantasy of transgression of laws along with a reassuring restoration of their authority and logic in the end, crime fiction tends to question the legitimacy of laws in the face of social inequalities, particular interpersonal situations, or contradictory principles.

The vast majority of criticism on crime fiction deals with authors from England and the United States. Edgar Allan Poe's "The Murders in the Rue Morgue" (1841) establishes the classic model in which the central figure is a detective (Dupin) who solves crimes. Amelia S. Simpson (1990) divides the evolution of that model into two strains: the *whodunit,* or puzzle-narrative, and the hard-boiled detective novel. The primary difference between them is their class focus. While the classic formula offers "an allegorical representation of the stability and continuity of the status quo . . . [providing] a reassuring view of society in the mechanistic crime-to-solution sequence" (Simpson, 11), the hard-boiled model resists elitism through its attention to the underclasses, its distrust of all institutions, and "its view of crime as all-pervasive" (12). In both the classic and the hard-boiled models, however, the process of detection takes center stage. Whether the criminal element is found hiding in the corridors of power or on the streets outside, the detective knows legitimate from illegitimate acts.

As every avid reader of either detective or crime fiction recognizes, the most compelling and clever criminals match wits with equally compelling and clever detectives or police. The pleasure for the criminal characters is in combining the thrill of transgression (the *jouissance* of abandoning discipline) with the game of avoiding detection (the *jouissance* of discipline itself). Games are fun because they have rules. In detective fiction of both the classical and hard-boiled types, readerly pleasure is produced when the distinction between criminals and legal authorities is blurred, but the rules of the game remain stable. The characters dance together on the boundary between good and evil, legal and illegal. Subject positions may be constituted across that line, but the reader's security and the pleasure of closure demand that the line itself be clearly marked. The pleasure of detective fiction is in its acknowledgment that we are all capable of a playful relationship to the law, but that the law will ultimately rope us in on the right side for our own good.

Crime narratives derive from and play off against the secure difference between right and wrong that grounds both types of detection fiction. Rather than compulsively reinstitute legal order in defense against criminal threats to its integrity, crime narratives rebelliously question that order. Through concentration on the criminal instead of on upholding the law, crime fiction "induces precisely the element of the irrational and anxious that the detective story is designed to outflank" (Hilfer 1990, 3). It becomes more difficult to assign clear guilt to characters when narrative structures sweep us up into identification with their psychology, life situations, and urge for liberation from societal constraints.

As twentieth-century derivations of the nineteenth-century classical detective fiction and psychological crime stories by "Godwin, Hogg, Poe, Dickens and Dostoevsky" (Hilfer 1990, 2), crime narratives are decidedly post-Freudian. They experiment with Freudian notions of identification and otherness. They underscore the threat of the other as an essential element in self-definition, not so much for the characters as for the readers, who are invited to understand and empathize with ideas and behaviors that are off-limits to law-abiding citizens in real life. The *characters* may remain securely on their appropriate sides as legal authorities or outlaws, but the difference between detective fiction and crime fiction as I define it here hinges on the readers' relative ability to stabilize loyalties in each type of reading experience.

Because murder fantasies bear considerable aesthetic power, the enjoyment of their representation in narrative poses a social and ethical dilemma. Subject status for the murderer in the crime novel is not just a question of deviance. It offers an interpretation of the dynamics of subjectivity for readers and also for nations. As Gilles Deleuze and Felix Guattari (1983, 30) put it, "Fantasy is never individual: it is group fantasy—as institutional analysis has successfully demonstrated." That is to say, violence and the wielding of power are indeed productive of social structures when exercised by either individuals or institutions. Crime narratives invite readers to identify with male aggressors' experience, complicating readers' abilities to vilify either criminality or misogynist violence. By relinquishing the control over morality, legal authority, and scientific knowledge that classical detectives wield, these texts place their characters and readers in an ambivalent relationship to the crime. Narrative structures in which no value is absolutely stable do not allow for any simple feminist condemnation of male attacks on women. That is not to say, however, that reading them celebrates violence against women uncritically.

In the case of the crime narratives in this study, the fact that the bodily integrity of women is violated along with the law calls into question the murderers' masculinity. Like the abstract category of femininity, the criminal subject is constituted as that which the dominant order—at least in the guise of legality—excludes. The murderers' attempts to "rise against power" falter on the boundary between identification with the masculinity of that power and identification with the feminized position of its victims. The first-level signification of murder in these texts bolsters a sexist hierarchy that promotes rhetorical and physical violence against women. By killing a woman, the individual man thumbs his nose at the law while also depending on its implicit bond with him as male. He believes he can kill the feminine element in his own subjection, establish his freedom to act by breaking laws, and still uphold the illusion that his possession of a penis grants him access to the phallic power of the law. The immediate result of his act, however, brings into sharp relief the difference between his subject status and that of ideal masculinity as figured in his newly exposed, contradictory vulnerability both to governmental laws and to symbolic law itself . . . in other words, to his own lack. The potentially salutary effect of such narratives arises in the aftermath of the crime. What happens when a man confronts *as his own* the lack which dominant fictions had always allowed him to project onto women? What happens to readers who simultaneously enjoy and condemn that character's violence against women and then identify with his reconstruction of masculinity?

By raising such questions, the texts I study here all partially participate in the general Western tradition of relating thantopoetics to femininity. In *Over Her Dead Body: Death, Femininity and the Aesthetic* (1992) Elisabeth Bronfen compellingly argues first that representations of dead women function culturally as symptoms of failed repression. She focuses on how the topos of the death of beautiful women mediates the observers' repressed knowledge of death and of the unstable opposition of self and Other. Then she develops a theory of how the sacrifice of women in art contributes to the reestablishment of imaginary social order for the "community of survivors" (xi). The Latin American narratives I have grouped together deploy the murder of women according to the same principle Bronfen describes, but they self-consciously resist the subsequent association of female sacrifices with increased social order. In fact, through their attention to the *false* promise of the restoration of order through female death, these texts provide counterexamples to Bronfen's "[c]ountless examples [that] illustrate how the death of a woman helps to regenerate the order of society, to eliminate destructive forces or serve to reaggregate the protagonist into her or his community"

(219). Rather than rehash literary attempts to secure masculine coherence through projection onto women of all traces of Otherness, these counterexamples activate Judith Butler's concept of *gender trouble* (1990). They try to "think through the possibility of subverting and displacing . . . naturalized and reified notions of gender that support masculine hegemony and heterosexist power, to make gender trouble, not through the strategies that figure a utopian beyond, but through the mobilization, subversive confusion, and proliferation of precisely those constitutive categories that seek to keep gender in its place by posturing as the foundational illusions of identity" (33–34). Borges, Somers, Lispector, Puig, and Arenas all employ shockingly predictable stories of violence against women to subvert, confuse, parody, and shuffle the conceptual and social divisions within which we understand masculinity. They engage readers' sense of self and gender identity in the indeterminacy of moral, legal, sexual, and power positions that crime fiction stirs up. Never producing a utopian reformation of the gender system, they nonetheless expose its most destructive effects and provide readers with an imaginative journey toward more flexible and sustainable fictions of identity.

Masculinity and Murder in Latin American Crime Fiction

Murderous fantasy in Latin American psychological crime narratives cannot be considered apart from the region's anticolonialist and antityrannical struggles for autonomy and legitimacy. Similarly to crime stories in the English-language tradition, Latin American texts explore individual deviant psychologies through the development of violent characters, but they often complicate the relationship between law and outlaw for populations which are profoundly skeptical of police authority. Both as experiments in projections of normative citizenship and as cautionary tales against illegitimate violence, fictional representations of killing pose a particular social and ethical dilemma in regions where breaking the law signals healthy autonomy on the part of (neo)colonized subjects as often as it indicates social pathology.

Mexican cultural critic Carlos Monsiváis asserts that, although crime stories and parodies of detective fiction proliferate, the classic model of detective fiction is fundamentally incompatible with Latin American colonial history and contemporary realities. Basing their plots on the illusion of stable, legitimated governance, such narratives find few readers capable of accepting the detective form unless the action is set in foreign urban centers like New York, London, or Paris: "If the aim of [detective] literature is to be realistic, [in Latin America] the accused would almost never be the real criminal and, unless he or she were poor, would never be punished. . . . The exception, the out-of-the-ordinary, isn't that a Latin American is a victim, but rather that he or she isn't one. We don't have any detective literature because we don't have any faith in justice" (Torres 1982, 14, quoting Monsiváis). Detective fiction is less appropriate to the region than crime fiction, which resonates with a general mistrust of the boundaries between the law-abiding and the outlaws, an awareness of the often arbitrary imposition of legal authority. The forms of that imposition in most Latin American countries, Monsiváis points out, are less mediated by the trappings of democracy and social order that facilitate reader enjoyment of detective fiction in more thoroughly postindustrial regions of the world.[15]

The tradition of narrative constructions of Latin American identity, whether they appear in letters from the Conquest, colonial legal papers, political essays, stories, or novels, offers a powerful combination of positively coded models for masculine behavior and dangerous examples of the reactive psychology which underpins it. In that tradition, the most often cited dichotomies which both produce and contest norms of male identity and conduct are typically ones associated with the founding of Latin America as a region that would combine New and Old World identities. They include the different forms of warrior culture (the indigenous "savage" or the murderous conquistador), the colonial debates regarding *civilización y barbarie,* the nineteenth-century ascendancy of *criollo* sons over Spanish fathers (which led to the independence movements), economic leaders defending *caudillismo* versus neoliberal reformers, and, most recently, the images of strong Latin American leaders resisting neoimperialist encroachments by the United States on regional markets and culture. While such competing ideals of strength pit men against men in the struggle to confer legitimacy on certain types of masculinity and to accuse opposing types as illegitimate, they obscure the question of masculinity's relationship to femininity.

The association of colonized people with women as a social category is not just an invention of the twentieth-century feminist movement of Europe and the United States. Rather, it appears overtly in a wealth of literature on the formation and analysis of Latin American identities at least since the independence movements of the early nineteenth century. Perhaps the most powerful and widely cited example is Octavio Paz's *El laberinto de la soledad* (1950). Paz generalizes about the ambiguous subjectivity of Mexican men, arguing that they are all sons of Cortes's Indian lover/translator doña Marina, the Malinche, La Chingada.[16] According to Paz, the historical figure of la Malinche represents the problem of Mexican identity in relation to the Conquest.[17] In this oedipal picture of Mexican identity, "los hijos de la Chingada" are post-Conquest Mexicans, whose mother(land) has been defiled and who repudiate her while seeking both identification with and independence from the father. Envisioning post-Conquest Mexican society within this paradigm of the family ensures "that national identity [is] essentially masculine identity" (Franco 1989, xix) because it allegorizes the nation as a son, and the nation's history as dependence on a traitorous mother who must be violently rejected in order to establish national autonomy. The feminine, understood as the "devalued, the passive, the mauled and battered, the violated, [that which is] screwed over, fucked and yet still . . . herself the betrayer" (Paz 1950, 72), embodies the conquered nation's dangerous inheritance and must be expunged in order to establish national strength and identity: a national masculinity, or a masculine nationality.

While the Malinche is a particularly Mexican figure, the paradigm of national identity that she symbolizes is not foreign to other Latin American countries. One can easily list numerous canonical images of the traitorous or defiled feminine in the context of independence and reformist social movements or in dialogue with European philosophical and cultural paradigms: the devouring Earth Mother of the *novelas de la tierra* (José Eustasio Rivera's *La vorágine:* Colombia, 1924), the savage mother/sexually dominant woman (Rómulo Gallegos's *Doña Bárbara:* Venezuela, 1929), the woman whose inaccessibility threatens the male ego (Ernesto Sábato's *El túnel:* Argentina, 1948), the innocent victim of irrational male violence (Graciliano Ramos's *São Bernardo:* Brazil, 1934), the eroticized victim sacrificed in atonement for men's sense of collective guilt or class inadequacy (Luisa Valenzuela's *Novela negra con Argentinos:* Argentina, 1991 and Armando Ramirez's *Violación en Polanco:* Mexico, 1980). Each of those forms of debasement, dismissal, or murder of women bears out its own logic of sexual difference in a particular national, economic, class, and ethnic situation, but they all exhibit the principle of violent rejection of femininity as a requirement of masculine subjectivity.

As long as simplified Freudian terms define masculine subjectivity (as they do for Paz in relation to Mexican men), it will be indistinguishable from domination and violence against women.[18] Yet, this drive to separate so violently from the mother resonates with the insistence of modern Latin American nations as well as many of their writers on breaking free of the colonial heritage to found the "newness of the New World." The problem arises, however, when the authority to found the New World is historically associated with illegitimate colonizing powers. When the promise of identification with the father—against the mother—appears both unconvincing and undesirable, how do men imagine the legitimacy and authority of mature masculinity?

González Echevarría (1990) eloquently argues that for Latin American countries, whose economic, political, and cultural self-definition has been established in narrative, literary production remains the site for reenvisioning and reshaping social realities: "The search for uniqueness and identity is the form the question of legitimacy takes after the colonial period" (10).[19] He unveils Latin American myths of origins by tracing the conflicting trajectories of literary projects which would establish national identities/histories and simultaneously subvert the requirement of legitimation in relation to European political and cultural authority. This is an important step to make toward freedom from cultural dependency, toward "a knowledge of self and collectivity that is liberating and easily shared; a clearing in the current jungle of discourses of power" (4).

Such knowledge, however, cannot be attained through cultural and critical production about nations alone; equal attention must be paid to the ways in which these very myths of origins affect relations between men and women at the level of individual psychology as well as with regard to socioeconomic forces and national identities. In relation to the question of "self and collectivity," Griselda Gambaro (1985) has addressed the lack of attention paid to the position of women by Latin American critical/political discourse:

> En América Latina hay un compromiso político visible donde se enfatiza la lucha de clases y la liberación del dominio extranjero—no se observa con mirada crítica el fenómeno de la situación de la mujer dentro de ese contexto. (472)

> [In Latin America there is a visible political involvement which emphasizes class struggle and liberation from foreign domination—but there is no observable criticism of the phenomenon of women's situation within that context.]

The "knowledge of self and collectivity" to which González Echevarría refers too often remains a knowledge based on masculine identity and masculinized group definition. As long as this is the case, the burden of "repeated attempts to discover or found the newness of the New World" is culturally parallel to the assumption that self-birth, or founding the newness and radical independence of the self, is possible or desirable. Giving birth to oneself not only requires overcoming the role of mothers as originary source; for men it also implies an ongoing resistance to women's agency in general, lest their powers of production and reproduction surface to destroy the illusion of male self-reliance. A feminist approach to regional identity formation must consider how the search for newness, when uncritically carried out within a masculinist imaginary, legitimates violence against women in the service of specifically masculine uniqueness and identity. In order to reach a "knowledge of self and collectivity that is easily shared," Latin American literary critics and theorists must both acknowledge and challenge paradigms for the expression of self-knowledge which have been received from European traditions. The general violent affirmation of the father to which Paz refers is just one problematic consequence of such cultural/political interaction.

In terms of nineteenth-century European literary paradigms for exploring expressions of male self-knowledge through crime fiction, we might take the example of Fyodor Dostoevsky's *Crime and Punishment* (published serially in 1866). Latin American narratives that use murder to highlight the connections between violence and the masculine ideal of autonomy necessarily share many elements of its themes and structure. Dostoevsky's work has been hailed as the first modern psychological thriller, the prototype of existential narrative and the crime novel, and a brilliant treatment of the problem of individual will versus social good. Even though this Russian text follows the classic realist paradigm in its drive toward closure and religious certainty in the epilogue, the novel exposes the contradictory investment of masculine subjectivity in eradicating the feminine other.[20]

The same attempt to expose and reassess the violence of the masculine drive to establish identity in opposition to femininity motivates the contemporary Latin American psychological crime narratives to which I turn. Borges, Somers, Lispector, Puig, and Arenas take up the theme of *Crime and Punishment* to focus on its central dilemma—the inadequacy of the notion that men must reject women's subjectivity in order to be free subjects in their own right. They exploit the dynamics of a man's murder of a woman to shed light on different possible constructions of masculine subjectivity and how they might relate to national and cultural identity for Latin Americans.

Each in its own way, these Latin American murder narratives revisit the scene of the crime in Dostoevsky's novel, where the narrator announces that upon killing an old female pawnbroker, the protagonist Raskolnikov was reborn.[21] My selection of the word "scene" here indicates the figuration of the murder of a woman by a male protagonist who is motivated, as is Dostoevsky's character, by a crisis in his experience of masculinity rather than by jealousy, severe mental illness, or self-defense. This crisis of masculine identity promises resolution in the murder of a woman but in fact leads readers to search for a more ethical, community-oriented, psychologically viable definition of masculinity itself. Like *Crime and Punishment,* the texts in my study portray the trite promise of virility in violence, and they position readers as male-identified seekers of an ultimately salutary narrative of healed masculinity. Unlike *Crime and Punishment,* though, the texts attend to the "search for uniqueness and identity [that] is the form . . . legitimacy takes" in contemporary Latin American social structures (González Echevarría 1990, 10). They question the ideal of accomplishing men's rebirth through the elimination of female agency. These twentieth-century crime fictions in which male protagonists seek freedom and power through the murder of women provide fertile ground on which to explore the frustrated equation of masculinity with political and individual autonomy in specifically Latin American contexts.

The murder of women in crime narratives illuminates the problematic intersection of the politically subversive declaration of radical individual freedom on the one hand and the ultimately self-destructive assault on the feminine which such existential celebration often carries with it for male characters on the other hand. Whereas Dostoevsky locates the resolution of that problem in Christian atonement, heterosexual union, and submission to the law, the twentieth-century Latin American murder texts I analyze find no single, utopian narrative with which to correct the flawed notion of masculinity that leads characters to murder in the first place. Rather, these narratives explore a broad range of available scripts for masculinity, as well as the contradictions among them.

In order to focus on complex literary investigations of masculinities, rather than on formulaic murder stories, I have excluded texts that might be considered examples of classical detective fiction or that do not include a metatextual, reflective, or critical dimension regarding male violence. In the fashion of *Crime and Punishment,* the works I have chosen part from the formulaic by regarding the relevant mystery not to be whodunit, but rather how, why, and to what end do men's murders of women promise (before realization) to bolster dominant notions of masculinity. These murder tales are ethically compromising when most thoroughly understood. They facilitate reader identification with the criminal (rather than with a detective or the law), question the status of the murder event, focalize through the male protagonist after the commission of the crime, and examine its social or political causal forces.

For all that, however, and unlike *Crime and Punishment,* they resist the second, textual erasure of the female victims that one finds in other Latin American texts such as Juan Carlos Onetti's *La cara de la desgracia* (1960), *El pozo* (1939) and *La vida breve* (1950), Sábato's *El túnel* (1948), Fuentes's "El día de las madres" (1981), Ramírez's *Violación en Polanco* (1980), and Juan Carlos Martini's *Los asesinos las prefieren rubias* (1974). Those works all maintain the consistency of narrative structure necessary to avoid reader identification with the female victims; they are focalized through the reactive male position in nonparodic fictions of violent masculinity; they do not foreground the contradiction in dominant fictions so much as the characters' direct inheritance of them. I am more interested here in texts that invite and problematize our identification with both victimizer and victim because they more directly engage the debate over hegemonic masculinity and its power to position us all, even in our enjoyment of transgressive fantasies. This unstable tension between the criminal as hero and the reader as judge constitutes both the enjoyment of the texts and their potential force as imaginary experiments in social change.

These experimental crime narratives posit individual accession to masculinity as violent repudiation of the mother in order to effect successful rebellion against the oppressive "no" of the father, where that "no" is associated with actual fathers, legal systems, compulsory heterosexuality, or the Spanish colonial heritage. The texts highlight the contradictions and impasses of male-identified national identities by focusing on the ambiguity of affirmation and negation inherent in the most definitive transgression of laws, murder. In the case of men's murder of women, that transgression confirms phallic privilege while challenging legal authority. It establishes masculine separation from feminine others and yet simultaneously performs the dependent and reactionary nature of that separation. Finally, it celebrates individual freedom even as it exposes the politically constructed nature of the discourse of radical individuality. The crime narratives in this study graphically represent the multiple forms of violence inherent in a cultural imperative for men to reject identification with women. They also question the distinction between justifiable and unjustifiable violence in political activity and/or revolutions.

Borges's "La intrusa," Somers's "El despojo," Lispector's *A maçã no escuro,* Puig's *The Buenos Aires Affair,* and Arenas's *El asalto* challenge the notion that coherent masculine identity requires the erasure of an other. In offering their distinct explorations of what might be viable ways of thinking masculinity differently, however, they all must also work from (both within and in resistance to) masculine opposition to, rather than recognition of, the other and the interpretive tradition which upholds it. By approaching these murder narratives as experiments with subjectivity, we clarify their connection to the construction of gender and power relations in the real world. These texts imagine masculine subjectivity for characters in ways that influence the interpretations readers can have of our own subjectivity, interpretations which we can support or contest only by carefully considering how they are produced.

CHAPTER TWO

Telling Secrets of Brotherly Love

Jorge Luis Borges's "La Intrusa"

Widely considered the first and most masterful Latin American expert on analytic crime fiction,[1] Jorge Luis Borges narrates the tale of two brothers who strengthen their bond to each other by sacrificing a woman in his short story "La intrusa" ("The Intruder"). Masculine subjectivity seems to achieve invulnerability when the men embrace over the dead body of the female lover they had shared, over whom they had fought, and whom they killed together. With her death the brothers assert their humanity against her object status, seal their unconscious pact to repress their homosexuality, reenclose their family unit, and consolidate their complicity with each other by keeping the murder secret.

While the crime appears to be a success from the brothers' point of view, the narrative structure threatens their attempted restoration of masculine stability. The narrator pits the brothers against each other when the tale is reconstituted from Argentine gossip. In the retelling, the brothers' bond reveals itself to be a futile form of competition in relation to women. Rather than successfully eliminating the female intruder from an ideal male universe, the murder actually exposes the fissures in the homosocial edifice it was meant to reinforce. Borges manipulates reader identification, narrative reliability, and his trademark metafictional codes to detect the flawed origins of masculinist community formation, the psychology of murderous males, and the pact of secrecy which keeps them dangerously dependent on one another.

Borges wrote "La intrusa" after a thirteen-year gap in his production of short stories. Unlike the author's better-known tales of intrigue, conundrum, and anxiety over the limits of representation, this story is a linear, realist text featuring grittier, more provincial and lower-class characters than the usual Borgesian cast. In spite of the presence of similar characters in Borges's earlier works such as *Historia universal de la infamia,* as well as attention paid to themes related to rivalry and physical prowess in other stories, "La intrusa" is the only tale in which misogyny and homosexuality appear as central issues (Keller and Van Hooft 1976).

Borges claimed in an interview with Richard Burgin in 1967, a little over a year after he had written it, that "La intrusa" was his best story because it was "simpler" than the others. He also mentioned that he had dedicated it to his mother, who reacted negatively to the story: "she thought it was awful" and "very unpleasant." Even though he claimed of "La intrusa" that "there's nothing personal about it" (Burgin 1968, 47), the dedication to his mother indicates an unusual level of personal investment in the effect of his writing on people close to him. In that regard it is curious indeed that "La intrusa" addresses masculinity more directly than any of Borges's other short stories.

"La intrusa" concerns male bonding between characters the author himself has called "hoodlums," in a tale he says offers no surprises: "It isn't a trick story. Because if you read it as a trick story, then, of course, you'll find that you know what's going to happen at the end of a page or so, but it isn't meant to be a trick story. On the contrary. What I was trying to do was to tell an inevitable story so that the end shouldn't come as a surprise" (Burgin 1968, 47). Although Borges claims the plot to be "inevitable," "La intrusa" evidences many of the formal characteristics of his better-known pieces such as the often-anthologized "El jardin de los senderos que se bifurcan" ("The Garden of the Forking Paths"), "El milagro secreto" ("The Secret Miracle"), "La muerte y la brújula" ("Death and the Compass"), "Emma Zunz," and "El sur" ("The South"). "La intrusa" shares their economy of style, embedded narration, and the presentation of a crime or a violent act which the story appropriates as a clue to explaining some mysterious aspect of human relations.

Even though many of his stories feature detectives as characters, or regular characters who assume the role of detectives, Borges always cedes to his readers the final responsibility of determining the significance of details and events in his fictions. He does not posit "the criminal case as a problem with a possible solution, but as a problem with philosophical and linguistic implications" (Holzapfel 1978, 53). This author's approach to crime fiction establishes a parallelism between the meanings, motivations, and consequences of two types of transgressive acts: violent crime and narration itself. Illegal acts require investigation and interpretation in order to be solved or settled, terms which typically refer to a lawbreaker's being found out and brought to justice. Stories, too, require attentive analysis and interpretation in order for readers to make sense of events that the stories narrate. Crimes and stories, Borges's oeuvre implies, invite the intervention of active readers to identify the motives and sources of transgression with an eye to making order. What sort of order can be constructed through the reading process, however, is open to question. And that returns us to the question of detection and justice: do investigators ever get to the bottom of any case, or do we just find the most comfortable stories to tell ourselves?

If, for Borges, stories are like crimes, what rules does "La intrusa," with its "simple" and "inevitable" structure, break? On the surface it seems to defend a rather obvious, or commonsense, principle of male bonding, namely, that the successful construction of male-centered worlds depends on vigilance against female intrusion. "La intrusa" illustrates the tragic extremes to which such a principle might be taken by two ignorant, particularly vulnerable men whom neither the narrator nor the readers are meant to accept as representative of men in general.

Because of the sense of inevitability that it creates, however, this story should not be understood to address two awful exceptions to some general model of healthy male psychology. Masculinity itself, not just for the main characters, serves as both the motive of the plot and the mystery to be solved in this short story. This text of less than two thousand words presents masculinity as a set of physical and behavioral characteristics, as a marker of class and work status, as a sex role, as a defense of family identity and integrity, and as the system of identification among men which ensures homosocial ties while repressing homosexual desires. The brief, feminine title, "La intrusa," invites speculation. Into what does she intrude? The "what" which could be interrupted signals a reactive masculinity that resists feminine otherness and its threat to the male ego. But as the narrative structure suggests, that version of masculinity also carries the seeds of its self-de(con)struction. Even as the plot establishes a seemingly solid loyalty between men that is based on the sacrifice of a woman, the telling of the story betrays their complicity with one another.

"La intrusa" relates how two inseparable brothers become jealous of each other over a woman with whom they both have sexual relations. After a period of secrecy in which the brothers each visit her separately, they finally kill "the intruder" and embrace over her dead body. The simple plot confirms a common understanding of friendship between men. In this dynamic, male-male relationships must be structured so that they are not adversely affected by men's desire for or love of women. While the men's heterosexual desires are required as a signifier of their similarity to each other, and hence provide that common bond upon which fraternal ties are predicated, male-male friendship must be kept separate—at least on the level of conscious interaction—from libidinal urges. When the homosocial and the sexual realms interfere with each other, individuals must choose between them. (Sedgwick 1985, 83–96).[2]

In Borges's story, the clear choice is the bond between the two brothers, which matters infinitely more to them than any other relationship. The main question, or mystery, of this crime story centers on the nature of that bond. From the beginning the brothers Nilsen appear inseparable; they share all the same characteristics deemed important by the narrator. The elder brother, Cristián brings Juliana Burgos home to live with him. The younger brother, Eduardo, brings home another woman but sends her away after a few days because he has fallen in love with Juliana. Cristián offers Juliana to Eduardo. The brothers share her for a few weeks; predictably, jealous tension between them mounts. They sell her to a brothel, but each one visits her in secret. Upon learning that Eduardo had been visiting Juliana, Cristián decides to buy her back and bring her home again. One day Cristián announces that they need to make a delivery. He and Eduardo ride out of town, and Cristián informs Eduardo:

> —A trabajar, hermano. Después nos ayudarán los caranchos. Hoy la maté. Que se quede aquí con sus pilchas. Ya no hará más perjuicios.
>
> Se abrazaron, casi llorando. Ahora los ataba otro vínculo: la mujer tristemente sacrificada y la obligación de olvidarla. (184)

> ["Now, brother, to work. Later on, the buzzards will give us a hand. Today I killed her. Let her stay here with all her finery, and not do us any more harm."
>
> They embraced, almost in tears. Now they shared an extra bond; the woman sorrowfully sacrificed and the obligation to forget her.][3]

The plot seems straightforward enough. Two brothers compete for a woman, but rather than maintain their rivalry or accept that one must win and one must lose, they opt to eliminate the source of competition. Insofar as they consummate their homosocial bond to one another through Juliana's body, however, the plot thickens. The solution to their problem, the sacrifice of Juliana, has two primary purposes. It eliminates the source of conflict, and it eliminates the physical evidence of the brothers' erotic bond to each other.

Featuring protagonists who exhibit all the same general traits, choose the same object of their sexual desire, and seem to share the same priorities, "La intrusa" is all about doubling. Although the title highlights singularity with its definite article and the divisiveness associated with intrusion, the embedded form of this story shifts focus to the reinforcing effect of doubles (the brothers) and of doubling back (the return to unity after Juliana's death). At the same time, however, it reveals the danger of such doubling: it will always betray itself.

Masculinity in "La intrusa" must therefore be read on two levels. First, the protagonists solidify and strengthen their masculinity through the sacrifice of a woman. In order to understand the portrait of unassailed masculinity and male-male relationship which their crime is meant to draw, a first reading of "La intrusa" requires a consideration of the protagonists' goals. They seek to reinforce their family unit and to seal their pact to repress homosexuality. They achieve those goals by asserting their (male) humanity over and against Juliana's object status and then by binding themselves to each other through the pact of a secrecy. Since, according to the closing words of the story, they both face "la obligación de olvidarla," they have found a new loyalty to replace the one that was lost in their rivalry over the intruder.

The second level of reading masculinity in Borges's story involves the instability of the narrative itself. The source of the story is in question from the start. The role of the narrator appears inconsistent with regard to access to information as well as to interpretive license. A series of points challenges the possibility of complicity between the brothers to keep Juliana's murder a secret. As we shall see, the text of "La intrusa" intrudes on the popular fiction of masculinity that guides its own male characters. The narrative structure offers ironic commentary on the myth that male integrity must or even can be founded on the sacrifice of women.

Brothers and Doubling

The plot of "La intrusa" owes its power to resonance with an old, familiar story: sacrifice produces and strengthens community. That power is complicated, however, by the distinct absence of any tragic dimension to the brothers' murder of Juliana. Since she never attains the status of a human being for them, they can experience her death only as a loss of property, albeit a piece of property that they load with symbolic significance. She does not function as an expiatory scapegoat in a Girardian sense of the term; rather, the brothers believe themselves empowered to use her and then discard her when her presence proves too costly to their hermetic fraternal system.

A basic feminist understanding of their logic hinges on the references to Juliana as "una cosa" [a thing], "la mujer" [the woman], "una sirvienta" [a servant], and on associations of her with "sumisión bestial" [animal submission] or *cueros* [animal hides]. By treating her as an object to be used, sold, bought, or killed at whim, the brothers consolidate their subject status in opposition to her. They negotiate with each other about her fate, and they never consult her on any matter whatsoever. From their point of view, killing her is the most efficient solution to their conflict because it removes nothing more than an object that had obstructed their perfect communication and sense of loyalty to one another. In spite of the brothers' nonanalytic understanding of the situation, the narrator signals to readers that Juliana's death is a barbaric expression of the problem of masculinity for the protagonists. This brief tale offers up a psychological analysis of murderous males, but its most disturbing aspect is the lack of moral accusation against them for their actions. While the narrator implicitly condemns the crime, he does so more because of the brothers' lack of insight into their own desires than because they kill a human being (Shaw 1992, 135).

The text exhibits a classic short-story form. It establishes the key elements of character and then moves to a simple chronology of events. After an opening paragraph in which the narrator relates how he came to learn of their story, he launches into the second paragraph by immediately describing the brothers Nilsen. He highlights the trappings of stereotypical masculinity which characterize them. Describing them as tall, with long reddish hair, he attributes their appearance and their love of fighting-whiskey ("el alcohol pendenciero") to their probable Danish or Irish blood. Greedy, conniving cheats and rustlers, these two inspire fear and are rumored to have killed—presumably other men—in disputes before. They have fought against the police and will defend each other against all enemies: "Malquistarse con uno era contar con dos enemigos" (183) [To cross one of them meant having two enemies]. In addition to their fame for threatening, rowdy behaviour, the brothers Nilsen are known for their spare lives. They spend all their time together, their only luxuries being "el caballo, el apero, la daga de hoja corta, el atuendo rumboso de los sábados" (182) [horses, riding gear, short-bladed daggers, a substantial fling on Saturdays]. Stereotypical slum dwellers, they live for the drama of barroom brawling.

Ironically, these two characters *taken together* embody the myth of the solitary man of action. The narrator is careful to point out that no one knew of their relatives or their family past: "De sus deudos nada se sabe ni de dónde vinieron" (182) [Of their ancestry or where they came from, nothing was known]. In fact, he points out that their last name, Nelson, was mistaken in their town for Nilsen. The misnamed brothers Nilsen proudly live outside of laws, whether those be laws of extended kinship structures or of police authority. Their family history a mystery, their physical characteristics atypical in their town, and their rebellious nature famed, the two men are inseparable. The narrator explicitly explains their close relationship as a defense against their feeling different from those around them:

> Físicamente diferían del compadraje que dio su apodo forajido a la Costa Brava. Esto, y lo que ignoramos, ayuda a comprender lo unidos que fueron. (182-3)
>
> [Physically, they were quite distinct from the roughneck crowd of settlers who lent the Costa Brava their own bad name. This, and other things we do not know, helps to explain how close they were.]

If *esto* refers to their difference from others of their social class, a difference constituted by their physical traits and their very public displays of extreme and destructive behaviors that are coded masculine (fighting, drinking, carousing, rustling), then "lo que ignoramos" hints at the flip side of that image, their vulnerability. They are so united because they feel threatened, perhaps because their love for one another borders on homosexuality, because individually they could not sustain their performance of hypermasculinity, or because the combination of a lack of social position through family history with a sense of beleaguered masculinity requires them to seek identity and strength in one another. At any rate, the result of their closeness is an absence of any genuine emotional attachment to other people.

Although the narrator calls the pair *calaveras* [womanizers] since they frequent bars and brothels in search of sex with women, Cristián's attempt to bring one specific woman into their lives proves disastrous. Her very presence destabilizes their carefully constructed sense of family. Since they are both attracted to her, they are forced to acknowledge that their absolute faith in fraternal unity is inadequate protection against threats to their identity as invulnerable males. Their desire for Juliana belies their illusion of self-reliance:

> Sin saberlo, estaban celándose. En el duro suburbio, un hombre no decía, ni se decía, que una mujer pudiera importarle, más allá del deseo y la posesión, pero los dos estaban enamorados. Esto, de algún modo, los humillaba. (183)
>
> [Without realizing it, they were growing jealous. In that rough settlement, no man ever let on to others, or to himself, that a woman would matter, except as something desired or possessed, but the two of them were in love. For them, that in its way was a humiliation.]

The narrator takes liberties here that he avoids in other parts of the text. He analyzes all the men of the area in one sweeping gesture, "un hombre no decía . . . que una mujer pudiera importarle," essentially claiming that their regional and class-based notion of masculinity enforced defensiveness against loving women. By omitting mention of the object of the Nilsens' love, however, the phrase "pero los dos estaban enamorados" allows for ambiguity of interpretation. The two brothers, unable to admit to love for a woman, felt love nonetheless—and that humiliated them.

The narrator leaves open the question of whether they were in love with Juliana or with each other. Combining that ambiguity with the way in which the brothers actually treat Juliana, the more plausible reading is that they were in love with each other and expressed those feelings through her. Their visits to her in the brothel do not differ from their former mode of relating to women except that they have now fixed on one specific woman. The narrator offers no evidence at all of any effects of her personality on the men—"By emphasizing her muteness and blankness, Borges highlights her role as a mere vessel or perhaps mirror: she is the recipient of the projected fraternal love which the brothers are unable to face, yet which, ultimately, they must come to grips with, since it is continually reflected in her presence" (Keller and Van Hooft 1976, 308). Many readers have noted this ambiguity in the text regarding the brothers' incestuous homosexual desires. Cristián and Eduardo think that they each desire Juliana, but they subconsciously use "la intrusa," both of them having sex with her, as a displacement of their physical desire for each other. Gary Keller and Karen Van Hooft's structuralist reading (1976) of "La intrusa" attends to the story's reversal of heterosexist expectation as the brothers learn through their adventures with Juliana that they really love only one another. In those critics' view, Juliana's murder allows Cristián and Eduardo to acknowledge and confront the prior sublimation of their desire. This interpretation leads, oddly enough, to the conclusion that the brothers have undergone a successful therapeutic moment through the murder of a woman:

> Borges has said that, for him, "La intrusa" is not a nightmare story, like "La muerte y la brújula," but rather a story in which things are awful but somehow real and very sad. We have tried to show that as a story of emerging awareness it is also, in spite of its tragic outcome, a hopeful story, and a psychologically plausible one. Pascal has stated that "Man is only a reed, the frailest thing in nature; but he is a thinking reed." Borges' "La intrusa" supports the verity of this statement by extending the attainment of other-awareness and self-awareness that it implies to the lowest stratum of society. (318)

While this understanding of how the brothers Nilsen benefit from their murder of Juliana shows extraordinary sensitivity to characterization in the short story, it fails to account for the moral problem of applying Pascal's observation to men only. Having experienced rivalry for the first time, the brothers do indeed progress to a higher awareness of their separate identities. Concluding that the story is hopeful for that reason, however, applauds Borges's extension of the description "thinking reed" from the culturally and economically privileged classes to lower-class men. It celebrates the brothers' psychological evolution at the expense of women in general.

The other-awareness and the self-awareness which the brothers may have attained at the end of the story is purchased with the life of a woman whom they never consider to be a subject in her own right. Whatever awareness of self and other they may have achieved operates for them only in a male-centered universe, and their successful eradication of female participation contains them all the more completely within a system of inescapable mirroring. Dependence on that mirroring caused Cristián and Eduardo's lack of moral perspective in the first place. This type of awareness, predicated as it is on the participants' blindness to male privilege, can never develop beyond the game of mutual contemplation and the basic separation required for the enjoyment of identification between like subjects. It can never reach an ethical stance toward others since such an ethics calls for enjoying, appreciating, or respecting difference.

Fortunately, the end of the "La intrusa" is open to another possible conclusion in defense of which readers do not have to ignore the horror of the brothers' crime. In this second possible reading, the murder of "la intrusa" accomplishes nothing more than a release of the sexual tension that had been building between the brothers before she was brought to live with them. With her death the brothers return to their apparently seamless fraternity predicated on blindness to their mutual desire. Juliana's death does not provide hope that they will become more reflective and ethical beings. Instead, it cements their now willful (whereas it was formerly unconscious) investment in *el olvido*, a state of manly unawareness of their relationship's complicated dynamics.

Keller and Van Hooft are right, though, that "La intrusa" is a hopeful story and a psychologically plausible one. It is plausible because it cites fictions of masculinity, fictions which still resonate with many readers' beliefs in commonsense definitions of masculinity and femininity as respectively active and passive, defensive and open. Also plausible are the lengths to which the violent, sexist, unreflective brothers Nilsen will go to avoid confronting their projection onto a woman of what they consider to be an inappropriate love for one another. The hope of "La intrusa," however, does not lie with the characters and their capacity for change. Rather, it emerges in the narrator's play on identification and differentiation between himself, the brothers Nilsen, and fictions of masculinity in general.

Narrators and Duplicity

"La intrusa" straddles the fence between crime fiction and detective fiction. As we have seen, when understood from the murderers' point of view, killing Juliana is "inevitable"; it is necessary and even generous. The brothers agree to lose an object of importance to each of them in order to avoid prolonged rivalry between them. This economical solution to an emotional problem works only within a misogynist world where women do not matter as people. The inevitability of the story depends on the brothers' as well as their peers' adherence to a rigid definition of masculinity. Any of them would lose face by admitting to loving a woman. In the Nilsens' case, the threat of that loss is magnified when their desire for the same woman interferes with their extreme loyalty to one another. Since their subjectivity is so intertwined, they must opt for murder rather than any other resolution which might diminish their dependence on each other.

As crime fiction focalized through criminals with complex motives and limited understanding of their situation, "La intrusa" overtly engages the pleasure and fear of transgression. Readers can consider the plot "inevitable" only if they—we—at least partially sympathize with the Nilsens' sense of vulnerability. Juliana's death is, indeed, restorative and strengthening for Cristián and Eduardo because it adds to their interdependence. Not only do they both now have "la obligación de olvidarla" insofar as she was a desired object, but they also must rely on each other to keep the murder secret. Having transgressed their own pact of unity, they punish themselves by sacrificing Juliana. Having transgressed laws against murder, they reward themselves by enjoying even greater complicity with one another. Their feeling of successful masculinity is linked even more tightly to their fraternal (homosocial) bond in combination with their outlaw status. The consolidation of those two principles so overwhelms them that, being manly, they *almost* cry: "Se abrazaron, casi llorando."

However convincing the unity between Cristián and Eduardo after Juliana's death, reading Borges is never as much about the characters and plots as it is about reading itself.[4] Through its treatment of masculinity, "La intrusa" may, at first glance, appear to be misogynist, but the story is open to interpretation and change. Approaching the text from a detective's point of view, we find abundant clues for discovering forms of transgression more subtle than murder, but no less essential to the story's critique of fictions of masculinity. These forms of transgression violate the rules of linear, realist, reliable storytelling.

From the first words of "La intrusa," the narrator introduces significant doubt regarding the sources and reliability of his tale. He then includes choice details which contradict his own presentation of the brothers' relationship. He interjects extradiegetic commentary inconsistent with his stated role as scribe for a story he heard fourth- or fifthhand. Finally, he adds a biblical reference as epigraph, which complicates the meanings and sources of the intrusion mentioned in the title.

The story opens with the impersonal verb *dicen,* indicating no particular source for the information: "Dicen (lo cual es improbable) que la historia fue referida por Eduardo, el menor de los Nelson, en el velorio de Cristián" (182) [They claim (improbably) that the story was told by Eduardo, the younger of the Nilsen brothers, at the wake for Cristián]. The phrase "lo cual es improbable" most logically refers to the notion that Eduardo was the original source of the story. No definitive explanation of why that should be improbable ever appears. Because of its placement, though, the phrase could also refer to the verb *dicen,* suggesting that the entire tale has been invented by the narrator rather than received from local lore.

The specific account of how the narrator came to hear of the brothers Nelson/Nilsen sheds little light on the tale's veracity:

> Lo cierto es que alguien la oyó de alguien, en el decurso de esa larga noche perdida, entre maté y maté, y la repitió a Santiago Dabove, por quien la supe. Años después, volvieron a contármela en Turdera, donde había acontecido. La segunda versión, algo más prolija, confirmaba en suma la de Santiago, con las pequeñas variaciones y divergencias que son del caso. (182)
>
> [Someone must certainly have heard it from someone else, in the course of that long, idle night, between servings of mate, and passed it on to Santiago Dabove, from whom I learned it. Years later, they told it to me again in Turdera, where it had all happened. The second version, considerably more detailed, substantiated Santiago's, with the usual small variations and departures.]

The chain of nameless sources and the mention of a long night indicate that the information about to be transmitted to us, the readers, is so diluted by fatigue, temporal distance, and lack of firsthand knowledge that its accuracy is impossible to guarantee.

Two points of apparent stability in that chain anchor the narrator's claim to authority: a specific source, Santiago Dabove, and the fact that his version was confirmed by others years later. Santiago Dabove is one of the authors whose writings appear in Borges and Casares's *Antología de la literatura fantástica* (1940). He died in 1951. Most readers of "La intrusa," even Argentine readers, would not recognize this reference to a relatively obscure writer. Insofar as Dabove is unfamiliar to readers, he functions as a placeholder, providing the structural support for the empty spot from which "La intrusa" originates. Insofar as readers accept him as an author of fantastic tales, however, the inclusion of his name as source suggests that "La intrusa" is not as realist a story as its author claims. At any rate, the narrator takes ultimate responsibility for "La intrusa," observing, "ya preveo que cederé a la tentación de acentuar o agregar algún pormenor" (182) [already I see myself yielding to the writer's temptation to heighten or amplify some detail or other].

The details that the narrator adds to complicate the story actually contradict his own claim regarding "lo unidos que fueron" the brothers. The elder of the two, Cristián, causes the crisis by bringing Juliana home in the first place. The brothers' rivalry over her begins only after Cristián invites Eduardo to use her as he will. Cristián's tone when he makes the offer is "entre mandón y cordial" [half commanding, half cordial], indicating his leadership position in the pair. Therefore, the presumed doubling that occurs between the Nilsens is incomplete. Only one of them initiates all the movement in the story. Cristián is the one who as much as orders Eduardo to have sex with Juliana; he finalizes her sale to the madam ; he decides to buy her back again; and he kills her without consulting with Eduardo beforehand. Cristián is also the only brother to speak in the text. Eduardo literally has no say in the situation.[5]

I argued earlier that Juliana's death provides an escape from the competition between the brothers, and that rather than win or lose, they both agree to put an end to their rivalry. During the period in which they shared Juliana sexually, however, the narrator indicates that Eduardo had already won Juliana's affection, such as it was:

> La mujer atendía a los dos con sumisión bestial; pero no podía ocultar alguna preferencia por el menor, que no había rechazado la participación, pero que no la había dispuesto. (183)
>
> [The woman waited on the two of them with animal submissiveness; but she could not conceal her preference, unquestionably for the younger one, who, although he had not rejected the arrangement, had not sought it out.]

While Cristián had the upper hand regarding decision making in the family, Eduardo garnered more female affection precisely because he did not instigate Juliana's servitude.

Another problematic detail concerns the fact that the brothers were known to fight each other's battles as if they were one person. The only reference to the townspeople's awareness of the odd arrangement in their home, of the fact that the two men were sharing one woman for weeks, involves Eduardo's defending Cristián:

> Una tarde, en la plaza de Lomas, Eduardo se cruzó con Juan Iberra, que lo felicitó por ese primor que se había agenciado. Fue entonces, creo, que Eduardo lo injurió. Nadie, delante de él, iba hacer burla de Cristián. (183)
>
> [One afternoon in the Plaza de Lomos, Eduardo ran into Juan Iberra, who congratulated him on the beautiful "dish" he had fixed up for himself. It was then, I think, that Eduardo roughed him up. No one, in his presence, was going to make fun of Cristián.]

Eduardo attacks Juan for suggesting that Cristián is being taken advantage of in the triangulated relationship between the Nilsens and Juliana. Curiously, Eduardo defends Cristián here against *himself.* "Ese primor que se había agenciado" is Eduardo's enjoyment of Cristián's lover. Just as the Nilsens project their love for each other onto Juliana, Eduardo projects onto Juan the role of dishonoring his brother. Eduardo's defensiveness in Cristián's name becomes necessary only because of Eduardo's perception that sharing Juliana diminishes his brother somehow. In this scene Eduardo enacts the separation and splitting of images which is precisely what the brothers seem unable to withstand. He takes Cristián's place in two ways, one of which establishes their difference (using Juliana for their separate pleasures) and one of which reasserts their single identity against external threat (each taking the other's battles as his own). Eduardo's aggression toward Juan exemplifies the unbearable tension between separation and unity introduced by the Nilsens' attempt to share a lover.

A final detail contradicts the notion that the brothers lived united against all intrusions. If in the end they shared the obligation to forget Juliana, that obligation functions in relation not only to their sexual desire but also to their need to keep her murder a secret. They must avoid the further separation that prosecution or entry into the legal system might cause. The question arises, then, of how the murder comes to be common knowledge. Who betrayed whom in revealing the secret of the brothers' pact? Since Cristián actually committed the crime, it seems improbable that he would have told the story. Yet, given that he is the only of the pair to speak, and that Eduardo always defends Cristián in public, it seems improbable (as the narrator points out in the first line) that Eduardo would have confessed his brother's crime. Since the narrator presents no evidence of witnesses other than the Nilsens, the only conclusion to draw is that one of them eventually betrayed the other. Perhaps it makes no difference which brother actually sang. The important thing is that they did not share equally "la obligación de olvidar [a Juliana]." At least one of them remembers her well enough to tell the tale.

In addition to the textual details that undercut the Nilsens' unity, the narrator also interjects periodic interpretations and assessments of events. They appear to be randomly dispersed throughout the story, indicating both that the narrator alters details for his own amusement and that he finds certain elements of the story more compelling than others; note, as earlier mentioned, his reflection on the causes of the brother's close relationship ("esto, y lo que ignoramos, ayuda a comprender lo unidos que fueron") and his depiction of men's inability to admit love for women. The other examples deal with reactions that he attributes to the whole neighborhood, reactions he could have validated only by interviewing many people who remembered the case: "[e]l barrio los temía" (182) ["the neighborhood feared them"], "[e]l barrio . . . previó con alevosa alegría la rivalidad latente de los hermanos" (183) ["the neighborhood . . . looked forward with malicious glee to the subterranean rivalry between the brothers"]. About Juliana he asserts that "[e]n un barrio modesto, donde el trabajo y el descuido gastan a las mujeres, no era mal parecida" (183) ["in a poor neighborhood, where work and neglect wear out the women, she was not at all bad looking"]. These are details and judgements which the narrator himself admits in the first paragraph he could not have confirmed as true. He intentionally constructs "un breve y trágico cristal de la índole de los orilleros antiguos" (182) ["briefly and tragically the whole temper of life in those days along the banks of the river Plate"] with his story, freely adding psychological observations, specific elements which seem irrelevant to the plot ("Había llovido . . ." (184) ["It had rained . . ."]) and privileged information which only the brothers could have known ("En Turdera, los Nilsen . . . quisieron reanudar su antigua vida de hombres entre hombres" (184) ["In Turdera, the Nilsens . . . sought to recover their old ways of men among men"]).

Although we have seen how the brothers might feel that their male-only universe is restored with Juliana's death, the narrator carefully exposes various fissures in their illusion. As part of his play with the predetermined feel of a tale which coyly claims to be a simple reflection of real events, the narrator includes a Bible verse as epigraph, citing David's eulogy for Jonathan from 2 Samuel 1: 26, "I am distressed for thee, my brother Jonathan: very pleasant hast thou been unto me: thy love to me was wonderful, passing the love of women" (King James Version).

According to Keller and Van Hooft, the epigraph suggests the motif of the "eternal return," positing that "this story is somehow a repetition of a previous one: Cristián and Eduardo are acting out a situation that has occurred before" (Keller and Van Hooft, 303). Employing just such a strategy of citation is certainly common in Borges's work in general. In this case, though, citing the well-known biblical account of extreme fraternal loyalty contradicts the narrator's stated goal of providing "un breve y trágico cristal de la índole de los orilleros antiguos" (182). The "cristal" suggests a window onto an isolated event, a glass through which observers watch others, yet it also refers to a mirror, or a glass in which observers see themselves. The narrator claims to portray an odd case of men in the poor outskirts of Buenos Aires; by relating their particularity to the ancient kings of Israel, however, he belies the specificity of region and class which might have seemed to afford him distance from the Nilsens' horrifying treatment of a woman.

As part of the introductory information in "La intrusa," the narrator mentions that the Nilsens had a Bible containing handwritten names and dates, presumably the record of their genealogy: "Era el único libro que había en la casa. La azarosa crónica de los Nilsen, perdida como todo se perderá" (182) [It was the only book in the house. The recorded misfortunes of the Nilsens, lost as all will be lost]. While not an unusual possession to find in any home, the fact that the Bible is the only written text mentioned in the story proper grants its citation in the epigraph more relevance as the record of inheritance for the men depicted. In the face of this loss of family ties, the models of masculinity, and especially of masculinity's relationship to fraternal love and crime, available to the Nilsen brothers came from patriarchal religion and local economic structures.

The Old Testament story of friendship between Jonathan and David clarifies the contradictory signs of legitimate masculinity which Borges addresses in "La intrusa." I Samuel recounts David's ascendancy to the throne of Israel. His relationship to Jonathan, King Saul's son, had been as that of a brother ever since the king took David into his own house after David defeated Goliath for the Israelites: "And Saul took him that day, and would let him go no more home to his father's house. Then Jonathan and David made a convenant, because he loved him as his own soul. And Jonathan stripped himself of the robe that was upon him, and gave it to David, and his garments, even to his sword, and to his bow, and to his girdle." Saul's increasing jealousy of David's successes in battle and the love shown the younger man by "all Israel and Judah" threatens the perfect friendship between the two younger men. When Saul plots David's murder, Jonathan warns David to leave. The two never see each other again.

Borges's use of the biblical reference to David's appreciation of Jonathan's love can be taken in two ways. If we privilege the isolated verse containing the eulogy for Jonathan, we concentrate on the notion of fraternal bonds that are tighter than any heterosexual union, the implication being, as it seems to work in Cristián's and Eduardo's minds, that neither any woman nor any interfering erotic desire could ever come between the two men.

On the other hand, if we privilege the whole story of David's relationship with Jonathan, we must note that no woman ever did come between them. "La intrusa" reflects this interpretation in that the brothers Nilsen are incapable of loving Juliana as a person, but only as a thing. In that sense, she is not really a woman in any position to love men actively anyway. She could never be the agent of the brothers' distress, but rather only the object that symbolizes it.

In the biblical story, the father figure, Saul, is the intruder. A woman participates in the episode, but only as an accomplice to David, never as the instigator of division between brothers. In fact, Saul made David and Jonathan legal brothers by giving his daughter Michal to David as wife. She was pivotal in resisting Saul's murderous rage toward David when, like Jonathan, she assisted in David's escape. The law of the father, Saul (who not coincidentally had been anointed king directly by God through the prophet Samuel), dictates that the brothers be separated. Saul's jealousy begins in the male-centered realm of battle, about which the people sang "Saul hath slain his thousands, and David his ten thousands" (1 Samuel 18:7), but it extends to male-centered family relations when Saul attacks Jonathan's love of David (who not coincidentally had been secretly anointed king by Samuel after God was displeased with Saul): "Then Saul's anger was kindled against Jonathan, and he said unto him, Thou son of the perverse rebellious woman, do not I know that thou hast chosen the son of Jesse to thine own confusion, and unto the confusion of thy mother's nakedness?" (I Samuel 20: 30). Saul pledges to kill David and to deny any inheritance to his own biological son until David's death. Two patriarchal authorities clash here over what is appropriate. The legal king, Saul, forbids the love between Jonathan and David, but the absolute ruler, God himself, approves of it as a source of increased strength and future legitimacy for his newly chosen king, David.

In Saul's story, earthly, legal, patriarchal authority recognizes fraternity through the accomplishment of great feats in war and through marriage to women. Male-male alliances for him must be grounded in identification with another's skills (one joins forces with equally great warriors) and mutual gain (one seeks marriages that increase family wealth and power, or inheritances that provide its continuity). However, God's sanction of David and Jonathan's friendship transcends those signifiers of masculinity and male privilege. He overrules Saul's attention to the secondary signifiers of masculinity and seems to smile on the young men's love for one another because they disdain the secondary signs of masculinity. They lose legal status in the king's eyes in order to defend their fraternal bond, a bond based not on mutual material gain but on empathy and mutual respect. This biblical story is quintessentially concerned with competing modes of legitimating masculinity.

Circling back to "La intrusa" and the Nilsens' desire to live a life "de hombres entre hombres," it becomes clear that murder serves as a catalyst to the brothers' achieving a transcendent bond. Having embraced in their most radical illegal act, they overcome their former dependence on the secondary signifiers of masculinity (overt heterosexuality) and establish a sublime link directly to the master signifier, Man itself, free of all threat from femininity. Because legal patriarchy (masculinist kings and laws) is so often confused with transcendent patriarchy (masculinist notions of God), the sublime moment for these characters will always carry with it the stigma of transgression. Their obsessive, mutual love brings them too close together for comfort in the social system, and yet the differences between them intrude, never allowing them to stay close enough in their search for transcendent masculine identity.

Borges closes "La intrusa" without returning to comment on its embedded narrative structure. After having peeled away the layers of access to the tale in the first part, the narrator simply leaves the story bare at the end. Readers have entered the Nilsens' scene and by the last line of the text have lost any of the distancing perspective which the narrator had so carefully set up in the introduction. Where does this shift leave us in relation to the distinction between crime fiction and detective fiction? What is the status of the crime, disclosed to us in/as the story's conclusion?

The association of Cristián and Eduardo with David and Jonathan makes kings of hoodlums insofar as they defend fraternal bonds in spite of laws against murder. They find a form of legitimacy of their mutual desire and identification, transcending their embeddedness in a social order which, while generally approving of misogyny, still promotes the degree of separation among men necessary for them to marry, procreate, and produce economically. The crime story of "La intrusa," focalized through the brothers' sublime devotion to one another, establishes their murder of Juliana as the successful resolution of an emotional problem. The detective story, relying on reader investment in challenging that notion of success, and focalized through a sense of justice that should apply equally to the brothers and to Juliana, seeks to reinforce conformity to legality. It attends to all the contradictions and gaps in the Nilsens' illusion of merged identities, and accuses their ignorance of the difference between love of self and other for motivating their horrific behavior.

When "La intrusa" ends in mythmaking fashion, with the murder that the author sees as inevitable and obvious, readers and the narrator are encircled in the brothers' desire to eliminate all barriers to what has become for the Nilsens an expression of pure masculinity : the uninhibited embrace of men. By never returning to question the validity of the story, however, the narrator reveals that embrace to be perilously deceptive. Although Juliana's death supports the possibility and desirability of a self-reliant male community, a community established in ancient religious lore, that community is suspect. The differential class, familial, and authoritative positions that men occupy, even men as identified with one another as David and Jonathan or Cristián and Eduardo, make transcendent unity impossible. Masculinity as these brothers define it, the detective reader in "La intrusa" discovers, provides no safe haven for vulnerable male egos. It offers the promise of security, but any attempt to express it unequivocally calls into question the collective origins of our social dependence on it. It becomes unsustainable by definition when it is placed in the realm of the sublime because it cannot be sustained in the face of differences among individual men. As we leave Cristián and Eduardo in their embrace and their "olvido," the narrator winks to the reader over the textual body. His ironic construction of an inevitable tale constitutes a metatextual embrace which sacrifices the veracity and emotional validity of the story itself in favor of a socially critical awareness of this type of masculinity's fundamental sterility.

Ostensibly a piece of crime fiction from the murderers' point of view, "La intrusa" actually offers a study in detection. Borges discloses the confused origins of the myth of pure masculinity, reveals the inherent contradictions of male-only community formation, and explores the psychology of murderous men. The Nilsens' story is predictable because it is a story of masculine defensiveness, told and retold across generations until it *seems* inevitable. "La intrusa," taken as Borges's metatextual commentary on the Nilsens' story, implies that their approach to defending against threats to masculinity, their sacrifice of women, is not inevitable; active reading reveals the old story's false promises regarding masculinity's enclosed self-reliance.

CHAPTER THREE

Fantasies of Erotic Domination

Armonía Somers's "El Despojo"

Armonía Somers's "El despojo" ("Plunder")[1] portrays masculine subjectivity as it passes through a variety of relationships with feminine figures. Narrated as a dream sequence, the story organizes itself around the memory of a murder; the sections of the triptych represent a regression through psychological stages, moving from homoerotic motivations for violence against women to the self/other opposition of rape and finally to a mother/son scene in which the protagonist's desire for return to the womb and his subsequent fear of penetration by an other (here, by a breast which feeds him) leads to his own death. The sections, "La araña" [Spider], "La violación" [Rape], and "El enjuiciado" [The Judged One],[2] each examine one type of male-female relationship. All of the relationships are defined by the male protagonist's obsession with separating his subjectivity from any identification with women. His encounters with women reveal the mechanisms of fantasies of erotic domination, and Somers's use of the "marvelous real" emphasizes the phantasmatic structure of violent forms of masculinity.

Somers (b. 1917), whose first novel, *La mujer desnuda*, was published in 1950, belongs by chronology to the Uruguayan literary generation of 1945. Her work is part of the "irrupciones experimentales" ("experimental irruptions") initiated between World Wars by the availability of Spanish translations of vanguard works by Eliot and Kafka, Joyce and Faulkner, and by a break with established aesthetic norms (Rama 1964).[3] Although Angel Rama lists Somers in a group of authors who together represent an Uruguayan shift to "invención fantasmagórica," he describes her work in a separate article as "insólito, ajeno, desconcertante, repulsivo, y a la vez increíblemente fascinante . . . la obra narrativa más inusual que ha conocido la historía de nuestra literatura" (Rama 1963 [uncanny, strange, disconcerting, repulsive and at once incredibly fascinating . . . the most unusual prose that the history of our literature has known]). Somers's combination of the charm of the fantastic mode with a more brutal (and implicitly more critical) focus on the cruel—sexual violation, the indifference of God, the visceral reality of human experience—sets her apart from other Southern Cone authors of psychological and existential narratives in the same period (Onetti, Sábato, Arlt, or even Borges). She effects this combination in unapologetically direct language within dense narrative structures.[4]

"El despojo" epitomizes Somers's particular—Rama would say "peculiar"—interests as an author with no desire to be categorized or anthologized along with the other recognized members of the "Generation of '45." A haunting portrayal of the causes and effects of a masculine subjectivity based on male fantasies of domination, it revolves around the protagonist's memory of having murdered a lover in the past. While other writers of the period—particularly Arlt, Sábato, Onetti, and as I argued in the previous chapter, Borges—have also addressed the topic of how masculine subjectivity is allied with hierarchy and violence, Somers' story is unique in that it points to the existence of an unexamined feminine reality, the recognition of which alone might provide a different way to conceptualize subjectivity.

"El despojo" is a particularly effective story in that it is written by a woman about the victimization of women, but from the male victimizer's perspective. Somers does not set herself up as a literary vindicator of women's suffering, but rather as the rational author of an irrational and violent dream sequence that follows an unnamed male protagonist's flight from a farm where he had been a laborer. Each of the three sections of the story describes an encounter with a different woman: "La araña" recounts the protagonist's sexual relationship with the farm owner's wife, introducing issues of homoeroticism and class relations; more directly addressing male/female power imbalances, "La violación" narrates the protagonist's rape of a sleeping young girl whom he encounters while seeking food; and finally "El enjuiciado" presents masculine responses to maternity, facing the main character with a sterile woman whose longing for a child has produced milk in her breasts, milk with which she nurses the adult fugitive.

The murder in this story occurs outside of the plot and is only referred to in the middle section, "La violación," as a memory whose most powerful visual images have been stirred up by the rape of the girl. The protagonist is walking away from the rape scene at the *panadería,* meditating on the tendency of women to leave things with him when they—for any reason—are separated from him: the farmer's wife left with him the image of her husband sexually assaulting her, and the *panaderita* left with him the guilt-producing image of her tightly belted waist as well as a vision of the earthy colors of the shop. He associates these traces with those left by the woman he had killed, apparently long before the episode at the farm

> Los colores del trigo, del pan, del gato, del pelo, todos la misma cosa terrible. Ese color se le incrustaría siempre en los huesos, en la fatalidad de los huesos que habitaban su carne. Había amado cierta vez a una mujer de ojos amarillos. Tenía con ella una especie de obsesión sumergida, no poderle permitir que los cerrara. Lo invadía el terror de que ella poblara su minuto con otra imagen que no fuera la suya, y la obligaba a vibrar con la mirada duramente abierta, en una dilatación sin tregua. Cierta noche de amor, después de haberla poseído en esa forma bajo una luz intensa, había terminado pidiéndole que dejara de mirarlo. Ella no pudo. El tuvo que bajarle los párpados con los dedos y sujetar sus mandíbulas con un pañuelo. Le quedaron tres pestañas doradas, en las yemas. La mujer se le había escapado no sabía él por qué misteriosa puerta. ¿Qué hacer con tres pestañas doradas, restituirlas, arrojarlas al fuego? Hasta cuando se van en esa forma insisten en dejar algo, piensa. (52)

> [The colors of the wheat, the bread, the cat, the hair, all terribly the same. That color would encrust itself forever in his bones, in the fatality of the bones which inhabited his flesh. He had once loved a woman with yellow eyes. He had a kind of submerged obsession for her, not being able to allow her to close those eyes. The idea that she might fill one moment with any image other than his invaded him with terror, and he made her vibrate while keeping her gaze cruelly open, in an unceasing dilation. One night of love, after having possessed her like that under an intense light, he had finally asked her to stop looking at him. She couldn't. He had to lower her eyelids with his fingers and tie her jaw shut with a handkerchief. Three golden eyelashes remained on his fingertips. He didn't know through what mysterious door she had escaped. What was there to do with three golden eyelashes? Put them back in place? Throw them in the fire? Even when they go away like that, they insist on leaving something behind, he thinks. (my translation)]

This death, having occurred during intercourse, represents the violence of male-female relationships in which the man feels free to demand that the woman serve his needs while he remains wholly unaware of and unresponsive to hers. Since this memory is focalized through the protagonist, there is no objective evidence with which readers might better understand the dynamics of his relationship to this woman. All that is known is that she died while having sex with him, and that he feels responsible.

In spite of the possibility that this woman's death was natural, the protagonist considers it an act of which others would probably accuse him, and the narrator's rhetorical approach to the topic—placing much of this segment within parentheses, as if it were simply a tangential episode in the character's life—actually alerts readers to the power and attraction of the repressed memories. The character supposedly had loved this woman, and yet the cause of her death, symbolized by the remaining eyelashes, is called a "bendito recuerdo" [blessed memory]:

> Siempre se le aparece en el momento en que irá a dormirse (la cintura de la hija del panadero), entreverado con las últimas cosas de la vigilia (la cintura se ensancha, desaparece), que es la mejor forma de evocar aquellas terroríficas pestañas. (La muelen a golpes y ella no responde. Luego se le hinchan los pechos, se vuelve enigmática, enorme y dolorosa como la luna llena. Quizá sea demasiado estrecha de huesos, y se les quede también a ellos entre los dedos, con los ojos endurecidos y sin pedirles nada. ¿Pero qué culpa puede caberle a él en todo eso, tan lejano, que ocurrirá después de tanto tiempo?) (52)

> [It always comes to him just when he is about to fall asleep (the baker girl's waist), glimpsed among the last wakeful images (the waist expands, disappears), which is the best way to evoke those terrifying eyelashes. (They beat her but she doesn't answer. Then her breasts swell, she becomes enigmatic, enormous and painful like the full moon. Perhaps her bones are too narrow, and she, too, ends up in their arms, with hardened eyes, without asking for anything. But how is he to blame for all that, so far away, after so much time?)

It is clear from the last question in this citation that the protagonist is preoccupied with his guilt about the death and with the strength of his need to have been seen by a woman. To be looked at so intently, a need later represented by the eyelashes, means being—for a time, at least—the exclusive object of the woman's attention. The fact that the woman had met this need is a comforting memory for the protagonist, but at the same time, the resulting death makes the memory *terrorífica* because it reveals the violence inherent in his demands.

The tripartite structure of "El despojo" offers an organized way to consider some of the factors involved in male violence against women. With each section centering on a particular manifestation of gender relations, the story implicitly explores the effects of the murder on the protagonist's subjectivity. The main scenes from each of the sections are so powerfully described that there is a sense of moments frozen in time, and the freeze-frame or tableau effect brings those scenes into the nonlinear simultaneity of psychological realism. These scenes are not just events through which the protagonist passes on his way to elsewhere; rather, they are emblematic of how his subjectivity is (has been) always already constructed through relationships with women.

Somers's protagonist passes through the stages of masculine development outlined in Jessica Benjamin's *The Bonds of Love: Psychoanalysis, Feminism, and the Problem of Domination* (1988). Basing her argument on Nancy Chodorow's description of the oedipal principle of masculine identity as rejection of the maternal figure ("I am nothing like she who cares for me"), Benjamin argues that patterns of adult erotic domination originate in this repudiation of the mother. She distinguishes between a healthy differentiation (the maintenance of tension between distinct, yet equally valued, subjects) and repudiation: "In the oedipal experience of losing the inner continuity with women [mother] and encountering instead the idealized, acutely desirable object outside, the image of woman as the dangerous, regressive siren is born. The counterpart of this image is the wholly idealized, masterful subject [father] who can withstand or conquer her" (164). "El despojo" portrays its protagonist's attempts to conform to this pattern of the development of masculine subjectivity. Each section of the story shows different effects of the repudiation of femininity in the service of establishing the "masterful male subject," revealing the mechanisms of what Benjamin describes as the fantasy of erotic domination: "Since the subject cannot accept his dependency on someone he cannot control, the solution is to subjugate and enslave the other—to make him give that recognition without recognizing him in return. The primary consequence of the inability to reconcile dependence with independence, then, is the transformation of need for the other into domination of him. For Freud and Hegel this is precisely what happens in the 'state of nature'" (54). In its focus on the violence and rigidity of fantasies of domination, this story cries out for readers to analyze, as Benjamin has done, the fallacies inherent in the cultural imperative that masculinity be equated with violence, absolute independence, and the objectification of feminine others.

"El despojo" is narrated in third person, with a sequence of preterite verb forms that tell of the protagonist's physical journey: "Huyó de la granja al amanecer. (42) [He fled from the farm at dawn]. ... Reptó un largo trecho entre las mieses (42) [He crawled a long way between the rows of corn]. ... Avanzó con dificultad" (48) [He moved forward with difficulty]. This progression is often interrupted, however, by an abrupt shift into the present tense. In "La araña" the shift signals a memory, the description of "el segundo de terror" in which the protagonist had waited for the *amo* (boss) to fall asleep so that he, the worker, could climb into bed with the farm owner's wife. In "La violación" the shift into present tense introduces the narrator into the protagonist's thought-world, and presents his suppositions about the girl's reactions to the rape. In the third section, which presents the mother figure, there is less use of tense change and more (although still not much) use of dialogue.

Throughout the story an element of indeterminability about the sequence and reality of events underscores the fact that they are interrelated by the protagonist's musings and because he refers frequently to a feeling of being in a dream:

> ... era demasiado nebuloso todo aquello, como si no le hubiera sucedido nunca. Estaba tan aclimatado en los hechos vulgares, que toda su vida había acabado acusando de ensueño ridículo a la maravilla. (59)
>
> [... it was all too clouded, as if it had never happened to him. He was so accustomed to ordinary events that all of his life he had accused wonderment of being absurd dreaming.]

The lack of transitions between sections unites the frozen moments not only within the movement of the story line, but also by having them function together to demonstrate various factors in gender relations which simultaneously contribute to and threaten the protagonist's identity as male. Although they should be taken as interconnected parts of a whole depiction of gender relations as seen by a male character, each of the three sections requires its own analysis for a discussion of the relevance of Somers's story to the construction of masculine subjectivity by way of the murder of women.

Homoeroticism

In the first of the three sections of "El despojo," the protagonist leaves the farm at dawn the morning after he witnesses his lover and her husband having sex.

For the previous four months, the main character had been sharing a bed with the two of them, hiding behind a chest in the room until the husband began to snore and then joining the wife who lay beside the sleeping *amo*. After making love in "una especie de evaporación de los cuerpos" [a kind of evaporation of bodies] the protagonist would return to his hiding place, wait until the husband left the room in the morning, and then leave himself—"pisándole las huellas al otro" [following in the other's footstep]—to do his work on the farm.

The night before he leaves the farm, however, the protagonist inadvertently makes a noise when shifting positions behind the chest. The husband wakes up, lights a lamp, and looks carefully around the room. The shadow created by his head as he holds the lamp is compared to a gigantic spider—"una araña sin medida." Finding nothing which might have made the noise, the husband turns his attention to the woman beside him. The narrator has already revealed that this is the only time that the married couple has sexual relations during the entire period of the protagonist's stay on the farm, and that the worker feels totally responsible for having wakened the husband and causing him to desire his wife:

> De pronto, los pelos del techo tuvieron un descenso brusco, y se empezó a proyectar hacia arriba una poderosa nuca rítmica. La araña había descendido sobre la mujer y se la estaba devorando, sexo a sexo. (46)

> [Suddenly the hairs on the ceiling descended brusquely, and a powerfully rhythmic neck began to be projected up above. The spider had descended onto the woman and was devouring her, sex to sex. (my translation)]

The man is left with an impression of an unexpected and violent attack by a powerful husband on a passive wife. He feels guilty for having created her suffering by his presence in the couple's room, and yet he quickly justifies his decision to flee rather than to continue making love to her in secret or to defend his honor against the amo:

> Pero, de pronto, cae en la cuenta de lo ridículo de sus cavilaciones. ¿Qué es una mujer, una sola mujer que va a morir de ser mujer, si todas las demás morirán de lo mismo? Noche a noche son devoradas en silencio, a grandes saltos, como ella. (47)

> [But, suddenly, he realizes the ridiculousness of his worries. What is a woman, just one woman who is going to die of being a woman, if all of them will die of the same thing? Night after night they are devoured in silence, mounted like her.]

The protagonist deserts his lover even though, refusing to release him from their last embrace, she begs him to comfort her:

> Cuando él intentó desasirse, ella lo apretó como nunca, casi hasta la asfixia. Tuvo que forcejar como un demente para volver al arca. (46)
>
> [When he tried to pull free, she held tight as never before, almost suffocating him. He had to shove like a crazy man to return to the chest.]

He rationalizes his choice to leave by generalizing her situation, by telling himself that all women are perpetually submitted to unwanted and brutal sexual assaults, by convincing himself that this state of affairs is unavoidable.

The second step in his effort to free himself from responsibility and guilt for the wife's desperation is to identify with the enemy. At first, when the protagonist had been hiding behind the furniture while the husband searched the room with his lantern, the humiliation was his alone. Crouching like a coward, terrified of being seen, the man had faced his own powerlessness. Later, however, he finds that by joining forces with the husband, by thinking of himself as a fellow despoiler of women, he gains the strength to leave his lover:

> Y de golpe, con la fuerza de un definitivo alumbramiento, comenzó a sentir que él y la araña habían sido los verdaderos en amarse en la sombra, formando una apretada unidad en torno a la víctima. Cada uno para despojarla a su manera, eso era todo. Y ella, la infeliz, optando por el mayor engaño, el más dulce. Fue precisamente eso, el saber que amaba al hombre, el confesarse que el hombre sólo se ama a sí mismo y en los otros hombres. (47)
>
> [And all at once, with the strength of a definitive flash, he began to feel that he and the spider had been the true lovers in the shadow, forming a tight unity around the victim. Each one to despoil her in his own way, that was all. And she, the unfortunate one, opting for the better deception, the sweetest. It was precisely that, knowing that he loved the man, confessing that man only loves himself and in other men. (my translation)]

This is a complex realization, with at least three major issues to be considered. The first sentence of the citation works in Spanish as a birth metaphor: "con la fuerza de un definitivo alumbramiento" in one reading relates to a flash of knowledge, enlightenment; however, it also recalls the phrase *dar a luz,* which literally means "to bring to light," but which idiomatically is "to give birth." That is, the thoughts which follow this sentence show the protagonist giving birth to himself, in this case as a man, not as a female-identified victim.

This birth involves two ways in which the protagonist unites himself to the amo. On the one hand, there is a link being made between men as companions in abusing women : "cado uno para despojarla a su manera" [each one to despoil her in his own way] implies that males are individuals but that they share the right to abuse women. On the other hand, the claim is made that the men actually are showing love for themselves through one another and by way of their use of women: "el hombre sólo se ama a sí mismo y en los otros hombres" [man only loves himself and in other men]. For the protagonist of this story, those two issues are inextricably united. He feels very strongly the class difference between himself and the married couple. The amo had routinely abused the worker in the fields: when, to recoup the rest he could not get while keeping vigil every night in the wife's bedroom, the worker observed "su gran siesta de holgazán" [his wonderful loafer's nap], it became a sleep "de la que despertó muchas veces en las puntas de las botas del amo" (45) [from which he was awakened many times by the toe of the boss's boot]). The worker, like the woman, is at the farmer's mercy. They belong to him as property to be used at will.

In order to distance himself from the position of victim, in order to maintain his power as a man, the protagonist had responded to the boss's wife's invitations to join her in the bed which would hold the three of them. The adultery, committed in the presence of the husband, was an equalizing gesture insofar as it placed the protagonist on the same level with the farm owner—literally (in the same bed together) and sexually (with access to the same woman). The *araña* scene, however, proved the fragility and precariousness of the worker's position. He was made small by his socio-economic lack of legitimate claim to the woman, and by his fear of the boss. The only way out of this identity as victim is to transfer his hatred of the amo onto the woman, and his love for her onto the amo. By shifting his identifications and loyalties, the protagonist joins forces with the powerful. He becomes a "real man" again by denying his concrete ties to women—to all victims. He privileges gender over class identity, and power over love or sympathy, in order to establish an image of an independent self.

Published more than a decade before Borges's "La intrusa," Somers's story captures just as effectively the libidinal economy in which men protect their relationships to other men at the expense of women's lives. In Borges' text, the seemingly absurd sacrifice of Juliana resolves the chaos introduced into the Nilsen household by her arrival. When she was present, the equilibrium was upset: authority, property, and truth were all challenged. The younger brother

Eduardo had every justification for being appalled that the elder would kill his lover, and yet he shows gratitude instead. Just as in "La araña," then, the issue is not one of simple self-defense or defense of one's property; rather, it is an issue of upholding masculine identity even within otherwise intolerable power (or class) differences.

By aligning himself with the older brother in "La intrusa" or with the farm owner in "La araña," the male who feels powerless before other males is able to construct an illusion of solidarity with the strong and superiority over the weak. The solidarity gives him the strength to kill, and it is his very need of such strength which reveals his violence as self-directed. He must "kill" the victim in himself in order to resist his fear *of other men* (best seen in the class differences of "El despojo") as well as his fear of *loving other men* (best seen in "La intrusa").

Rape and Differentiation

During the *araña* scene, the main character concludes that women are made to suffer sexual assault and men are made to commit it; the *violación* segment of Somers's story follows that conclusion by narrating the protagonist's assault on another woman. "La violación" represents an effort to consolidate and solidify identification with the amo at women's expense. The effort, as will become evident, does not work; indeed, it cannot work.

Rape is the attempt to establish male rights over women's bodies regardless of women's desire. It is a violent act against the body but more so against the person. A physical manifestation of the rapist's need to establish masculine identity through disregard of feminine subjectivity, rape demonstrates the perpetrator's imperviousness to the other's demands for recognition. Every assault on women designed to deny their subjectivity, however, inherently validates the importance of women in the construction of masculine subjectivity; the strength of the need to erase feminine subjectivity indicates the power of its existence in the first place.[5]

The rape of the panaderita is described in graphic detail, beginning with the man's physical arousal upon seeing her sleeping on a pile of empty bags amid inviting loaves of bread (he has been travelling now for some time, and is very hungry):

> Desde los tobillos hasta la nuca, los runruneos de la muchacha y el gato le están caldeando por dentro, en una especia de monstruoso sinapismo que se le extiende y aprieta hasta desollarle vivo. Y ya no más batalla. (48–49)

[The girl and the purring cats are heating him up inside from his ankles to his neck in a sort of monstrous upheaval that extends all over and presses until it skins him alive. Enough fighting.]

The experience of arousal is described here as passive. The phrase "Y ya no más batalla" [enough fighting] indicates a degree of resistance on the protagonist's part to the "heat" produced in him by the sleeping girl. In this sense, the rape scene is similar to the murder in Dostoevsky's *Crime and Punishment;* Raskolnikov feels led to kill while in a dream state, or suffering from a feverish condition which excites his senses at the same time that it dulls his will to resist violent impulses. In "La violación" the rape results from an irresistible impulse to erase the young girl's subjectivity. The rapist thinks of her as a hated object, not as the object of sexual desire:

[E]l nunca ha sentido un deseo tan feroz de aniquilar a alguien y una incapacidad tan total de defenderse de sí mismo. . . . Es necesario ese furor, aun a trueque de olvidarse de muchas cosas. La está odiando mientras la despoja, la odia cada vez más adentro, va a atravesarle las vértebras y a dejarla clavada con su sexo sobre los sacos. (48–50)

[He has never felt such a fierce desire to annihilate someone and such a total incapacity to defend himself from himself. . . . That rage is necessary, in exchange for forgetting many things. He is hating her while he despoils her, he hates her more and more inside, he is going to pierce her vertebrae and leave her pinned against the sacks by his sex.][6]

The rapist's motives are caught in an unresolved contradiction; in his desire to "annihilate" the girl, he reveals susceptibility to her presence. He rapes her in order to deny the strength of emotion which her peaceful sleep had aroused in him. His hatred for her seems to result from his own subjectivity, split between a desiring self and a self subject to desire. The unexamined impulses from which he cannot defend himself, then, indicate a divided subjectivity for which the hatred offers unification. In "pinning her by his sex" against the sacks of bread, the man recovers an effectivity at the girl's expense.

A disruptive thought immediately challenges his recovery of a unified subjectivity, however:

Mas ¿qué le ha hecho ella? Fue al cabo de esa pregunta cuando dio en mirarle el rostro."(50)

[But what has she done to him? It was after this question that he looked her in the face.]

Although the rape is an attempt to deny the girl's effects on him, the main character cannot ultimately free himself of the ethical obligation to recognize her as a fellow subject. In an effort to apologize, he begins to kiss her pubis, trying to introduce passion and awareness of her pleasures into the scene. The only explanation for this behavior—in relation to the urge he has just followed to erase her—is that not atoning for the rape would be to remain in the state of denial, which would be yet another form of being controlled by the desire (sexual or violent) the girl has created in him.

This sequence of actions—the rape described as stabbing, and uninvited oral sex meant to soothe—is impossible to explain except in terms of the search for control in self/other relations. Wielding his penis to "annihilate" a virgin offers power, but not an unchallenged one; implicit in any rape is that the victim has power over the perpetrator, being the subject which he feels must be denied. Therefore, by attempting to atone for the violent attack through soft kisses, the man hopes to forestall that conclusion. By counteracting his denial of her subjectivity, he seeks a double erasure of her effects on him; in admitting guilt before being accused, the rapist regains control over the rape itself. The attempt to deny his own denial, however, makes the girl's presence even more present:

> Iba sintiendo un gusto metálico bajo la lengua y cierta humedad expesa en los labios. Se pasó el dorso de la mano y vio la sangre que le habían ofrendado. . . . Ya se había sorbido toda la sangre de la muchacha y empezaba a sentir necesidad de escupir su propia saliva, verla fuera de él hecha una bolita en el suelo. (51)
>
> [He felt a metallic taste under his tongue and a certain heavy wetness on his lips. He passed the back of his hand across them and saw the blood which they had offered him. . . . He had already swallowed all of the girl's blood and he was beginning to feel a need to spit his own saliva, to see it outside of himself, made into a little ball on the ground. (my translation)]

The girl leaves traces—the image of her waist and the taste of her blood—with the rapist, who would like to be rid of her when he leaves the panadería, but the mixture in his mouth of her blood and his saliva remains as evidence of an indestructible link between men and women.

Somers's use of bodily fluids to highlight the impossibility of absolute distinctions between subject and object parallels Julia Kristeva's explication (1982) of the abject. The subject's dependence on the object for identification is exposed by the abject, that type of object which the subject tries to ingest or expel. The abject includes blood, saliva, tears, waste, vomit, and so on, and is neither wholly a part of the subject's self-defining body nor distinct from that body. Since the abject is both inside and outside of the subject's body, it threatens the subject's identity and boundaries by making ever present the possibility of dissolving the integrity of self/other distinctions.

In "El despojo" the protagonist's urge to spit on the ground reveals his continued and still unfulfilled desire to separate his masculine subjectivity from any traces of femininity. In wanting to see saliva expelled from his own mouth, the character demonstrates the futility of the kind of othering the rape was meant to achieve; he might spit out the traces of the girl's blood, but that act would simultaneously be the expulsion of his own fluids. The feminine other exists, then, both outside and inside him.

The Desire of the Mother

How can masculine subjectivity be (re)constructed once this principle of mutuality has been exposed? The last section of Somers's triptych depicts a return to the pre-oedipal state and, at the same time, a progression forward to a reassessment of the mother/son relationship in terms of the mother's desire. Because the protagonist's death follows his encounter with the mother figure, this section can be understood positively as a final lesson in reforming gender relations, or negatively as the ultimate impasse caused by human differences.

"El enjuiciado"(The Judged One) opens with the same man who fled the farm and raped the *panaderita* being awakened by a third woman, a *campesina* "de edad indefinida" [of an indefinite age]. She calls him "chiquillo" (little one) and invites him to ride on top of the hay in the wheelbarrow she is pushing. The man, looking at her from beneath the bridge under which he had been sleeping, finds her image comforting, and he walks up to meet her. Joining her on the path, however, he realizes the absurdity of her invitation, given the size of the wheelbarrow. None of his disbelieving smiles seems to affect the woman, so he finally gets into the wheelbarrow, forcing his adult body to conform to the small space. The man's acceptance of a passive role is surprising, given the violence of the first two sections of this short story. His approximation of a fetal position, his contentedness in being carried along, and his willingness to obey the campesina's will in spite of his own doubts all seem to contradict this character's drive to obtain control.

In another sense, however, this passivity confirms Benjamin's thesis that male subjects display contradictory impulses toward the mother when she is seen as all-powerful: they simultaneously want to annihilate her and to establish union with her. The fear of losing her governs both of these desires; annihilation ultimately denies her difference, appropriating her power for the self, and absolute union incorporates her into the desiring subject's identity.[7] The larger frame of "El despojo," which contains all three sections, reflects this masculine ambivalence toward the mother; that is, the scenes of the story occur as a man flees the horror of the "spider" on the farm. His abuse of women must be understood within the context of the unexamined fear of his own "smallness" in relation to the idealized power of the amo (here, as idealized father).

The narrator describes the protagonist's impressions as he rides in the cart, enjoying giving himself over to being led, even if the situation requires him to sacrifice comfort and freedom of movement. Soon the woman stops walking and prepares a place for the two of them to lie down in the grass together. Crying silently, she unbuttons her blouse to free a breast and begins to feed the man as she would an infant. The protagonist continues in his passive state, accepting her actions and conforming his own to complement them.

As the narrator, focalizing the description through the protagonist, observes, the rhythmic adjustment with which the two characters accommodate each other is made by their bodies without the intervention of conscious will. This encounter is clearly in the realm of the preverbal, approximating that undifferentiated, fully physical space occupied by mother and child that Kristeva (1980, 133) calls the *chora*, the "receptacle, unnamable, improbable, hybrid, anterior to naming, to the one, to the father and consequently maternally connoted."

Given that both figures in Somers's nursing tableau are adults and strangers to each other, however, the man's thoughts continually interrupt the scene; even though his desire to resist this experience of the chora is momentarily overcome, it is signaled nonetheless: "esa forma de olvido tan desigual para cada uno de los dos y que jamás podrían transferirse" (55) [endless forgetfulness that is so different for each of them and never to be shared]. The reference to an insurmountable difference in mother/child roles, especially in relation to what must be forgotten, introduces a concept very close to Kristeva's notion of the semiotic: the set of presignifying (in this case of development in reverse, perhaps, unsignifying) impulses working in and through the infant's body—defined in the maternal relation but located in/on the child.

This scene offers more than just a wish-fulfilling return to an undifferentiated relation with the mother, for at the moment of his most complete surrender to being nursed, the protagonist's thoughts return to resentment; he feels penetrated, and so he begins to summarize the event as if it were really he who had made demands of the woman, and as if his sucking at her breast had been an active effort to rob and debase her. The shift to a consideration of who makes demands on whom, who possesses, who penetrates, signals here the unavoidable repressions effected with entry into the symbolic, which both Kristeva and Lacan understand to be the ordering system whereby hierarchy, dichotomy, and social and power relations are articulated.

The man is shocked not only that he would be subjected to an invasion of liquid from an other's body, but also that he could be led to accept and even enjoy it. This reaction exemplifies the semiotic as both precondition and sporadic accompaniment of subjectivity and symbolic functioning (Kristeva 1980); the semiotic overflows its symbolic containment. At this point of the reestablishment of the symbolic, the man begins to reconstruct a description of the breastfeeding as if it had been a demand on his part that the campesina open her shirt in the first place; his revised account exposes his determination to dominate even in the face of his own potential enjoyment of unity with the maternal.

The same pattern, in which his interpretation of events serves to bolster the dominant fiction of masculine power and independence, is evident in the first two sections of "El despojo" with the protagonist's cold self-interest when he leaves the farmer's wife and the savagery with which he rapes the panaderita. This drive to domination, however, proves absolutely self-destructive in the end because the man is so determined to understand all relationships with women in terms of power struggle that he is unable to accept, much less enjoy, any expressions of feminine desire.

The spontaneous production of breast milk introduces aspects of magical realism into the narrative. The campesina recalls the Earth-Mother, in relation to whom the male protagonist momentarily relinquishes his obsessive hold on division, difference, and domination. She brings him back to the earth, to a recognition of his own materiality, through her milk. Somers's magical realism is the presencing of a quintessentially feminine desire which has been denied expression in the male Symbolic. When the protagonist asks how she produces milk without having had a baby and the campesina responds that "Ocurrió de tanto desearlo" (58) [It happened because I wanted it so badly], the man then wonders why other men had not helped her satisfy the desire to be pregnant: "¿Es decir, pues, que no te adivinaron ellos tampoco, que no te amaron nunca?" (58) [You mean, they didn't guess either, they never loved you?]. The campesina explains in a few words the problem and why the magical "solution"—the nursing scene—had to occur: "No saben, no pueden—contestó con dureza, quitándole el pecho y escondiéndolo" (58) [They don't know, they can't," she answered firmly, taking her breast away from him and hiding it]. The protagonist realizes that the "magical" power of feminine desire has "invaded" him (through the milk); he also sees that, along with the anonymous masculine *ellos* [they], he has denied that desire through ignorance combined with the will to have power over it. At the moment of this realization, however, the campesina closes her blouse, withholding her breast and leaving the male character wanting, lacking.

This last scene of the story, in which the man is confronted with the campesina's desire, also includes his death. His altered relationship to the flute which he has been carrying and playing throughout his journey symbolizes his progress toward death. The flute has represented continuity among scenes in the short story, appearing first as he flees from the amo's farm. Clearly a phallic symbol, the flute relates closely to the protagonist's fear of losing masculine control over life situations: "no podía liberarse nunca del terror de haberlo perdido" (44) [he was never free from terror at the thought of losing it]. He cleans it more carefully than he does his own body, and while playing music on it, he fantasizes about the destruction of his enemies.

In the final scene of the story, after the encounter with the mother figure, the flute is described as being "fiel como su sexo" [as loyal as his penis], explicitly illustrating the connection this character has made all along between penis and phallic power. Right after the nursing scene, however, the man drops the flute while considering the changes that all of the women have made in him:

> Aquellas míseras mujeres lo habían transmigrado a tantas formas. Aquellas mujeres . . . Quiso volver a pensarlas a todas, desde el primer deseo de la vida. Pero en ese instante su caramillo le resbaló a lo largo del muslo y cayó sordamente en la hierba.
>
> —Extraño: no quiero, no puedo levantarlo. (59)
>
> [Those awful women had changed him in so many ways. Those women . . . He tried to think of them all again, from his very first desire. But in that instant his flute slid down along the length of his thigh and fell dully into the grass. "Strange: I can't, I don't want to pick it up." (my translation)]

Lack of desire and lack of strength to pick the flute back up signals impotence. The protagonist voluntarily relinquishes his connection to phallic dominance.

Tragically, in the face of his recognition that the campesina has the power to leave when the nursing situation no longer satisfies *her*, the man has no basis upon which to know himself as a subject. He cannot recognize feminine desire and be a man at the same time because of his unrelenting faith in the necessity of patterns of domination. He has been defeated by the mother's desire—a desire that does not always depend on him.

The protagonist dies at this moment, and the narrator offers a simultaneously critical and sympathetic epitaph:

> Era, en realidad, un huésped vulgar para la muerte. Tenía aún en las uñas la tierra y el estiércol de la granja. (59)
>
> [He was, really, a vulgar candidate for death. He still had the dirt and grime of the farm under his fingernails.]

In addition to the traces left to him by the women, the farm filth he still carries signifies the traces not only of his subordinate relationship to the amo, but of his final submission to the materiality of physical dependence (on earth and mother). He is just another person lacking the power with which he had formerly assumed his penis (and flute) would endow him. The physical presence of a penis had supported his imaginary phallic power throughout, but the campesina's lack (Freudian lack of the "penis" that her nonexistent baby would have been for her) is transformed, simply by her overwhelming desire, into the material, maternal presence of breast milk.

The impotence of Somers's male character, who desperately holds on to an imaginary power, contrasts to the plenitude of the peasant woman, whose imaginary motherhood produces the milk with which she feeds him. Only within a logic of domination would the feeding scene have to be interpreted as an attack; penetration (by breast or by penis) does not, Somers suggests, have to be understood as invasion. In the psychology of her protagonist, however, there is no other form of human interaction than attack and defense, and that is the tragedy of masculine subjectivity as it is so often imagined.

The protagonist's projections of his own victimization onto women, his violence against them in complicity with what he understands to be other men's privilege, and his inability to maintain a nondominating relationship with the campesina's desire to feed him all result in his own death. Ironically, he had killed a woman by demanding her recognition of him (keeping her eyes open) regardless of her own need, and finally his own recognition of the (m)other as a desiring subject kills him. "El despojo" exposes the (ph)allacy of an independent and dominant masculine subjectivity by confronting it with the materialization and transformative power of a distinctly feminine desire. The story graphically enacts the risks *for men* of rigid adherence to a simplified master/slave model of defining masculinity against femininity. First, Somers suggests that the pursuit of male dominance in gendered terms will always backfire because the Hegelian master/slave dialectic depends on sustainable *mutual* recognition, while her protagonist's notion of dominance insists on his own unsustainable control over all forms of recognition. Finally, as the opening nightmare of "La araña" illustrates, class differences among men preclude the realization of the fantasy of universal male privilege or universal male bonding over and against women's desire or their very existence. Somers's protagonist dies because of his inability to disassociate his subjectivity from an impossibly rigid and defensive definition of masculinity. His story indicates that acquiescence to and unfettered enjoyment of the *other's* desire would have saved him if he had been able to recognize that desire outside of the limits of domination and submission imposed on him by his own sense of masculinity.

CHAPTER FOUR

Crime and Punishment Reconsidered

Clarice Lispector's *A maçã no escuro*

We have to become murderers in order to experience ourselves as real . . . isn't that horrible?

Gregor von Rezzori, *The Death of My Brother Abel*

Published in Brazil nearly a century after *Crime and Punishment* (published serially in 1866), Clarice Lispector's *A maçã no escuro* (*The Apple in the Dark*, 1961)[1] cites and reworks the components of conversion and salvation in Fyodor Dostoevsky's text, arguably the most widely read crime novel of the modern period.[2] It is impossible to verify Lispector's intention regarding the intertextual resonances of her novel with Dostoevsky's; yet, the thematic and structural similarities that her entire text bears to the epilogue of *Crime and Punishment* call for comparison, especially by readers attentive to murder and masculinity as the central dilemma of each work. Dostoevsky stages a successful murder, describing physical violence committed by a perpetrator with no typical motive such as self-defense, revenge, or passion which might immediately reveal his guilt to the police. Narrated early in the novel, *Crime and Punishment*'s double-murder scene frees readers from such concerns as legal detection and the conventional solving of a mystery in order for the text to undertake its study of a fundamentally sensitive and moral character who is nevertheless misguided by his own criminal mind and crisis over masculinity. Although two women must be sacrificed in the process, Dostoevsky's Raskolnikov ultimately overcomes his trangressive tendencies in the novel's epilogue, and Christian atonement helps him transcend lack by founding his identity in the absolute subject.

A maçã no escuro comments on that sacrifice of female victims by experimenting with what might structure masculine subjectivity when the attempted murder of a woman is unsuccessful. Two elements of Lispector's text frame the failure of the murderous project: first, the female victim, presumed dead throughout the novel, reappears alive and well in the conclusion; second, the murder never confers, even in the protagonist's imaginary, the existential benefits he had hoped for. This complex of failures illustrates the limited imaginary value of the sacrifice of women in the search for masculine self-determination. It further compounds that critique by exposing the contradictions at play even within the imaginary realm. Lispector's protagonist Martim finally welcomes his interpellation into only provisional social structures when faced with the impossibility of shoring up a unitary self through murdering his female other. Parodying the religious conversion which concludes *Crime and Punishment*, *A maçã no escuro* directly addresses the constructedness of gender, the materiality of language, and the violence of social relations in its reconsideration of viable masculinity.

Like Dostoevsky's Raskolnikov, Lispector's Martim seeks freedom in one radically trangressive act. By attempting to murder his wife, he believes he is escaping the bonds of societal control, breaking free from the "language of other people." He retreats into what is, for him, the unknown "heart of Brazil," into a self-imposed silence.[3] Martim initially rejects social interdependence and longs to define himself in terms for which he alone can accept credit. In his sermon to the stones, the first explanation of what he has accomplished through murder, he gives three possible reasons for having expressed through crime his rage at living a passive life. First, he asks the stones to imagine "a person who did not have the courage to reject himself" and who therefore commits an unpardonable act so that others will reject him. Next he argues from the position of Nietszche's pale criminal from *Thus Spake Zarathustra:*

—Imaginem uma pessoa que era pequena e não tinha fôrça. Ela na certa sabia muito bem que tôda a sua fôrça reunida, tostão por tostão, só seria suficiente para comprar um único ato de cólera. E na certa também sabia que êsse ato teria que ser bem rápido, antes que a coragem acabasse, e teria mesmo que ser histérico. Essa pessoa, então, quando menos esperava, executou èsse ato; e nêle investiu tôda a sua pequena fortuna. (40)

["Try to imagine a person who was small and had no strength. Of course he knew very well that all of his strength, piece by piece, would only be enough to buy a single act of rage. And of course he also knew that such an act would have to be quite quick before his courage petered out, and it would even have to be hysterical. That person, then, when least expected, executed that act, and in it he invested his whole small fortune." (31)]

Finally, he invests his violent assault with religious meaning:

—Com um ato de violência essa pessoa de quem estou falando matou um mundo abstrato e lhe deu sangue

. . . Desta hora em diante teria a oportunidade de viver sem fazer o mal porque já o fizera: êle era agora um inocente. (42)

["With an act of violence that person of whom I spoke killed an abstract world and gave it blood."

. . . From that time forward he would have the chance to live without doing evil because it had already been done; now he was innocent. (33)]

In this conflation of the philosophical, psychological, and spiritual motives as well as consequences of the murder, Martim articulates the phases of self-explanation through which Raskolnikov also passes in Dostoevky's text. These characters' destructive acts promise personal victory because they change the images that other people have had of them. In breaking the social contract, Martim and Raskolnikov at first feel free to create themselves anew, rebuilding what they believe to have been constructed inauthentically by collective power, whether that power takes the form of other people's notions of their identity or of a generalized feeling of guilt and inadequacy.

For both characters, however, the solitary project proves unbearable. Internal contradictions compel them to rely on other people. Raskolnikov, for example, seeks encounters with the police examiner Porfiry Petróvich out of a psychological imperative to validate and yet simultaneously undermine his successful crime. Martim's case develops that impulse through philosophical reflection. Just after proclaiming, "Yes! Courageously, he had done what every man has to do once in his life: destroy life in order to rebuild it on his own terms," his own understanding of the human propensity for self-deception requires him to recognize that "his truths did not seem to be able to bear attention for a long time before they became deformed . . . (without realizing it, his reconstruction had already begun to gasp)" (133). He needs others to agree to his new terms in order to trust them himself. In both novels, then, the protagonists ultimately devalue their experience of self-creation. They first deny the significance of their crimes (both as violent transgression of social norms and as signifiers of their individual freedom), of their ensuing isolation from society, and of their extended contemplation of freedom and self-awareness. In the end, Raskolnikov and Martim actively seek submission to the very forces from which they had previously sought liberation.

The most controversial aspect of these texts is the apparent incongruity between their investment in existential character development and their endings. Just as with *Crime and Punishment*, *A maçã no escuro* has caused readers to struggle to interpret the surprising ending. Some critics read it as a failed existential project, suggesting that Lispector uses Martim's submission to the law (as represented by a professor, a detective, and two policemen) as a symptom of his inability to maintain his newfound freedom, of the failure of his will to support authentic being. In such a reading, Martim fades away into the background of the society he had tried to escape. He cannot sustain the personhood he had acquired during the silence of the first two sections of the novel. In his *Clarice Lispector,* Earl Fitz adopts this position by appealing to a Sartrean notion of freedom: "Although Lispector's characters often attain a state of authentic freedom for themselves, they also realize that they will have to live out their lives alone, that freedom, while it can be given, cannot be shared. Like Sartre Lispector understood that we are indeed 'condemned to being free . . .'" (39). If Fitz understands Lispector correctly, then Martim's docile acceptance of society's laws and language must be read as a failure to accept the conditions of freedom, implying that his having committed murder in the first place constituted—at least in an immediate sense—freedom rather than a prior dependency.

Other critics have focused on the success of Martim's project, arguing that the mystical nature of his surrender to the authorities celebrates a triumphant epiphany, the realization that freedom entails a chosen submission to the fact of our dependency. Benedito Nunes (1989, 69) takes this position as he describes the division of the novel into three sections: the existential ("How a Man Is Made"), the romantic ("The Birth of the Hero"), and the mystical ("The Apple in the Dark"). Nunes's identification of two separate trajectories in the novel—the existential one that fails and the spiritual one that triumphs—allows him to affirm Martim's spiritualized (though not theologically developed) identity.

By referring to the idea of a real self, though, Nunes, like Fitz, limits Martim's existence to a series of either/or decisions between self and society, even though he defends the idea that a decision for society is really a decision for the self. This emphasis on the failure or success of finding oneself, which is evident in both Fitz's and Nunes's readings of *A maçã no escuro*, echoes the bulk of intrepretive approaches to Raskolnikov's surrender to the authorities and to Christian values at the end of *Crime and Punishment*. A clear example of such an interpretive approach appears in William Hubben's summary (1952, 38) of Kierkegaard's definition of the totality of life in relation to Dostoevsky's epilogue: "It must transcend itself in faith. The philosophical existentialist inverts Descartes's 'I think, therefore I am' by stating, 'I am, therefore I think.' But the religious existentialist will have to say, 'I believe, therefore I am.'" In contrast to this description of Dostoevsky's conclusion, Lispector's protagonist Martim repeats "I don't believe. . . . I don't believe. . . . Halleluia, Halleluia, I'm hungry again" in the last pages of *A maçã no escuro*. Viable subjectivity hinges on radical doubt and lack rather than humble belief and plenitude in this reexamination of *Crime and Punishment*'s existentialist and religious projects. The ambiguous use of a religious ("Halleluia") doubt ("I don't believe") presents a subjectivity defined by Althusserian interpellation which also involves desire and choice on the part of the individual.

While critical responses to their endings have been uncannily similar, there are significant differences in the narrative structures of *Crime and Punishment* and *A maçã no escuro*. Whereas Raskolnikov kills a woman he barely knows, Martim tries to kill his own wife. Raskolnikov contemplates the implications of his action before committing murder. Martim seems to have murdered impulsively, without any plan. Whereas readers witness the killing in *Crime and Punishment*, they meet Martim only when he is already a fugitive. Raskolnikov goes through a psychologically draining cat-and-mouse game with the authorities, but Martim's struggle is more private. While Raskolnikov's submission to judgment is based on Christian faith in salvation through sacrifice, Martim's is overtly pragmatic and social. Lispector's character exploits religious discourse to express his mystical experience of submission to the language and judgment of other people, but not to represent any essentially spiritual or even moral salvation.

Perhaps the most intriguing difference in the way the experiments in subjectivity are designed in these two novels is that unlike in *Crime and Punishment*, in Lispector's novel the exact nature of the crime is hidden from readers until the final section of the text, when it is revealed that Martim had tried to murder his wife. Ironically, the same section of the novel which explains that he tried to kill her out of boredom and frustration with the world of (l)imitation she represents, also reveals that Martim, in fact, failed to kill her. Throughout most of the novel he only *thinks* he has committed murder, and is therefore free to define himself apart from his wife's world. The distinction between the novelistic fact of murder in Dostoevsky and the novelistic illusion of murder in Lispector affords an understanding of the ways in which subjectivities are founded as much on imaginary social relations as on the psychological effects of real events.

Hélène Cixous (1990, 66) addresses the series of illusions and doubles in Lispector's work, asserting that *A maçã no escuro* "is a most deceptive book. It is presented like a novel, but it is the opposite. It is a mystical path of such density that it becomes perhaps even more unreadable than *The Passion* [*According to G.H.* (1964)]. The book is double." Cixous does not elaborate on what she means by "the opposite" of a novel, but certainly *A maçã no escuro* is "double" insofar as it always harks back to Dostoevsky. Cixous's comment, however, is based on two couples figured in the work: Martim and Ermelinda, on the one hand, and Martim and Vitória on the other. Her reading of this novel focuses on the "questions of sexual difference and of different libidinal economies" (60) which these pairings raise.

There is, however, another way to address doubling in the text without ignoring the wife whom Martim had tried to kill, without reading her as no more than a foil for the subsequent exploration of Martim's own femininity. The novel explores different libidinal economies to mirror the impasses of *Crime and Punishment* back onto themselves, and to open them to reconfigurations of the protagonist's attempts to escape the mundane by way of murdering women. Lispector's reconsideration of Dostoevsky's Christian humanist masterpiece on the fragmented self seeking unity is especially powerful in that it uses a male protagonist with goals similar to Raskolnikov's to develop a notion of masculine subjectivity not grounded in the real or fantasized eradication of women.

Both novels show that any hope for unity of the self requires participation in a community of sufferers. But what, really, *is* this unity of the self, who are the sufferers, and what defines the community? Lispector's theoretical experimentation with Martim responds to Dostoevsky's work with Raskolnikov, reconstituting the category of subjectivity to focus on gender and language as the sites of the greatest contradictions between subject positions. Martim's project begins like Raskolnikov's, as a test of existentialism and religion, but it ends with a post-Althusserian play on masculinity and social power.

Cixous (1990, 62) argues that Lispector's novel shows that "femininity is more capable of otherness" than one would initially assume masculinity to be, and that the fact that Martim happens to be male is deceptive: "In the ordinary world thousands of reasons explain why a man would kill his wife. Given the nature of his crime, one could think that Martim is a real man. In fact, everything is reversed. A close reading shows that he is the most feminine of all the characters." In a reading of Lispector's novel which regards it as an answer to Dostoevsky, however, Martim's biological masculinity and his masculinist crime—the attempt to disrupt social ties with women in favor of extreme individualism—are precisely the elements which make his ultimate reintegration into the social so complex.

If we read *A maçã no escuro* as literary heir to *Crime and Punishment*, its motive is to depict a male protagonist learning that, although nondominating engagement with others checks his creative power, it simultaneously offers the only possibility for his exercise of it. Of course, this lesson requires an exploration of what was killed off in the original *Crime and Punishment*, what Cixous would call the "feminine," but it never requires a loss of gender difference, as Cixous suggests, or a war waged for the supremacy of either men or women. Rather, it acknowledges power relations between state and individual (represented by the police and Martim), between boss and worker (Vitória and Martim), and between characters whose desire is in flux; only by first recognizing the effects of the principle of domination in such relationships can we imagine new relations between men and women.

Crime and Punishment is narrated at a dizzying pace, inviting—indeed, forcing—readers to share in the effects of Raskolnikov's moral and psychological illness. Readers experience a desperate delirium as they suffer with Raskolnikov. Only in the epilogue, the section which introduces a hope for psychological peace, does the narrative pace slow down. In this brief account of Raskolnikov's life in a Siberian work prison, the feverish confessions and fears of the first six books do not appear. The narrative of the epilogue is clear and precise, outlining the character's behavior but seldom entering his mind as does the narration of the rest of the work. This rupture in narrative style has led critics to call the epilogue an awkward and unnecessary addition to an already complete story.[4] If, however, one reads the novel's six books as a representation of one person's conflicting subject positions, and the epilogue as an acknowledgment of the impossibility of representing the unitary (but still ideal) subject he has become, then the terse style of Dostoevsky's epilogue becomes allusion. It carries Dostoevsky into the postmodern as it "puts forward the unpresentable in presentation itself" (Lyotard 1984, 81). The catch here, of course, is the persistence of the unitary subject, clearly the point of difference between the postmodern as literary *style*—which we can attribute to Dostoevsky's epilogue—and the postmodern as an understanding of decentered subjectivity—which *Crime and Punishment*'s ending denies with Raskolnikov's conversion to Christianity and the establishment of spiritual certainty for him.

Although the epilogue to *Crime and Punishment* is quite short (14 pages of the 465–page edition I cite here), its pace and its suggestions prefigure those of all 321 pages of Lispector's novel. *A maçã no escuro* maintains an even discursive flow from beginning to end. Paced to match its protagonist's slow and deliberate creation of himself, the entire novel parallels the structure of Dostoevsky's epilogue in its elaboration on and critique of the earlier text. Four aspects of Lispector's novel most obviously appropriate elements of Dostoevsky's epilogue: the protagonist's retreat into silence, the centrality of manual labor, the relationships with women, and the submission scene. Through imitation, appropriation, and subtle alteration of the terms of the argument, *A maçã no escuro* radically questions the goal of defending the protagonist's unitary, masculine subject position.

Silence and Confession

Silence is central to both novels. The first six books of *Crime and Punishment* deal with the problem of expressing authentic experience in language. After having been summoned to the police station because he had not paid his rent, for example, Raskolnikov is overcome with fear of being found out to be a murderer, and he realizes that the world of normal social functioning is closed to him. He experiences emotions and conflicts which he believes are inexplicable to other people:

> Something new and unexpected, something hitherto unknown and undreamt of, had taken place in him. . . . He did not so much understand with his mind as feel

> instinctively with the full force of his emotions that he could never again communicate with these people in a great gush of feeling, . . . or in any way whatever. . . . He had never in his life before experienced so strange and desolating a feeling, and the most painful thing about it was that it *was* a feeling, an immediate sensation, and not knowledge or intellectual understanding. (87)

Having sought authenticity through murder, he can now experience feelings as "immediate sensation" or in a "great gush," but he cannot communicate them. To avoid detection, he must keep all exchanges guarded and artificial, denying the "full force of his emotions." Consequently, in the epilogue, after having confessed to murder, having succinctly reported to the police his exact actions, and having been sentenced to eight years of hard labor in Siberia, the protagonist throws off even the language in his mind. Internal debate is absent at this point. We read of Raskolnikov's self-questioning—"What should he strive for? To live in order to exist?" (458) or "Why had he not killed himself?" (459)—but not of any answers he might be able to offer.

In the epilogue, Raskolnikov discards language out of frustration over his inability to maintain the illusion of transparent language. Martim, on the other hand, wants to escape language altogether in *A maçã no escuro*. The stages of Martim's progressive identification with rocks, then rats, then cows, then the hilltop view of nature, all revolve around his desire to free himself from the constraints of the "language of other people"; each separate stage involves its own epiphany, or moment of silent recognition of Martim's physical presence in the world. Because he wants to make himself over "in his own image," this character rejects a system of communication that relies on imitation, repetition, and relation.

When resting alone in the wasteland during his flight from the hotel, Martim is first struck by the pleasurable impossibility of speaking about his situation:

> "Perdi a linguagem dos outros," repetiu então bem devagar como se as palavras fôssem mais obscuras do que eram, e de algum modo muito lisongeiras. Estava serenamente orgulhoso, com os olhos claros e satisfeitos. . . .Porque alguma coisa estava lhe acontecendo. E era alguma coisa com um significado. Embora não houvesse um sinônimo para essa coisa que estava acontecendo. Um homem estava sentado. E não havia sinônimo para nenhuma coisa, e então o homem estava sentado. Assim era. O bom é que era indiscutível. E irreversível. (32)

> ["I have lost the speech of other people," he then repeated slowly, as if the words were more obscure than they were, and in some way more praiseworthy. He was serenely proud; his eyes clear and satisfied . . . .Some thing was happening to him, and it was something that had meaning. Even so he had no words for what was happening. A man was sitting down. And he had no words for anything. Therefore he was sitting down. That is how it was. The best part is that it was indisputable. And irreversible. (23)]

This silence does not refer to impotence. In fact, it signals the sublimity of criminal escape; secure in his identity as transgressor, Martim experiences a momentary freedom from social constraints. In rejecting language, Martim tries to validate his perception of sovereignty. Of course, the liberating effect of transgression is bound to a respect for the law which one has broken. The word crime signifies only for those who agree to its meaning; without the shared concept of what constitutes a crime, the murderer cannot long enjoy the sensation of having transcended his subjected status.

Lispector complicates Martim's expected enjoyment of the extralinguistic experience in two specific ways: she introduces the need for writing, and she uses Martim's interior voice to narrate the confession scene. The question of writing, appearing roughly in the middle of the novel ("Birth of the Hero," chapter 8) highlights the ambiguities attendant upon any notion of private experience or knowledge. One evening Martim sets out to organize his thoughts on paper, thoughts which had seemed to him just hours earlier, after having sex with Ermelinda, to be clear, whole, and relevant to the external world. As soon as he begins to write, however, he realizes the futility of trying to express in words anything one has experienced so intensely. The experience seems to disappear as Martim realizes that the words for it have escaped him. He writes simply, "Things I must do," and then, finding that phrase too ambitious, writes, "Things I must try to learn: Number 1." Next to this line, he writes only "That."

At first Martim is satisfied with his ability to allude to a wealth of knowledge and experience which he has begun to feel is available to him. Then, however, he continues to "Number 2: how to link 'that' which I may know with the social state of things." The drive to write at all becomes inseparable from the drive to understand the relation between his own existence and the "social state of things." The process of writing forces Martim to realize his already social condition. Martim discovers that "putting into words" involves a splitting of the unitary "grandeur" of the writer's supposed subjectivity in that it requires him to listen to himself, to read his own messages. He finds them absurd insofar as they claim to communicate any private truth.

In the confession scene, Lispector poses her second challenge to the sanctity of silence as refuge for the consistent subject. Raskolnikov's confession in *Crime and Punishment* relieves readers of the responsibility of his secret. We may have hoped he would not be caught, but we do not doubt that his moral crisis will now achieve closure. Readers know that a murder did indeed occur, because the murder scene is graphically described in the first chapter. When Raskolnikov says, "It was I who killed the old woman and her sister, Lizaveta, with an axe, and robbed them" (1964, 450) readers take the role of objective listeners with direct access to the protagonist's thoughts. The determination with which Raskolnikov declares himself guilty does not allow for any speculation about his sincerity or conviction.

Later, in the second part of the epilogue, the narrator states, "But he did not feel remorse for his crime." After his confession, Raskolnikov questions the meaning of the word *crime,* but he does so using the same argument that he used before he murdered: an appeal to historical heroes who transgressed the law, but who thereby brought about social change beneficial to certain majorities. "This was the sole sense in which he acknowledged his crime, that he had not succeeded and that he had confessed." Raskolnikov perpetually makes claims with determination and then questions those claims. Dostoevsky's project in the end, however, illustrates the conditions under which a man learns to accept his absolute dependence on a higher order. Raskolnikov may not understand all his motives in their complexity, but he does come to see that his self-contemplation and declarations will always ring false in relation to spiritual truth: "He tortured himself with these questions, unable to realize that perhaps even while he stood by the river he already felt in his heart that there was something profoundly false in himself and his beliefs. He did not understand that that feeling might have been the herald of a coming crisis in his life, of his coming resurrection, of a future new outlook on life" (1964, 459). By insisting that there *is* a truth to Raskolnikov's experience, even though the character may not comprehend it, the narrative creates an acceptance on the reader's part of this reference to resurrection. The possibility of his resurrection is predicated upon the believability of Raskolnikov's spiritual death, his profound guilt.

In *A maçã no escuro* a shift in focalization deconstructs this certainty with regard to the reality of the murder and the question of guilt. Readers are not gratified that the murderer has come to accept his criminality; instead, they are called upon to acknowledge the artifice involved in any confession:

> —Matei minha mulher, disse Martim . . . —Porque estava quase certo de que minha mulher tinha um amante. . . .
>
> O que, se não era a melhor verdade, era afinal uma verdade que tinha valor de troca. . . . Com curiosidade, com o pêso no peito, êle estava de novo trocando, comprando e vendendo. (334–35)
>
> ["I killed my wife," Martim said. . . . "Because I was almost certain that my wife had a lover." . . .
>
> Which, if it were not the best of truths, was at least a truth that had the value of exchange for something. . . . With curiosity, with the weight on his chest, he was exchanging once more, buying and selling. (321–22)]

Readers of *A maçã no escuro* must rely on Martim's understanding of the murder. He never clarifies the event, and any "authorial" interpretation of the crime remains unspecified. The only principle defended here is one of social exchange value: "buying and selling." Martim's confession involves a complicated series of assertions, denials, and compromises. Focalization through Martim presents his confession as a self-conscious attempt to control the social reception of his message.

The presence of the four men who come to arrest Martim would seem to introduce other, more objective accounts into the readers' store of information about the protagonist. The physical relations among the men, however, actually belittle the authorities' version of events. Martim's physical size dwarfs the tiny figures of the mayor of Vila Baixa, two detectives, and the professor. While Martim himself feels at a disadvantage (and perhaps because he feels that way), readers are invited to assume the position of arbitrator between, on the one hand, the protagonist with whom they have suffered through various personal epiphanies, and on the other hand, the representatives of social control. Although Martim may feel incomplete, this contrast brings readers to his defense, putting them in the position of arguing that in some ways he actually is a "giant among men." The physical incongruity of Martim's surrender to the "band of armed midgets" parallels the suggested verbal incongruity of Martim's confession. Martim tries to believe in trite explanations in order to make the words he has used bear meaning for the others, whose authority is credible only because Martim chooses to submit to them.

Readers here are caught in the trap of the notion of unitary subjectivity: we want to defend Martim's experiment with autonomy, and so support a defiant confession of the murder; at the same time, we recognize that the desire to confess reveals a dependency on others' reception of the information, and their subsequent power to position Martim as they choose. Readers who had identified with Martim's desire for radical individuation must necessarily feel betrayed by his willingness to be reintegrated into the social system. The question hovers between character limitations and readerly desire: under what conditions is the murderer able to restore a viable masculinity in relation to others?

Readers sensitive to the contradictions inherent in Martim's search for independence throughout the novel (the scene of writing) see that the hero-giant created through private meditations finds no spiritual retreat from the contradictions of social exchange. There is perpetual compromise ("even if not the best of truths") and negotiation ("buying and selling"), even within the silences.

Labor

The contribution of physical labor to the experiments with subjectivity is another similarity with which Lispector subtly questions the oppositions set up in Dostoevsky's novel. Each of their protagonists has different motives for discarding language, but each takes pleasure in the physicality of hard work. Whereas manual labor in the Siberian work camp successfully enforces Raskolnikov's identity as conscious and physical subject in relation to the object world, Martim's phenomenological experience actually resists that kind of separation. Raskolnikov's initiation into real work and fresh air occurs in isolation from family and friends, establishing his body as separate, whole, and masculine—this last in relation to his friend Sonya's feminine work of serving many of the other prisoners' social needs through letter writing or making conversation. Only after "becoming himself" through manual labor and noncommunication does Raskolnikov feel ready to unite his life with Sonya's. That is, Raskolnikov enters into adult relations with a woman only after his spiritual and physical initiation into an isolated existence.

In *A maçã no escuro* Martim's initiation period actually moves him away from an obsession with distinguishing his masculinity from the object world and the femininity he initially attributes to it. His progress is measured by the degree to which his status as masculine subject includes feminine elements. This process occurs most obviously in the shifts in his relationship to his work on Vitória's farm.

Martim vacillates in almost every chapter between an initial impulse to oppose himself and his body to other elements of the physical world, and the impulse to become one with those elements. His relationship to the cows exemplifies various aspects of this dynamic. Vitória demands that he clean the cowshed, and Martim initially resents the interruption of his work with the plants. The moment he enters the cowshed, however, he becomes open to a new sensation. To gain admittance from the cows themselves, he must abandon the subject/object relationship to nature:

> Imitando as vacas, num mimetismo quase calculado, êle ali em pé não olhou para parte alguma, tentando êle também dispensar a visão direta. E numa inteligência forçada pela própria inferioridade de sua situação, deixou-se ficar submisso e atento. Depois, por um altruísmo de identificação, foi que êle quase tomou a forma de um dos bichos. E foi assim fazendo que, com certa surprêsa, inesperadamente pareceu entender como é uma vaca. (106)

> [Imitating the cows with an almost calculated mimicry, he stood there not looking at anything, in fact making an effort not to look at anything. And with an intelligence brought on by the very inferiority of his situation, he let himself remain submissive and attentive. And then, through the altruism of identification, he almost took on the form of one of the animals. And by doing just that he suddenly seemed to understand, with surprise, what it was like to be a cow. (95–96)]

As Martim's work on the farm takes him through evolutionary stages of identification with lower forms (rocks and rats), then higher forms (horses and cows), he repeats this pattern over and over: he first opposes himself to the other, then integrates the experience of the other into his own, and finally reestablishes the self/other distinction in a more sympathetic way.

A disturbing example of the transitions made in this dialectic occurs in the chapter immediately following Martim's initiation into "what it was like to be a cow." He approaches the *mulata* on the farm, a nameless character who never speaks and is granted only a few appearances in the novel. Martim applies his new skill of "not looking":

> E ficou de pé sem olhá-la. . . . Êle a pegou sem pressa como um dia pegara um passarinho. —Você é forte como um touro, riu a mulher. (118)

> [And he stood there without looking at her. . . . He grabbed her slowly, the way one day he had grabbed a bird. "You're strong as a bull," the woman laughed. (108)]

These references to animals forge a link between Martim's experiences with nature and his brief contact with this woman. The bird mentioned here is the one he had killed on the first day of his flight into the "heart of Brazil" after having committed his crime.

Martim may now understand how to be a cow, but by calling him "strong as a bull," this nameless woman signals the dangers of difference and power imbalances. The associations of people with animals, and of this particular woman with animal victims, caution readers that the question of identity must be formed anew in each relational situation and that language, labor, and love are intertwined social phenomena.

Postmurder Relationships

Relationships with women after the commission of the murders figure prominently in both Dostoevsky's epilogue and Lispector's novel. In *Crime and Punishment*, Sonya, the ex-prostitute who loves Raskolnikov, refuses to let him slip away completely from contact with other people. She follows him to prison in Siberia, visits him daily, worries over his physical and spiritual illnesses, and writes faithfully to his family in St. Petersburg. Even when Raskolnikov seems unresponsive to her love, she continues reaching out to him, and her persistence becomes a powerful force in his rebirth.

In *A maçã no escuro* the self/other dialectic evident in Martim's relation to the natural world through his work on the farm is complicated further in his interactions with the two principal female characters , Ermelinda and Vitória. Ermelinda provides him with a masculine physical/sexual identity in contrast to her feminine softness and passivity. Because their relationship is strangely lacking in emotional content, it validates individuality rather than union. In contrast to Ermelinda's feminine need for a man, Martim begins to see himself as complete, as a self-constructed being who, when looking into a mirror, takes pride in his own masculine image.

Vitória, however, represents a different kind of relationship for Martim. Although they love each other in mutual identification rather than in their difference, they never have any physical contact. As owner of the farm, Vitória has controlling power over Martim. It is ultimately she who betrays him to the authorities through her friend the professor. When Martim finally comes to see that she understands his own inner turmoil, he is disconcerted:

> Mas qualquer coisa no rosto da mulher fêz com que êle pestanejasse numa sensação de desconfôrto. Como viciados que se reconhecessem, êle acabara de ver nela êle próprio. O que foi desagradável. Nela havia aquela coisa que também nêle existia, e que êle só não acusou porque nêle próprio também doía, e porque, quem a tinha, disso sofria. Martim desviou os olhos. (289)

> [But something on the woman's face made him blink with an uncomfortable feeling. Like addicts who recognize each other, he had just seen himself in her. Which was disagreeable. There was in her that thing which also existed in him, and which he did not accuse her of because it also hurt within himself, and because a person who had it suffered with it. Martim averted his eyes. (277)]

Martim's contact with the *mulata* was initiated with an aversion of the eyes. Then, sexual contact with Ermelinda led his admiring gaze back onto himself. When Martim averts his eyes in Vitória's presence, it is out of a respect and pity that arise from his ability to be empathetic. Ironically, Martim and Vitória are more alike than different in their attempts to found identities in solitude.

The presence of women during Martim's and Raskolnikov's postmurder search for selfhood provides an identity for the men in their difference and offers hope in their ability to understand the struggle between the need for freedom and the need for submission. Martim's experience is much more problematic, however, in that he consciously addresses the unresolvability of similarity and difference. Raskolnikov's relationship with Sonya is strictly spiritual. *She* offers understanding because her history of prostitution and destitution parallels his history of criminality and spiritual depravity. *He* turns to her for help, though, because, whereas her situation was caused by family and social dynamics completely beyond her control, his was supposedly caused by spiritual arrogance and desperation. Her absolute victimage is presented as an edifying counterexample to his self-imposed anguish.

Lispector responds to Dostoevsky's use of Sonya as a virginal prostitute and spiritual guide by fragmenting Martim's relationships with women. His desire for interaction with the other is mostly split between Ermelinda and Vitória, but it is also evident in the more animalistic scene with the mulata. This splitting disallows any transcendent salvation through love between men and women because it asserts the variability and contextuality of each relationship. Raskolnikov resolves his conflictual relationship to the self/other dichotomy through his contact with only one person, Sonya, whose difference from him is essential. In contrast to that one emblematic relationship, Martim's contact with others spreads to multiple relationships whose simultaneous exercise of similarity and difference forces him to realize his more complex boundedness in the social.

Rebirth as Women's Labor

The last scenes of these two novels dramatize their most extraordinary point of correspondence. The men physically kneel before the virgin purity of the women they love. Remarkably, the protagonists assume a position of repentance and humility before women against whom they have committed no crime. Their repentance is for an offense against other women, and their humility is before the power of an abstracted feminine love to re-create them. On the morning of his rebirth, Raskolnikov is resting from work but feels disturbed by some unnamed, anguished longing. His transformation requires Sonya's quiet presence:

> Suddenly Sonya appeared at his side. She had come up almost soundlessly and sat down beside him . . . she gave him a joyful welcoming smile, but she held out her hand as timidly as ever . . . this time their hands remained joined. . . . How it happened he himself did not know, but suddenly he seemed to be seized and cast at her feet. He clasped her knees and wept. For a moment she was terribly frightened, and her face grew white. She sprang up and looked down at him, trembling . . . (463)

Although stunned at first, Sonya immediately recognizes the import of this moment for the two of them. "Love had raised them from the dead, and the heart of each held endless springs of life for the heart of the other" (463). Because Raskolnikov has finally allowed love to exert power over him, the narration indicates that he has stepped into a new life, and he and Sonya have become inseparable in a spiritual, eternal future.

Martim's kneeling before Vitória does not introduce a new life for the two of them, but rather just for him; his motivations for asking for her forgiveness, however, can be attributed to the same need that Raskolnikov feels. Both men must be humbled before an external power in order to be freed of the burdensome responsibility of self-creation. They must ask a woman to give them a new birth:

> Então Martim se ajoelhou diante dela e disse: —Perdoe. . . . Mas a mulher de repente segurou num movimento incoercível o ventre com as mãos, lá onde doi uma mulher,

sua bôca estremeceu atingida, o futuro era um parto difícil . . . e a alegria era tal miséria. (366)

[Then Martim kneeled down in front of her and said: "Forgive me." . . . But the woman with a sudden irrepressible movement clasped her stomach with her hands, there where a woman pains, her mouth trembled, touched, the future was a difficult birth . . . and the joy was such a misery. (352)]

Even before he asks, Martim knows that Vitória does not want to forgive him. The narrator describes her resistance to his request but asserts the inescapability of mutual obligation: the man is at the mercy of the woman who will allow him entry to the world.

Oh, não era coisa de que se pudesse escapar—assim já tinham sido esculpidas imagens de mulheres e de homens ajoelhados, havia um longo passado de perdão e amor e sacrifício, nao era coisa de que se pudesse escapar. (366–67)

[Oh, it was something impossible to escape from—sculptors had already done images of women and kneeling men, there was a whole long past of forgiveness and love and sacrifice, it was something from which it was impossible to escape. (353)]

Neither Martim nor Vitória comprehends the scene they enact. She resists with words, but the physical result is inevitable: he is raised up, granted life. She grants her forgiveness but does not know why or for what. He accepts it but does not quite understand what made him ask for it. The best they can do is to allow the transformation of the man to take place.

Martim's epiphany clearly reflects Dostoevsky's conviction that renewal of the spirit must come in submission, but for Lispector it is a submission to the lack of control we have over our own births. Language creates us precisely by placing us always in relation to other people, as a "whole long past" of "images of women and kneeling men." While for Dostoevsky obedience to God necessarily engenders humility before others, for Lispector's narrator God is created in the shared experience of two human beings' recognizing that only impotence results from the solitary search for selfhood.

Raskolnikov and Martim subject themselves to the objects of their desire, and they become sons—objects of the mothers' desire. Lispector challenges Dostoevsky's uncritical representation of the mothering function, however. In *Crime and Punishment* Sonya is taken aback by Raskolnikov's sudden change, but she immediately and joyfully accepts it. In Lispector's novel the shock of labor makes

Vitória react, but she also recoils from the recognition that, as a woman, she has no choice but to let the man be born through appeal to her. The key difference is that Martim has also already realized the same for himself. As Cixous (1960, 63) puts it, "Martim is being born and gives birth simultaneously at the extremity of himself. He gives place, body, and existence to the other, but others have also given him that which, had he stayed alone, would not have been accessible to him. The others while being born become body for him." The exchange of labors does not have to make Martim into the "most feminine of all the characters," as Cixous had argued prior to this more complex observation. Birthing in this scene begins with a woman's physical pains, becomes spiritualized through the association of rebirth and atonement, and ends discursively as Martim's new awareness of mutuality. This awareness opens space for Vitória and the four men to exist both within him as the otherness necessary for his self-identification, and externally to him as the social limits to his freedom. Subjectivity here is more like a wordless conversation between subject positions *in particular contexts* than like an articulated, self-imposed identity. Lispector's arrangement of this scene deploys the conventionality of gender constructions in order to demonstrate the structural necessity of otherness—whether it be a difference of gender, of profession, or of purpose in any given instance.

Individuation and the Murder of Women

As long as ideal masculine subjectivity (sought in the beginning by both Raskolnikov and Martim) is predicated upon rejecting the feminine, then fantasies of domination and murder will continue to control the male imaginary. Differentiation initially occurs in relation to the mother (or primary caretaker), through a child's experiences of the mother's departure and return. As the child perceives that gratification of its own needs depends on the mother's presence and attention, it learns that its existence is separate from the mother's. For Chodorow (1978), successful differentiation for the child involves not only its perception of its own individuality, but also the perception that the mother has individuality of the same kind (Eisenstein and Jardine 7).

For Raskolnikov, adequate differentiation is quite problematic. At the beginning of *Crime and Punishment*, he conflates his negative self-images and his negative feelings toward women, and projects them onto the figure of the pawnbroker before he murders her.[5] Then, as part of his redemption process in the epilogue, he projects all of his positive feelings toward women onto Sonya, leaving the impression that the two of them will live in a mature, husband-wife relationship. His personal and spiritual renewal is accomplished through his ability to separate *self*-image from a conglomeration of images of the feminine other, a connection that, it is often argued, had caused his psychological splitting in the first place; the murder was a desperate attempt to rid himself of identifications with the feminine. In the epilogue his Christian rebirth and acceptance of Sonya's love are presented as the first steps along a healthy, philosophically consistent path to individuation as opposed to the chaotic path of murder.[6] Based on experiences with God and guilt, though, Raskolnikov's ability to be with Sonya does not result from social interaction. It comes from Raskolnikov's spiritualized transcendence of his psychological splitting.

Martim, on the other hand, achieves no such closure in his individuation process. Because the women in *A maçã no escuro* are shown to have their own interests in dealing with him, he cannot rely on free associations between images of mother, boss, sister, wife. For Martim, each category maintains a certain integrity because the novel develops female characters who themselves occupy subject positions in relation to him. The contrast between Dostoevsky's and Lispector's work on the nature of the protagonists' ties to the social is evident in parallel scenes from each text which portray the men's relation to these women through their hands. Sonya, like an ideal mother for a son, is always reaching for Raskolnikov. He reserves for himself the choice to respond: "She always stretched out her hand to him timidly, sometimes even half withdrawing it, as if she feared she would repulse him. He always grasped it reluctantly, always greeted her with a kind of irritation, sometimes remained obstinately silent all through her visit" (463). Vitória, however, is a reluctant mother figure for Martim. She willingly engages only when it can be on her own terms, but she is also pulled to respond to his needs, however hesitantly:

> Martim estendeu uma mão impulsiva. Mas como a mulher não esperara o gesto, atrasou-se espantada em estender a sua. Nessa fração de segundo, o homen recolheu sem ofensa a própria mão—e Vitória, que já agora adiantara a sua, ficou com o braço unútilmente e dolorosamente estendido, como se tivesse sido iniciativa sua a de procurar—num gesto que se tornou de repente de apêlo—a mão do homem. Martim, percebendo a tempo o braço magro estendido, precipitou-se calorosamente os dedos gelados da mulher, que não pôde conter um movimento de recuo e mêdo. (364–65)

> [Martim stuck out his hand impulsively. But because the woman had not expected the gesture, she drew back frightened as she put out her own. In that fraction of a second,

the man withdrew his own hand without offense—and Vitória, who now had hers outstretched, stood there with her arm uselessly and painfully extended, as if hers had been the initiative of reaching out—with a gesture that suddenly had become one of appeal—for the hand of the man. Martim, perceiving in time the thin outstretched arm, ran forward emotionally with both of his hands uplifted, and he warmly squeezed the icy fingers of the woman, who could not restrain a movement of retreat and fear. (351)]

Martim and Vitória do not relate in the same terms as Raskolnikov and Sonya. A subtext of anger and fright with regard to assumptions they each have made about gender relations challenges the give and take. Martim is not the misogynist one would expect a wife-murderer to be, and Vitória is not the passive, pleading female one might expect a reluctantly aging virgin to be. When Vitória stands in as mother to Martim, she is not the ideal, all-giving mother whom Sonya represents for Raskolnikov. Martim knows he must appeal to Vitória, a woman whose angers, frustrations, and desires perpetually assert themselves just as do his own.

Returning to consider the origins of these relationships, we must remember that Raskolnikov does indeed kill the person onto whom he had projected his image of the "bad mother" (among other things). His new stable identity requires the sacrifice of a woman. Martim's reworked subjectivity, on the other hand, requires failure in his attempt to murder his wife. She simply will not die as fulfillment of his desire for an autonomous identity. Her return at the very end of the book, although it is a return only reported by the authorities and not verified by her appearance as a character, calls into question any fixed identity for Martim (both as husband and as criminal). It accomplishes for him the "adequate differentiation" which Chodorow defends: he finally becomes a man by relinquishing his hold on separation and othering as these are developed at the end of *Crime and Punishment.*

If the other refuses to be killed or victimized, as do the women in *A maçã no escuro*, then she must be recognized as another actor in the world who makes demands and who responds to demands made on her. Whereas *Crime and Punishment* discovers the spiritual center of identity, Lispector's novel is about the return of the margins, especially with the return of the supposedly murdered wife. The text works with the materiality of language to show the social construction of identities and events. It combines that notion with a representation of gender relations which denies fixed and autonomous masculine identity through the continued presence of multiple, varied women who refuse victim status.

Martim's thoughts at the moment of his confession recall Althusser's formulation of how subjects are hailed into serving dominant ideology; this character assumes that the mayor, the professor, and the policemen, as representatives of politics, education, and law, respectively, have the power and the right to accuse and arrest him:

> —Vamos, disse então aproximando-se incerto dos quatro homens pequenos e confusos. Vamos, disse. Porque êles deviam saber o que faziam. Êles certamente sabiam o que faziam. (376)

> ["Let's go," he said then, going uncertainly over to the four small and confused men. "Let's go," he said. Because they must have known what they were doing. They certainly knew what they were doing. (361)]

In an ambiguously parodic twist on Althusser's analysis of how ideology constructs subjects, however, Lispector shows Martim to be the director of his own interpellation. That is to say, there is no element of illusion or deception here. Martim consciously demands that the social order define him because he is too tired and needy to be the existential hero he had earlier imagined himself to be:

> Em nome de Deus, eu vos ordeno que estejais certos. Porque tôda uma carga preciosa e podre estava entregue nas mãos dêles . . . (376)

> [In the name of God, I command you to be sure. Because a whole precious and putrescent weight was being given into their hands . . .(361)]

This confusing vacillation at the end of Lispector's novel displays the difficulty of dismantling the ideal of an autonomous and unitary masculine subjectivity without a reductive move to social determinism. Martim still desires, but the nature of his desire—or at least of what he now recognizes it to be—has changed. He now believes that the task of self-creation in an absolute sense is intolerably violent and lonely, and he seeks to enjoy a newfound faith in intersubjectivity:

> Por mais liberdade que tivesse, êle só poderia criar o que já existia. A grande prisão. A grande prisão! Mas tinha a beleza da dificuldade. Afinal consegui o que quis. Criei o que já existe. E acrescentara ao que existia, algo mais: a imaterial adição de si mesmo. (363)

> [No matter how much freedom he might have, he would only be able to create what already had existed. The great prison! The great prison! But it had the beauty

> of difficulty. Finally he had got what he wanted. I have created what already exists. And he had added something more to what had existed: the immaterial addition of himself. (348–50)]

Lispector shrewdly revisits the central questions posed throughout both *Crime and Punishment* and *A maçã no escuro*. Martim's "Halleluia" both pessimistically and euphorically declares the difference between the materiality of sexual difference upon which identity is predicated, and the immateriality (the abstraction as well as the nonimportance) of fantasies of masculine domination. In Lispector's existentialist frame, sustainable and nonviolent masculinity *is* the joyful citation and circulation of multiple and contradictory *pre*-scripts for men's identities.

CHAPTER FIVE

Genre, Violence, and the Mystery of Masculinity

Manuel Puig's *The Buenos Aires Affair*

Manuel Puig's *The Buenos Aires Affair* (1973) registers multiple types of violence: it describes physical and psychological violence perpetrated by both individuals and the Argentine state; it parodies discursive violence through the self-consciously overdetermined use of psychoanalytic categorizations of personality and behavior; finally, it exposes the violence inherent in the conventions of detective fiction, blatantly seducing readers into identifying with the abuse of power by appealing to our desire to "solve" a crime. In exploring the self-destructive, masochistic tendencies of a male victimizer of feminized others in the context of oppressive military regimes, *The Buenos Aires Affair* is ultimately concerned with how violence in individual, political, theoretical, and literary manifestations of masculinity might be resisted or overcome.

Set in Argentina between 1934 and 1969, the novel presents its protagonist's struggle to find a viable masculine subjectivity in the climate of increasingly militarized control over individual actions. *The Buenos Aires Affair* makes explicit references to Juan Domingo Perón, police brutality and particular historical dates, signaling itself as a comment on the effects of Argentine political instability during the latter part of this period. Its primary focus, however, is on an individual man, Leopold Druscovich, and his experience of subjectivity as well as on prevailing psychological/sociological explanations of it.

Between the fall of Perón and the Guerra de las Malvinas (from 1955 to 1982), Argentina experienced sixteen changes of government and a cycle of inflation and recession.[1] Two of the governments during this period (Frondizi, 1958–62; Guido, 1962–63) launched massive *campañas moralizadoras* which produced a form of police surveillance of the private activities of Argentine citizens. At the same time, societies for the defense of rigid morals proliferated. The main characters in *The Buenos Aires Affair*, Leo and Gladys, exemplify the social and psychological effects of this authoritative gaze, whose goal was to control the popular response to economic and political problems through disciplining individual behavior. Appropriate channels for sexual expression and mutual respect among subjects are difficult to find in an environment of fear about one's social-political identifications in relation to the different factions competing for governmental power.

Although subtitled *una novela policial* [a detective novel], *The Buenos Aires Affair* belongs to the genre of crime fiction (as I define it in chapter 1) because of its consistent citation of and deviance from classical detective fiction. It invites readers to participate as detectives, but in a case which far exceeds the rational problem solving of standard examples of the genre. Leo, the male protagonist, has a compulsive fascination with his own crime, and readers have access to a broad range of interpretive discourses that pretend to offer explanations for his actions. As with *Crime and Punishment*, murder and its aftermath for Leo are presented more as a psychological experiment than a mystery to be neatly solved. Stephanie Merrim highlights this connection, arguing that *The Buenos Aires Affair* "is a rewrite of *Crime and Punishment* in the light of modern Freudianism" (148). Merrim acknowledges that in her essay the term "modern Freudianism" refers to popular appropriations of Freud, not necessarily to sophisticated readings of his theories, and her claim thus trivializes the effects of the psychological elements of the novel. She argues that "Puig has, in effect, used the detective story format to give us a dime-store version of a Freudian case study" (148). She is certainly correct in that *The Buenos Aires Affair* offers reductive psychological histories of the two protagonists, Leo and Gladys; however, by limiting her discussion to "modern Freudianism," she largely misses the parodic nature of Puig's appropriation of Lacanian and Freudian psychoanalytic categories as a form of detection.

The case studies, "Acontecimientos principales de la vida de Gladys" [Principal Events in Gladys's Life] and "Acontecimientos principales de la vida de Leo" [Principal Events in Leo's Life], sport subheadings such as "Madre e hija" [Mother and Daughter], "Padre e hijo" [Father and Son], "Primeros bailes" [First Parties], "Problemas de adolescencia" [Teenage Problems], "Conciencia política" [Political Awareness], "Actividades políticas" [Political Activity], and "Faz estacionaria" [Stationary Phase]. The categories and subsections focus primarily on the Oedipus complex, the origins of sadomasochism, and the effects of social relations on individual psychology and career choices. The fact that they are given such self-conscious headings, however, indicates that they are not unquestioned categories of analysis in the novel; they elicit laughter from readers familiar with psychoanalytic studies which presume to simplify complex psychological structures into narrow scenarios of observable cause and direct effect.

In his discussion of parody and the Latin American baroque, Severo Sarduy, a contemporary of Puig,[2] addresses the function of quotation, the practice of inserting either direct citations from other texts into one's own, or of adopting the codes and structures of other texts in a more generalized way—intertextuality. It is this last type of quotation which is exemplified in Puig's use of the psychological biographies of Leo and Gladys

> The signs are used here but only in order to reveal them as arbitrary, as pure formal simulacrum. Citations which are inscribed within the domain of the baroque because upon parodying it, deforming it, emptying it, employing it uselessly or with the aim of misrepresenting the code to which they belong, reflect only upon their own artificiality. Neither distance, nor the scale of objects in perspective, nor volume: everything "fails" here, when only the falsely natural procedures may be found which we employ to give the illusion of them, to deceive.... The parodic use of the code to which a work belongs, its apotheosis and mockery—the coronation and dethroning of Backtine—the interior of the work itself are the best means for revealing that convention, that deceit. (Sarduy 125)

Puig achieves a similar parodic effect with regard to psychoanalytic strategies in his next novel, *El beso de la mujer araña* (1976, *The Kiss of the Spider Woman*). As the two main characters discuss their different philosophies of life (the homosexual Molina is a true romantic, and the macho revolutionary Valentín is a staunch realist), the narrator intervenes with footnotes which paraphrase various theoretical accounts of the origins of homosexuality. The footnotes suggest that the expert analysis should be read simultaneously—or interwoven—with the characters' dialogue. The disjunction between the two forms of discourse, however, creates the parodic effect: the analysis satisfactorily explains neither Molina's experience nor Valentin's homosexual encounter with his cellmate. Even though the narrator displays no specific disagreement with the psychoanalytic explanations, their scientific tone always falls short of the character. Molina himself displays an intimate and ongoing interaction with the factors that shape his identity. He does not classify, bracket, or sort the components of his sexuality as much as he lives them; his self-presentation is ultimately privileged over the footnotes because the fictional text is inherently more attractive to the novel's readers. The explanatory nature of psychoanalysis is parodied in this structure, then, by being juxtaposed with a character who demands to be listened to as something more than the result of certain categorizable events.

In *The Buenos Aires Affair,* however, the case studies are not footnoted; they are included in the text of part 1 of the novel. Their presence in the body of the text integrates them into the fiction whereas *El beso de la mujer araña* maintains an apparent dichotomy between fictional text and scientific text with the use of the footnotes. The case studies in *The Buenos Aires Affair*, then, seem to impart authorized knowledge to the reader, who is invited to play the role of detective in this psychological mystery. They offer, however, only partially valid clues to the mystery of why Leo must reenact a murder, and why Gladys is his willing victim.

Less sophisticated and more centered on Freudian complexes than the footnotes in *El beso de la mujer araña*, these categories appear as pseudoscientific explanations for characters' adult behaviors. Their simplistic subheadings seem to be decoys, clearly naming them as limited categorizations of life stages which only sometimes legitimately account for (and sometimes misconstrue) the characters' experiences. They throw back onto the reader the task of *dis*-covering a reality more complicated, more powerful, more mysterious. The novel never offers closure for that task, however, showing the psychoanalytic tradition—as well as its own conventions—to be participants in the creation of narratives that protect and conceal the real trauma which always lurks behind them.

Puig's combination of the form of the detective novel with the psychological case studies produces an intriguing ambiguity with regard to those two discourses. Validated as foundational structures of the text, they are violated when they are used self-consciously and too frequently. Lucille Kerr's (1987, 137) reading of *The Buenos Aires Affair* points out the seductive effect of that ambiguity on readers: "Puig's characters are as much the protagonists of a play on a psychoanalytic or psychiatric case . . . as they are the main actors in a criminal one. . . . And the novel's readers are as much the investigators of a crime of desire as they are the conventional subjects of a desire for crime." To point out the ambiguity in Puig's use of psychoanalytic and detective conventions is not, however, to dismiss their importance as investigative tools. It merely underscores their limitations as fully explanatory systems. Since there is no authorized detective assigned to investigate the apparent crime which opens *The Buenos Aires Affair*, the text leads its readers to adopt that identity, seducing us into desiring the crime. We want there to be a case so that we can solve it. The status of crime itself, then, is under investigation. As Celeste Fraser Delgado (1994, 71) argues, Puig displays "the intersection of the discourses of sexuality and criminality" in the years following the first Peronist presidency by "unmooring violence from any isolated act, [unsettling] the mechanism by which classic detective fiction disavowed the complicity of social relations and the discourses that sustain them in the production of 'crime.'"

Incorporating elements of popular detective fiction into a complex parody not only of that genre but also of psychoanalytic discourse, the novel presents additional sources of information. The inclusion of police reports, newspaper headlines, an autopsy report, a murder scene, and a missing person clearly places this work within the genre of the crime novel, and, as we will see, there is a displacement of the usual case which detective fiction purports to solve. However, like typical detective fictions (as understood through Todorov's [1977] analysis of the temporal duality of the detective form), Puig's novel moves backward from a crime scene to the situations in the past which led up to it, and finally returns to a reenactment of the crime based on the detective's (in this case, the reader's) increased knowledge. In this sense, *The Buenos Aires Affair* fulfills its announced role as *novela policial*.[3]

Puig's novel also subverts the notion of detective fiction, however, by the way in which it returns to the past. The past is presented through the collage of Freudian categories already mentioned, Lacanian psychoanalytic principles, and political references; the text's present contains only an intentional reenactment of an earlier crime, and solving the mystery is not about identifying the criminal; rather, it is about determining why Leo restages a murder twenty years after its occurrence.

The mystery that must be solved according to the conventions of detective fiction is the one with which the novel begins, which in this case is a simulacrum.

The kidnapping and expected murder of Gladys turns out to be a staged event; the real crime was committed twenty years before the opening scene of the text, and involved Leo's rape and murder of another man. Although this murder is first chronologically and is revealed to be Leo's only real crime in story, it is marginalized in the detective structure by being completely disclosed to the readers; it is presented along with Leo's biographical information, becoming one of the clues about why Leo has abducted Gladys with the apparent intention to rape and then kill her.

I use the term simulacrum to describe the novel's opening crime scene in a different way than that in which Jean Baudrillard employs it in "The Precession of Simulacra," where he argues that the neutralization of reality occurs in mass media first through reflecting it, then masking it, then masking its absence, and finally through relinquishing all relation to reality. The simulacrum at work in *The Buenos Aires Affair* is more akin to that which Linda Hutcheon (1988) describes in her critique of Baudrillard:

> [P]ostmodern art works to contest the "simulacrization" process of mass culture—not by denying it or lamenting it—but by problematizing the entire notion of the representation of reality. . . . It is not that truth and reference have ceased to exist, as Baudrillard claims; it is that they have ceased to be unproblematic issues. We are not witnessing a degeneration into the hyperreal without origin or reality, but a questioning of what "real" can mean and how we can *know* it. The function of the conjunction of the historiographic and the metafictive in much contemporary fiction . . . is to make the reader aware of the distinction between the *events* of the past real and the *facts* by which we give meaning to that past, by which we assume to know it. (223)

The Buenos Aires Affair works with intertextuality and indeterminacy to comment on the effects of various disciplinary controls over the individual body and psyche, and it simultaneously creates a new form of (anti)detective fiction through its exposure of the contradictions inherent in available methods of solving crimes and psychoanalyzing subjects. Like Leo's troubled masculine subjectivity, detective fiction itself is displayed in the novel as a site of lack through the use of the misleading opening crime scene.

The text begins on May 21, 1969, with Clara, Gladys's mother, discovering that her daughter has disappeared from their vacation beach house. Gladys's absence is the setup for the criminal investigation which the reader is invited to undertake, and the following chapter describes in vivid detail what the conventions of detective fiction lead one to believe is the crime scene: a man wearing only a towel listens for sounds outside the door of his apartment, which is decorated tastefully with international art objects (especially sharp objects—scissors, knives, swords, acupuncture needles); a woman is tied up and gagged on the bed; and in the kitchen are a syringe, some injection vials, and pieces of cotton soaked in alcohol. The narrator anticipates reader expectation by slyly mentioning that

> no se vislumbran huellas de violencia, tales como hematomas violáceos o heridas con sangre coagulada roja oscura. Tampoco hay rastro alguno de violencia sexual. (18)

> [there are no signs of violence, such as purple bruises or wounds clotted with dark blood. Neither is there any sign of sexual violence (on the woman's body).] (Puig 1976, translation by Suzanne Jill Levine)

By indicating the absence of violence, the narrator both validates and exposes the conventions to which the text is appealing in these first two chapters. That is, it lays bare the assumptions that if a woman is missing, she must have been kidnapped; if she was taken by a man, sexual assault must be involved; if sharp weapons are present, they will be used against her. These assumptions are, necessarily, those of the reader, and in providing a typical description of a crime scene, the narration manipulates its readers into actively desiring—choosing to interpret the description such that—the scene will produce violence against the woman.

In this novel, the immediate past of this supposedly criminal scene, introduced in the first two chapters, is not a past filled with criminal motives at all. It is a past within which are hidden the real crimes. The present (1969) crime scene is a reaction to previous violent events which prove to be much more traumatic and transgressive. The temporal postponements in *The Buenos Aires Affair* do not simply increase suspense; they do not just retard the progress of the story. They change the story, fundamentally altering the case to be solved. The first temporal shift of the narrative occurs in chapter 3, which contains Gladys's biography. This chapter postpones the story's progress by returning to May 29, 1934, the day she was conceived. Chapter 4 continues Gladys's story up to June 1968. Then chapter 5 deals with May 1969 and an anonymous phone call to the police reporting a possible murder. Chapter 6 returns to the distant past by reporting Leo's biography, followed by two chapters which offer stream of consciousness narration by Gladys and Leo, respectively, in April 1969. Part 2 jumps back three days before the last date referred to in part 1 (April 24, 1969) and then follows a strictly chronological order, covering only one month—late April to late May 1969—in the last eight chapters of the novel.[4]

As readers learn more about the personal histories of Gladys and Leo, it gradually becomes evident that they (the readers) have been duped by the text's introduction of the classic crime scene: the abduction and probable rape and murder of a woman who had been recovering from a nervous breakdown. This simulated crime, with which *The Buenos Aires Affair* opens and closes, retains its position as the privileged mystery scene in the novel. Given all of the temporal leaps made to accommodate the histories of the two main characters, however, that scene is marked as not the "real thing."

In traditional detective fiction, the significance of the crime scene is taken for granted: a murderer transgresses the law and must be identified and punished. In *The Buenos Aires Affair* the significance of the crime scene is precisely that it is a scene, a reenactment of an earlier crime, the details of which have been clearly explained by the time the present situation's resolution is narrated. The question for the detective-reader, then, is what does the reenactment accomplish for the characters? Thus, the detective function is displaced from catching a criminal in the present to determining the significance of the characters' actions. The novel becomes a psychological mystery rather than a criminal one.

In fact, according to information included in the biographies, Leo's masculine subjectivity requires a much more complex reading than the opening chapters indicate. He is not simply a male subject who attacks an objectified female in order to reinforce his masculinity. The rape/murder scene between Leo and Gladys is shown to be a repetition of an earlier event in Leo's life, and to conform to patterns of desire set up in Gladys's childhood. It evokes a series of conflicts inherent in both of their subjectivities.

The earlier event is narrated in the biographical subsection called "Juventud de Leo" [Leo's Youth]. One afternoon, having recently lost an erection while having sex with a girlfriend (because he had come to find pleasure in intercourse only when his partners offered resistance), Leo visits a female prostitute who had once complained that his penis was too large. The prostitute refuses to accept him, and he begins walking home. On the street, a young gay man offers to perform oral sex on Leo. The protagonist gladly accepts, eager to release his sexual frustrations. They enter a vacant lot, and Leo soon desires to penetrate the other man, who refuses after seeing the size of Leo's member. Leo rapes him, covering the victim's mouth with his hand in order to silence the screams of pain. The victim bites the hand just as Leo's pleasure is increasing, and Leo smashes a brick into the other man's head. Leo's pleasure subsides when the unconscious victim can no longer resist, and he abandons the gay man in the vacant lot, assuming him to be on the verge of death.

Leo considers himself a murderer. His greatest guilt is now associated not only with sex, as it had been before (due to his father's prohibitions on sexual games Leo had played with his sisters when he was younger) but also with homosexuality. This event is the motivating factor in Leo's subsequent impotence with women and increasingly violent temperament. The incident is never established as a murder by the narrative itself, however. There is only the strong suggestion that the gay man eventually died:

> A la mañana siguiente entre las noticias policiales del diario figuraba el caso de un amoral encontrado en fin de vida en un baldío, por aparentes motivos de hurto. Nunca apareció crónica referente a la captura del culpable. Tampoco se publicó la noticia de la muerte de la victima. (92–3)

> [In the following morning's paper among the police chronicles there was a notice about a pervert found near death in a vacant lot, the apparent motive robbery. A report referring to the capture of the guilty party never appeared. Neither did the notice of the victim's death.]

The lack of a death notice highlights the importance of Leo's interpretation of and reaction to the event. He must live with an absence of resolution and with the fact that the victim was anonymous. His need eventually to confess to murder indicates Leo's certainty that he had, indeed, killed the young man, and that the event haunts him; he cannot, however, make restitution for a crime against a man with no name.

Kerr (1987, 151) traces the implications of that certainty in Gladys's abduction and in Leo's reaction to his stay in prison (he is arrested for political involvement) and the torture to which he is subjected there

> [T]his criminal version of Leo's actions—the image of Leo as a murderer still undiscovered and unpunished, but already pursued—begins to inform his interpretation of material reality as well. In the section entitled "*Actividades políticas . . .*" Leo's experience in prison is transformed into a painful punishment and pleasurable purgation. Having been tortured, Leo confesses the political secrets he is "guilty" of possessing but is finally unable to keep. He not only suffers but also analyzes that suffering so as to make himself pay (through both pain and pleasure, it seems) for his various, and now superimposed, crimes.

Although I will return to Kerr's analysis of the "painful punishment and pleasurable purgation" which inform Leo's experience of violence as both victim and victimizer, her description of Leo's self-image—"a murderer still undiscovered and unpunished, but already pursued"—connects, within Leo's psychology, the rape of the gay man with the need to stage Gladys's murder. Leo seeks punishment and closure for the earlier event by creating an occasion in which he will be seen to be a criminal and will be pursued as one. The staged assault on Gladys, however, includes a curious shift from the male homosexual to a female heterosexual as victim; the reenactment of the original crime is made to conform to a pattern of male sadism and female masochism, and this restructuring of the components of the original crime is an attempt to simplify them into accordance with a fiction of masculine mastery over the feminine other.

The key to subjectivity in this novel is the ambiguity of the penis in relation to power (which is established by the recognition of others) and psychological structures. The psychological histories of both Leo and Gladys reveal a fascination with the penis in its conflation with what more properly should be called the Lacanian phallus—symbolic and social power. The confusion of the two is the central problem of subjectivity in *The Buenos Aires Affair*.

The two murders which shape this novel display that confusion: the murder of Gladys, which turns out to be a staged murder; and the *crimen del baldío,* which is revealed to be the only real murder in the story even though, because it is completely disclosed to readers, it is not central to the novel's detective structure. Leo confesses the crimen del baldío to María Esther, an older artist whom he recommends for a national art award. He confesses, however, without giving the details and by including misleading information; for example, that the victim was a young woman. When María Esther reports to the police that Leo is possibly a murderer, the police question him and conclude that the informant must have been lying. Then, in an attempt at removing María Esther's suspicions and keeping her from further contact with the police, Leo kidnaps Gladys, who is the older woman's rival for the art award; he drugs her and pretends to plan her murder. This performance of criminal acts is staged in order to convince María Esther that Leo's vague confession to murder had really dealt with an intention, not a past action. It is important, also, that his intent be seen by María Esther as a heterosexual (that is, "normal") encoding of violence, so that the contradictions in Leo's gendered subjectivity not be revealed.

Leo wants María Esther to believe that he had planned to kill Gladys, and that she (María Esther) prevents him from committing murder. That way, the suspicions he had aroused in her by discussing the original murder would be discounted. María Esther would consider the case closed; she would be convinced that she had saved both Leo and Gladys from the crime, and it would never occur to her that Leo had really been talking about a different murder when he confessed to her.

The reader, like María Esther, is seduced by Leo's performance of an abduction and planned murder. Although the abduction of Gladys is ostensibly the central crime mystery in the novel, the crime scene itself—Gladys bound on the bed—is just a cover-up. The striking aspect of this structure is that it is such a plausible scene, given the pervasiveness of representations of men establishing personal power through assaults on women. This pervasiveness is acknowledged by the text itself. As the novel opens, Gladys's mother suddenly realizes that her daughter has disappeared from their vacation beach house. The mother absentmindedly recites a poem (Bécquer's *Rima 72,* which is about a young girl's death) as she goes through the house noticing clues related to Gladys's absence. Kerr (1987, 44) observes:

> The poem, a fiction that fills in much of Clara Evelia's thoughts while she conducts her search for her daughter, whose body is nowhere to be found, fills not only part of the chapter's text and Clara Evelia's mental ramblings, but also the criminal space created by the whole chapter. In that poem it is a female corpse that fills a funereal niche. . . . It supplies the text with a body, a potentially criminal figure, that seems to fit perfectly into and fill the empty space created by Gladys's disappearance. . . . The text fills its perplexing voids with a dominant fiction: the image of death solidified in the corpse of the young girl seen in the poem of chapter 1 and in the body of Gladys found in chapter 2. Though this fatal image seems to be a possibility too horrible for Clara Evelia's imagination, it is, we must remember, the very fiction toward which she is drawn and with whose complete representation she is finally so satisfied.

There is a pleasurable moment for Clara Evelia amidst the suspense of finding her daughter missing: the chapter ends with her finally remembering the conclusion of the poem:

> . . . cuando las maderas / crujir hace el viento / y asota los vidrios / el fuerte aguacero, / de la pobre niña / a solas me acuerdo. / Del húmedo muro / tendida en un . . . / tendida en un . . . "—cómo seguía? [. . .] ¡qué no hubiese dado por saber dónde estaba su hija en ese preciso momento! ". . . allí cae la lluvia / con un son eterno; / allí la combate / el soplo del cierzo. / Del húmedo muro / tendida en un . . . en un . . . ¡hueco! /

> acaso de frío / se hielan sus huesos . . .," logró por fin recordar, con satisfacción. (*Buenos Aires* 15–16)
>
> . . . when the wind makes / the rafter creak, / when the violent rain / lashes the windows, / lonely I remember / that poor girl. / Stretched in the . . . in the . . . "what came next? [. . .] what wouldn't she have given to know where her daughter was at that very moment! "there falls the rain / with its noise eternal, / there the north wind / fights with the rain. / Stretched in the . . . in the hollow! / of the damp bricks, / perhaps her bones freeze with the cold . . . ?" finally she remembered, to her satisfaction. (Kerr 1987, 143; translation of the lines from the Bécquer poem by John Masefield, *Anthology of World Poetry.* Edited by Mark Van Doren. New York: Halcyion House, 1939, p. 650)

A body is needed as evidence for a crime, but is also desired by the detective function itself. That is to say, Clara Evelia as well as the readers actually hope to see Gladys's dead body because the spectacle will relieve the tension created by the mysteries—the mystery of the poem's conclusion, that of the novel's opening scene, and that of the story of Gladys and Leo. The pleasure of closure in a crime story is simultaneously a pleasure in violence. Clara Evelia, María Esther, and the readers are likely to understand Leo's desire to kidnap, rape, or even murder Gladys, because the scenes to which they are respectively exposed lead them—as detectives—to desire that resolution.

This dominant fiction, produced by Leo himself and by the text's teasing of our reader-detective tendencies, resists the complex implications of Leo's violent, homoerotic history. Even though *The Buenos Aires Affair* offers only a series of partial clues and dead ends, an examination of masculinity in the novel requires further investigation of Leo's subjectivity. Why does he need to reenact his crime? And why does he do it with a female victim rather than with a male one?

The crime scene with Gladys is the culmination of a plan, one that results in physical (sexual) pleasure for Leo, but in a way that only reproduces Leo's splitting. He sets up the scene, but it is María Esther who initiates the sexual activity to which it leads. Leo first becomes aroused because she, the mother figure, touches him. This sexual experience provides a pleasure counter to Leo's possible masculine self-images, images necessarily based on dominance and violence according to his personal history. Leo's subjectivity-in-crisis is intensely bound to gender and his inability to appropriate for himself any viable definition of masculinity. Leo uses his former lover Gladys to perform a fictional murder in which he wants María Esther to believe. He combines sexuality, murder, and being seen by a mother figure—an attempt to recreate and resolve his internal conflict. Leo reenacts the murder of the gay man as a way to compensate for his various forms of sexual repression.[5]

Thus, Leo's plan to convince María Esther of his intention to murder Gladys suits his cross-purposes. Roberto Echevarren (1986) reads *The Buenos Aires Affair* as a narrative of traitors and spies, suggesting that Leo feels himself to be a traitor (both of his gay rape/murder victim and of the political group he denounces under torture by the Peronist police). The protagonist is motivated by a dual purpose: to hide his identity as traitor, and to be seen and punished for his traitorous behavior. He wants to protect himself and yet still find a way to free himself from guilt. He desires to be labeled a traitor-murderer by others so as not to bear the burden of that designation in isolation, but he does not want to face the social consequences of the revelation of his crimes. This dual goal is partially accomplished when, through the simulated crime against Gladys, the real crime—at the very moment when Leo is supposedly found out—is successfully hidden. María Esther is led off track. Even though María Esther sees only a misleading spectacle, she fulfills Leo's need to be seen.

Leo simultaneously validates his passivity as an observed object (which implicitly grants Gladys, María Esther, and readers the power to position him within their own interpretive structures) and his controlling power as the orchestrator (artist) of the crime scene when he is caught in the act. Not surprisingly, Leo's performance leads to sexual activity, with his penis taking center stage. He is caught *in the act* in many ways: his guilt is exposed, the act is sexual, the simulation of a crime is shown to be acting, and all of the characters in this Sarduyan postmodern moment are caught—ensnared—by the fictive web of the text itself.

The portion of the novel that addresses these multiple aspects of the *act* is narrated in sections representing the characters' separate thoughts. Each section begins with a heading that describes the action with which the thoughts are connected:

> Sensaciones experimentadas por Leo, al verse en el espejo junto a Gladys, inmóvil en la cama, y junto a María Esther, la cual de pie en el centro del cuarto, bajo la amenaza de su revólver según lo previsto por el plan de acción, exclama "Por favor no hagas una locura."
>
> [Sensations experienced by Leo, upon seeing himself in the mirror next to Gladys, motionless in the bed, and next to María Esther, who, standing in the middle of the room, under the threat of his revolver according to the plan of action, exclaims "Please don't do anything crazy."]

> Sensaciones experimentadas por Leo al notar que el ojo de Gladys le mira el bulto curvo que su sexo forma bajo la toalla arrollada . . .
>
> [Sensations experienced by Leo when he notices that Gladys's eye looks at the curved bulk formed by his sex organ under the towel]
>
> Sensaciones experimentadas por Leo, al notar que también María Esther mira en dirección del lugar ya señalado . . .
>
> [Sensations experienced by Leo when he notices that María Esther, too, is looking at the same place]
>
> Sensaciones experimentadas por Leo, ante el movimiento sorpresivo de María Esther, la cual le toma bajo la toalla el miembro viril (llevada por un confuso intento de conciliación) y le dice "¿Qué tenés acá? ¿un pajarito?" . . . (185–87)
>
> [Sensations experienced by Leo, upon María Esther's surprising movement when she takes hold of the virile member under the towel (led by a confused attempt at reconciliation) and says "What do you have here? a little birdie?"]

The ensuing sexual activity is narrated so that all of the action is attributed to Leo, and most of the reactions are the women's. Leo sees that María Esther smiles at him. Then he caresses her cheek, sets the revolver on the bed next to Gladys's feet, takes off his towel, turns on a lamp, leads María Esther to the bed, lays her down beside Gladys, caresses María Esther's pubis, kisses her on the mouth, and then "compasiva pero dolorosamente" [compassionately but painfully] penetrates Gladys.

Kerr (1987, 157–58) addresses the fact that this scene is the mirror (reverse) image of the "original" crime from 1949.[6] Whereas Leo's sexual aggression is rejected and leads to extreme violence in the *crimen del baldío*, Leo's penis is finally the main attraction toward which events and other characters are drawn in the murder/rape performance with Gladys. After touching Leo in her conciliatory gesture, María Esther fantasizes about a science-fiction film in which an intelligent, mature woman is announcing some international upheaval related to a new transmitting satellite and is being ignored by a group of "baratas muchachas echadas sobre el camastro" [cheap girls lying on the broken down cot]. She imagines the satellite's transmitting antenna to be the vehicle of contact between enemies, a mighty uniting phallus. The concavity of the structure in María Esther's fantasy is in contrast to its having been "lanzado desde la tierra" [thrust from the earth], which makes it a symbol both of Gladys's exposed genitals and of Leo's penis. The references to "ciertas potencias extranjeras" [certain foreign powers] and the "baratas muchachas" indicate a sense of rivalry between the two women, a rivalry that Leo's sexual prowess purports to overcome (192–93).

Gladys, on the other hand, experiences the scene in a haze induced by sleeping pills Leo had put in a drink for her. She seems unaware of María Esther's participation in the sensuality of the moment. Her impressions are indistinct, tinged with a sense of foreboding, until Leo penetrates her without foreplay. At that moment, she fantasizes that he is a farmer thrusting his plowshare into the earth. Her thoughts, shown to cause genuine pleasure for Gladys, reflect the discourse of the Latin American tradition of *novelas de la tierra*, which make earth a metaphor for women (and vice versa) and which portray female pain as a necessary sacrifice for the founding of nations:

> La reja del arado es afilada y tosca, imperfecta, hecha en la fragua a golpes de martillo. El labrador avanza decidido, con fuerza clava el arado. La tierra se abre, el arado avanze. ¡Oh buen hombre! labras con tu sudor el porvenir de nuestra patria. . . . Yo, la tierra, estoy herida, sin quejidos me desangro, y en cebada, centeno, trigo y maíz doy mi vida. Quizá en tu modestia y virtud no alcances a comprender de tu labor la magnitud ¡tú siembras la semilla del amor y la amistad! ¡Gloria a ti labrador! ¡tú forjas con tu rudeza de mi país la grandeza! (194)

> [The plowshare is sharp and rough, imperfect, forged by a hammer. The farmer moves forward with determination, he forcefully thrusts in the plowshare. The earth opens, the plow advances. Oh good man! with your sweat you till the future of our nation. . . . I, the earth, am wounded, without moaning I bleed, and in barley, rye, wheat, and corn I give my life. Perhaps in your modest and virtuous attitude you will not comprehend your labor's magnitude, you sow the seed of love and friendship! Glory to thee, farmer! you forge with your toughness our beloved country's greatness!]

Gladys's fantasy removes her from the crime scene and elevates the rape to the level of patriotic discourse. Identified with the fertile earth, she comes to embody nature and nation in a self-sacrificing song to masculine *rudeza.* To the degree that this recitation helps her to transcend the sexual reality of the moment, Gladys participates in a world of pre-given words which structure her experience, even to the point of metaphorizing her humanity out of the picture.

Gladys's mental oration during Leo's assault and the nationalist poem her mother had forced her to recite in her childhood (and which she had been unable to remember on stage) indicate her retreat into conventional poetic imagery to account for (produce?) her own pleasure in forced intercourse with Leo. These recitations curiously resolve her repressed contradictions. In her most degrading sexual situation, Gladys fulfills her mother's hopes for her, namely, that she remember a nationalistic poem (Colmeiro 1988, 184).

Gladys had always resisted her mother's love of recitation because she considered it inauthentic repetition, or bad art. Ironically, in this inauthentic murder scene, Gladys expresses more pleasure than at any other point in the novel, and she does so through the stylized, stereotyped recitation which Sarduy has defined as the parodic display. Gladys is fully realized in her role as consummate masochist because Leo uses his penis to act out the dominant fiction of the cruel male who nobly opens the earth and women in order to create good. The blatant sadomasochism of this scene exposes the perversity of the nationalistic discourses of Latin America's foundational fictions, especially through the equation of women and earth that has been prevalent since Romanticism and particularly overworked in the realist fictions of the early to mid-twentieth century (Sommer 1991).

However, Leo's role as masculine aggressor evokes the nationalist and naturalist myths of the founding father/farmer. The male sexual organ functions in this scene as a savior for Gladys and María Esther. They grant it the power to resolve their internal conflicts, to choose between them, and to represent their value as women insofar as it seeks them out. In this sense, Puig has parodied female characters whose excessive acquiescence to the cult of machismo relegates them to an inevitable social and sexual masochism.

For Leo, however, the penis is an even more problematic presence. It cannot serve him as an exterior symbol of the healing of internal divisions. For the male protagonist, the penis makes self-definition difficult. Even in this adult scene designed and produced by Leo himself, in which his genitalia are the focus, the penis is most painfully the symbolic site of his psychological conflicts. Leo's thoughts during this scene are a condensed version of the fantasies which continuously subvert his masculine ego ideal throughout the novel. He has achieved success in terms of career and reputation: he acquired a great deal of money and an education in art when he was an ambassador's assistant in Scandinavia, and he is now the renowned editor of Argentina's premier magazine for the arts. His idea of responsibility and stability led him to marry at age thirty-one, but his impotence and a violent sexual attack on his wife resulted in a permanent separation. In contrast to his public persona, his private life is haunted by the guilt of his aggression and by his inability to invest in personal relationships other than casual sexual encounters and meetings with prostitutes.

The crime scene with Gladys and María Esther serves as a microcosm of the desires and fantasies which structure Leo's experience of masculinity as almost pure conflict. His thoughts range widely, periodically interrupted by descriptions of the action of the scene as well as by passages focalized through the two women. Read in the order in which they appear in the chapter, and understood in relation to the interaction among the three principal characters, however, the sections representing Leo's fantasies highlight his contradictory identifications and incompatible subject positions.

When he sees himself in the mirror and hears María Esther's admonition, "Por favor no hagas una locura" ["Please don't do anything crazy"], he imagines in great detail the birth certificate of a privileged boy. Then, registering the fact that both Gladys and María Esther direct their gaze to his crotch, his thoughts are transformed into an embedded narrative about a blind mother who is horrified to discover while bathing her infant son that he has the sex organs of a grown man. This sequence reveals quite clearly the guilt caused by Leo's repression of aggressive sexual impulses. As a privileged member of the social elite and as an intellectual, he sees his identity printed out on the formal birth certificate. When he is begged not to do "anything crazy," the contrast between his social position and his most immediate desires and fantasies is laid bare.

The story of the blind mother reinforces that sense of Leo's being an impostor. The male infant laughs gaily during his bath, innocently enjoying the attention of his mother, but the reality is that he is a sexual monster, assaulting her sensibilities and even her motherhood with his unnatural anatomy. Her blindness is further indication of Leo's conviction that he is forever hiding the ugly reality of his deformity—located at the site of his penis. In Leo's psychic structure, his penis is too large for him. Imagining himself to be a baby with a man's sex organs, he feels that his stature as a person does not measure up to the biological evidence of his masculinity.

Two sets of relationships are at play in this sequence. On the one hand, there is the issue of the equation of penis and phallus; on the other hand, there is the problem of the gaze of the Other. When images of masculinity conflate the penis and the phallus, they doom the male subject to failure (Silverman 1992, 42). No male can approximate the power of the phallus because it is out of reach by definition. In the patriarchal confusion of the Law of Language and the Law of Kinship Structure as outlined by Althusser (1977) the phallus, which in Lacanian terms actually insures lack in the subject, comes to represent masculine access to power through the penis.

For Leo, who is marked in *The Buenos Aires Affair* as an overendowed male, the penis-phallus equation reduces his subjectivity to the level of a helpless infant denied access even to maternal care because of his own unwitting/unwilling participation in the power of a Law identified with the male sexual organ. As Leo perceives that Gladys and María Esther gaze at his partially covered penis, the blind mother in his imagination is horrified by what she discovers there. The narrative builds tension around her discovery of the unexpected deformation by following the progress of the bath: the mother begins by washing the baby's head, then his dimpled arms and armpits, "the nipples and little belly button." The child's nurses try to take the sponge away from the mother before she has reached his genitals, but she persists. Had she been able to see, the story would not have the power of a repression. Leo's fixation with the size of his own penis is a symptom of his fear of being exposed as a boy whose being does not inhabit the physical structures it ought to occupy. The revelation of that which is hidden from view is dreaded because there is nothing to support it, no foundation for it.

This sense of being an impostor is carried over into the next passage of the novel. When María Esther grabs Leo under the towel and asks "¿Qué tenés acá? ¿un pajarito?" [What do you have here? a little birdie?], Leo's fantasy turns to Praxiteles' Hellenic statue of Hermes, whose right arm and penis are missing, but whose testicles and pubic hair indicate the former presence of a large penis. María Esther's question, one more appropriately addressed to a child, alerts readers immediately to the connection with Leo's older sister Olga and the games she used to play with him until he was seven years old:

> El juego consistía en lo siguiente: Olga decía "había una vez una hormiguita que iba paseando, paseando . . ." y con las yemas de sus dedos índice y mayor tamborileaba desde la muñeca hasta la axila del niño y allí le hacía cosquillas, el niño se contorsionaba y ambos reían, pero la culminación del juego venía después, cuando Olga empezaba a tamborilear por el pie del niño e iba subiendo por la rodilla, donde hacía una pausa, para después continuar el ascenso por el muslo hasta llegar a la rosada ingle infantil donde los tamborileos se multiplicaban y Olga exclamaba ". . . y la hormiguita encontró un ratoncito y asustada se escapó . . . ," a lo cual seguían cosquillas en la barrriga, ". . . pero después la hormiguita volvió y vio que no era un ratoncito, era una campanita, y empezó a tirar de la campanita, tilín, tilín, . . . ," y Olga tironeaba del diminuto miembro viril, haciendo reír convulsivamente al niño. (84–85)

> [The game was as follows: Olga would say "Incey wincey spider, climbed up the water spout . . ." and with the tips of her middle and index finger she would drum upon the child's wrist all the way to his armpit and there tickle him, the child would twist and turn and both would laugh, but the climax of the game would come afterwards, when Olga would begin to drum along the child's foot and then go up to the knee, where she would pause, to then continue her climb along the thigh until reaching the pink infantile groin where the drumming would multiply and Olga would exclaim ". . . and the incey wincey spider found a little mouse and cried wee wee wee, all the way home . . ." to which the tickling on the belly continued, ". . . but then the incey spider came back again and saw that it wasn't a little mouse, it was a little bell, and she began to ring the bell, ring-a-ring-a-ring . . . ," and Olga would tug at the small virile member, making the child laugh convulsively.

That game is recorded in the section of Leo's biography called "Olga y Leo," which follows "Padre e hijo." These two categories comprise the period of Leo's young life in which the absence of his parents led to a particularly difficult and concentrated oedipal conflict, the details of which are so well fitted to a Freudian schema that it is impossible for Puig's readers to ignore their self-conscious implications for Leo's adult problems.

The father left the children in the care of a maid after Leo's mother died due to weakness caused by the boy's birth. When Leo was born, his sister Amalia—who later became head of the household—was fourteen years old, and Olga was seven. Not until he himself is seven does Leo meet his father, and then only for an afternoon. Leo tells him that he wants to marry Olga when he grows up, and the father makes clear his disapproval of that desire. Later that day, Olga refuses to play the game with Leo anymore, saying that "Daddy would get angry." The next day, Leo looks through the bathroom keyhole and sees Olga naked. He reports to the maid his discovery that "Olga has a little plant." Amalia punishes Olga, who in turn slaps the boy. Amalia says to Leo, "You deserve it, with poor Daddy so sick and you still behaving like a bad boy. Oh, Leo, you're very little but we all have to pray for Daddy to get well."

In concert with this accusation, Leo's father dies a week later. The boy's guilt complex is well entrenched: not only has he transgressed against the no of the father (which is introduced late and with no forewarning), and the prohibition of incestuous desire, but Leo's discovery of female anatomical difference is now related to the real death of the father—not just to his symbolic power. Leo's being a "bad boy"—spying on his naked sister—is connected, through

Amalia's rebuke, to his father's disappearance. The boy's discovery of sexual difference is tied in this case to the loss of the parental prohibitions on desire and to the actual loss of the father.

The oedipal period for Leo combines Freudian notions with Lacanian ones to confuse the site of lack. If in Freud it is anatomical observation of the female body which introduces the fear of castration, in Lacan it is the name/no of the father that becomes the productive symbol of patriarchal law and gender differentiation. By identifying with the father's symbolic power, Leo might successfully have entered into the order of signification without the perpetual sensation of lack which imaginary access to phallic power is supposed to gloss. The death of his particular father, however, removes the very presence which is supposed to offer symbolic compensation for Leo's acquiescence to the prohibitions of patriarchal law. For this character, then, the father condemns without offering the delayed access to that same power which supposedly would facilitate the boy's entry into masculine identification. In Leo's imaginary structure, the specter of death is the result of masculinity, but resistance to the No of the Father in the form of sexual transgression of patriarchal norms (homosexuality or incestuous desire) is no solution either because of the unbearable guilt produced through its association with the father's death.

Since Leo's masculine subjectivity cannot be based on identification with his father, he is compelled to confirm it by soliciting the validating gaze of any other. Echevarren (1986, 57) understands this character to be caught in a cycle of repetitions of scenes in which he must be seen as masculine in order to hide his pleasure in passivity:

> El yo transgresor, culpable, agresivo de Leo es meramente un agente (héroe) de un goce que surge al concebir en otros ojos la restitución del símbolo fálico al objeto pasivo. Los ojos de un tercero recogen el simbolismo fálico, en su ambigüedad pasivo-activa, sin poder descubrir la raíz pasiva del goce de Leo. Así, al representar engaña, mientras que su goce es verdadero. La castración esencial del yo coexiste en él con la represión de un fin sexual pasivo que se desliza insatisfactoriamente en la masturbación y retorna en el revés de una agresividad y en la intolerancia frente al gozo de la mujer.

> [Leo's transgressive, guilty, aggressive "I" is merely an agent (hero) of a pleasure which appears upon conceiving in other eyes the restitution of the phallic symbol to the passive object. The eyes of a third party take in the phallic symbolism in its passive-active ambiguity, without being able to discover the passive nature of Leo's pleasure. Thus,

> when representing, he deceives, although his pleasure is real. The essential castration of the subject coexists in him with the repression of a passive sexuality which is expressed unsatisfactorily in masturbation, and which returns in aggression and intolerance in the face of women's pleasure. (my translation)]

Leo's changing fantasies in reaction to María Esther's gaze in chapter 13 support this explanation of the relationship between the phallus and the other. Moving from the mental image of the castrated statue of Hermes, Leo pictures a Michelangelo fresco of the Last Judgment as he slowly gets an erection under María Esther's touch. He identifies with Saint Sebastian in the painting, whose penis he considers to be definitely larger than that of Michelangelo's other figures, and who stands with the other saints beside Christ as the sinners are dragged down to hell. The connection here is clearly that Leo's ability to reach penile erection validates him physically and spiritually, linking him with the strong and the good, as long as his erection is seen.

Immediately his thoughts shift again, this time to Wagnerian opera and an identification with Siegfried's waking the sleeping goddess:

> Es entonces cuando ella despierta del letargo y mira en derredor el mundo que le fuera quitado, por mandato divino. Un hombre invencible la ha devuelto a la vida. (191)

> [It is then that she wakes up out of the lethargy and looks around at the world that had been taken from her, by divine command. An invincible man has returned her to life.]

Imagining himself "invincible" and in concert with a "mandato divino," Leo removes the real towel from his own body. This hero of Norse myth, however, is instantly turned into a frightening rapist in the eyes of the opera's audience, who—in Leo's fantasy—see him penetrate the goddess-cum-mortal woman against her will:

> El público se siente ultrajado por tal obscenidad y quiere hacer abandono del teatro, pero Sigfrido lo impide, las salidas habituales no se hallan donde siempre, insensiblemente el teatro de ópera se ha convertido en otro recinto, a la vista no hay salida alguna, y ese lugar ahora se parece más a la carpa de un circo gigantesco. (191)

> [The audience feels outraged by such an obscenity and tries to leave the theater, but Siegfried prevents it, the usual exits are not where they should be, imperceptibly the opera house has turned into another enclosure, there is no exit in sight, and that place now looks more like the tent of a gigantic circus.]

This passage contains the conflict inherent in Leo's inordinate dependence on the gaze of the other for his ability to perform sexually. He himself, as Siegfried, keeps the audience hostage to the performance, yet the presence of others is precisely what cheapens his myth of heroism and turns it into a circus. Even in his own fantasies, Leo cannot be the hero and be observed at the same time; without being seen, he remains unrealized as a subject, but as soon as he is observed, his lack is on display.

The pattern of this impossible relationship to the gaze of a third party begins, as mentioned earlier, with the father's late intervention into Leo's games with Olga. Virtually the only contact the boy has with his father is the paternal admonition not to desire the sister. Leo's masculine identity requires the prohibition, but his subjectivity never comes to occupy the place of the father since the father is dead and gone. This fascination with the simultaneously constraining and defining gaze continues through his adolescence, and is especially relevant in his first sexual relationship.

Although the young Leo believes that images of his girlfriend's vagina produce his orgasms when masturbating, it is actually the fantasy of being seen by her grandmother which produces his pleasure. His sexual relationship to Susana is predicated upon her resistance to his advances. As soon as she begins to express desire as well, Leo is unable to perform—unless the grandmother is in the house, representing the possibility of a witness to the couple's intercourse. Leo imagines a violent visual confrontation:

> Al alcanzar el orgasmo imaginó que la abuela de Susana abría la puerta cancel del zaguán donde la pareja estaba fornicando, y debido a la sorpresa Leo sacaba su miembro de la vagina para espanto de la anciana que miraba dicho objeto como un arma del diablo. Apagado el orgasmo Leo tuvo la impresión de haber gozado plenamente por primera vez en su vida, y decidió que la vagina de Susana había sido la fuente de su satisfacción. (88–90)
>
> [Upon reaching orgasm he imagined that Susana's grandmother opened the hall door of the vestibule where the couple was fornicating, and due to the surprise Leo took his member out of the vagina, thus frightening the grandmother who looked upon said object as a weapon of the devil. The orgasm over, Leo had the impression of having enjoyed it fully for the first time in his life, and he decided that Susana's vagina had been the source of his satisfaction.]

Echevarren (1986) notes the similarity of this scene to the central scene of the novel, in which Leo waits for María Esther so that she can witness his intended rape/murder of Gladys. That scene becomes a sexually rewarding one because of the older woman's willingness to look

> La abuela de su compañera ocupa aquí el lugar del espectador (en su infancia sería la hermana mayor, que prohíbe el acceso a Olga; en la "representación" del capítulo XIII, la madura María Esther.) (58)
>
> [The girlfriend's grandmother occupies the place of the spectator here (in his childhood that would be the older sister, who prohibits access to Olga; in the performance of chapter 13, the mature María Esther) (my translation)].

The requirement of a spectator implicates Leo's subjectivity in the social realm. His masculinity does not exist as such without the gaze of a third party.

The repetition-compulsion acted out in the crime scene appears to solve Leo's problems. He convinces María Esther that he is not a murderer, he is able to maintain an erection and produce pleasure for two women at once, and he is assured of a masculine subject position in their eyes. Chapter 14, however, unravels those successes. Most readings of *The Buenos Aires Affair* to which I have had access maintain a complete silence regarding that chapter, which follows the crime scene. Chapter 14 contains the account of another witness, the doorman of Leo's apartment building. He uses his master key to enter Leo's home at the request of María Esther's son, who had been outside waiting for his mother. He sees Gladys nude on the bed, Leo quickly covering himself, and María Esther adjusting her clothes; he also notices the revolver in Leo's hand. The doorman exits quickly but returns later to apologize:

> Le toqué el timbre y dije que era yo solo. . . . El me abrió, estaba sin vestirse nada. . . . El tipo ahí desnudo y una mujer con un ojo como lastimado, que no lo podía abrir, la que estaba todavía en la cama. . . . Y en eso se empieza a reír y le dice a la mujer que estaba seria en la cama siempre callada, nunca dijo nada, que a mí tampoco se me paraba, que no era él solo. . . . Y me dijo que si ella no se hubiese soltado cuando les golpeamos la puerta, hubiesen terminado lo que tenían que terminar, pero que ahora todo se había jodido y ella tenía la culpa. . . . [M]e empujó contra la cama encima de la mujer . . . pero yo ahí le dije que me tuviera un poco más respeto . . . y ahí me dio un manotón a los huevos y casi me doblo del dolor, y me dijo que lo que pasaba era que a mí no se me paraba. (197–98)
>
> [I rang the bell and said that I was alone. . . . He opened it, he had nothing on. . . . The guy there naked and a woman with one eye sort of wounded, that she couldn't

> open, the woman that was still in the bed. . . . And then he starts laughing and says to the woman who was looking serious in the bed, keeping her mouth shut, she never said a word, he says that I couldn't get a hard-on either, that he wasn't the only one. . . . And he said that if she hadn't let go when we knocked on the door, they would have finished everything they had to finish, but that everything was fucked up now and it was her fault. . . . He pushed me against the bed on top of the woman . . . but then I said that he should have a little more respect for me . . . and right then and there he grabs me in the balls and I almost double over with pain, and he said that my problem was that I couldn't get it up].

Like Leo's father, this witness invalidates Leo's desire by interrupting it. The protagonist blames the doorman for making him appear unable to complete the sex act. In fact, however, Leo's desire for Gladys and María Esther was a result of his own artistic production; it was a desire produced in the service of a plausible fiction. The doorman's appearance on the scene poses as the reason for the interruption of intercourse, but it only enhances the cycle of crimes and witnesses which Leo has set in motion. The goal is always to present himself in a state of masculine wholeness and virility, but the result is always to expose himself (literally) to the risk of detection (of his impotence, both physical and psychological).

This unending cycle of repetitions, exhibitions, and violence leads to Leo's self-destruction. Because he clings so tightly to the equation of penis and phallus, Leo cannot develop his own pleasure. To achieve the dominance expected of himself, he must deny his own desire for reciprocal relationships with feminine figures. Jessica Benjamin (1988, 164) critiques the oedipal model's goal of complete individuation for the male:

> His adult encounter with woman as an acutely desirable object may rob him of his own desire—he is thrown back into feeling that desire is the property of the object. A common convention in comedy is the man helpless before the power of the desirable object; . . . he is overpowered by her attractiveness, knocked off his feet. In this constellation, the male's sexual subjectivity becomes a defensive strategy, an attempt to counter the acute attractive power radiating from the object. . . .

Leo's fantasy of himself as Siegfried parallels Benjamin's reference to the man's being overpowered by the desire which he perceives to be the property of the woman. Just before entering Gladys, Leo thinks of the hero:

> Por fin sabe lo que es una mujer. Lo embarga una emoción para él totalmente desconocida. Tiembla. Una mujer le ha enseñado lo que es el miedo. Una mujer dormida. (190)

> [He finally knows what a woman is. He is seized by an emotion totally unknown to him. He trembles. A woman has taught him what fear is. A sleeping woman.]

Domination and submission, when culturally aligned with masculinity and femininity respectively, result from the failure of self and other to meet as equals in self-assertion and mutual recognition, a failure often initiated in the mother/son relationship. *The Buenos Aires Affair* addresses the same problem, but with a twist. The male protagonist must function in a world and within discourses structured by domination and submission, but his psychological formation has denied him access to either side of the dichotomy. He seeks interaction with women, but the cultural imperative (Law of Kinship Structure) to separate his desire from feminine desire makes him passive-aggressive. He seeks participation in patriarchal domination by objectifying sexual others, but he feels too much guilt and fear in doing so, largely because his first victim was also a man, a mirror of himself relegated to victim status before the Law of Language and the No of the Father.

Ironically, and in concert with that notion of mirroring, the only corpse to appear in *The Buenos Aires Affair* is Leo's. Although he is set up as the problematic victimizer, it is finally his—the murderer's—body that receives the legal/medical gaze usually directed to feminine (or feminized) murder victims in detective plots. Just as the gay man's body is not recovered in the text except in Leo's memory, Gladys's body is similarly marked by absence: signs of Leo's having injured her are mentioned only because they are not there. After the staging of his intended murder of Gladys, and the sexual scene involving the two of them with María Esther, Leo goes for a drive away from the city. When the police begin chasing him for speeding, he assumes he is being pursued for the murder of the gay man twenty years earlier. Out of fear he increases his speed, loses control of the car, and dies in a ditch. The autopsy report reveals the *murderer's* body as the only evidence of the crimes investigated in the text. This strange passage turns the tables on the standard detective novel plot. It is not the victim whose wounded body is examined scientifically, but the victimizer's:

> Declaración médica: cadáver de hombre joven, en rigidez generalizada, piel blanca, cabello castano, abundante en cabelludo: escaso panículo adiposo. Por palpación y percusión el examen exterior del cadáver revela: heridas traumáticas en el rostro, profundas, cortantes y sangrantes; una de ellas en el labio superior, con hemorragia de encías; gran hematoma con escoriaciones en la piel a nivel de la región frontal

derecha; otro del mismo tamaño y forma a la altura del hueso temporal. Múltiples contusiones en la pierna derecha, fractura del femur en su porción media, de la rótula y huesos que forman la garganta del pie. . . . Dada la herida posterior craneana, sin extraer la masa encefálica se observa una fractura de la base del cráneo continuada hasta el hueso temporal. En la masa encefálica hay múltiples estallidos de vasos sanguíneos. Efectuado un pequeño corte vertical de la masa encefálica, se verifican exudados hemorrágicos. (201–2)

[Medical Statement: corpse of a young man, in rigor mortis, skin white, hair brown, abundant on scalp, scanty fatty membrane. By palpation and percussion the gross inspection of the corpse reveals: traumatic wounds on the face, deep lacerations; one of them on the upper lip, causing a hemorrhage in the gums, a large hematoma with flayings of the skin at the level of the right frontal region; another of the same size and form at the level of the temporal bone. Multiple contusions on the right leg, fracture of the femur in its middle portion, of the kneebone and of bones which form the instep of the foot. . . . Considering the posterior cranial wound, without extracting the cephalic mass, a fracture at the base of the skull continuing to the temporal bone can be observed. In the cephalic mass there are multiple ruptured blood vessels. Effecting a small vertical cut in the cephalic mass, one can identify exuding hemorrhages.]

On one level, Leo's death in a car accident represents a trite resolution to the Freudian conflicts addressed by his biography (Merrim 1984, 154). However, with the autopsy report and the general information about dead bodies which follows it, "Referencias omitidas en la autopsia médico-legal" [References omitted in the medicolegal autopsy], another effect is achieved. Leo is stripped (literally) of identification with the masculine symbolic and made (merely) flesh. The autopsy is the medical enactment of the cutting which the sharp objects so meticulously described in the simulated crime scene had promised. Rather than being the masterful director of crime scenes, now Leo is the one whose body is cut into. The subjectivity he had so desperately clung to in his machismo and violence is ultimately shown to be inaccessible. Masculinity in *The Buenos Aires Affair* is a dangerous performance, and the main player knows it to be illusory. Leo only partially inhabits too many subject positions, and is unable to resolve them, even in syncretic moments.

Therefore, Leo's death is the only resolution he could "live with." Stephanie Merrim's conclusion (1984, 148) about the difference between *Crime and Punishment*'s Raskolnikov and *The Buenos Aires Affair*'s Leopoldo Druscovish is that the former strives to be a Nietzschean superman while the latter strives to be a supermacho: "In telling the tale of Leo's self-punishment and eventual death, Puig places a *supermacho* in the suit of a 'superman' and exposes the fallacy of such an equation. Thus, the movie-inspired *macho* stereotype receives another, demythifying blow." The relevant characteristic of Leo as a supermacho, of course, is his impotence; it reflects the inadequacy of the penis/phallis equation. Because of that equation's promise, Leo's most distinguishing characteristic (his large penis) is the most psychologically damaging, and it is this point which Puig drives home about the contradictions inherent to machismo cults and political dictatorships. On the individual level, Leo's attempts to conform to his exaggerated notion of masculine subjectivity lead tragically to the death of another man, the perpetuation of violence (in the real and in representation) against Gladys, and his own death.

An important element of *The Buenos Aires Affair* has been marginalized in this reading so far: the excerpts of dialogue from Hollywood films. The atmosphere of political repression which pervades the novel and situates Leo's self-destructive, masochistic, and yet outwardly aggressive tendencies is countered by the epigraphs which head each chapter and which suggest the possibility of cinematic escape from masculine fantasies of domination when film connotes identification with strong female stars. The quotes from the Hollywood films are another way to contextualize the novel, but they do so along the lines of an imaginary centered on female movie stars. Their inclusion contrasts the dated references to national upheaval in that they provide a pleasing escape from conflict while still offering themselves as models for alternative identifications. The cinema of the United States invades the novel, introducing each chapter with a film scene which readers only later recognize to have been a commentary on the contents of the chapter.

The images and stereotypes of Hollywood's legendary leading ladies—Greta Garbo, Joan Crawford, Marlene Dietrich, Jean Harlow, Greer Garson, Norma Shearer, Hedy Lamarr, Susan Hayward, Bette Davis, Mecha Ortiz, Ginger Rogers, and Rita Hayworth—offer prepackaged reactions to the sections of the novel, and in doing so they rival the psychoanalytic references and the political context for the reader's favor as interpretive categories. As the cinematic intervention into the text indicates, Puig's novel is as much about the need to find nonviolent interpretive strategies as it is about the inherent conflicts in masculine subjectivity within the dichotomy of domination/submission.

In keeping with the offering of cinematic alternatives to the enactment of crime scenes, *The Buenos Aires Affair* does not end with Leo's death. Rather, there are two subsequent chapters which describe Gladys's plans for entering the Buenos Aires art scene on her own terms. Puig's juxtaposition of the powerful female personalities of the silver screen with the masochistic, compliant individuals in the real world of the novel produces a certain melancholic hope in the end. If the masculine subjectivity represented by Leo and repressive military regimes must eventually turn its violence onto itself, then there will be something left—an as yet undefined, though not unquestioned, feminine principle—from which to rebuild.

In contrast to the use of simulacra throughout the novel (in Leo's attack on Gladys, the inclusion of cinematic figures, and Gladys's celebration of the woman/earth equation, for example) the final scene of *The Buenos Aires Affair* is oddly realistic. Also, as opposed to the violence and raw language of the rest of the text, this section is gentle and idyllic. It is not related to Leo's crisis; in fact, it concerns an encounter between Gladys and a female neighbor while Gladys, ignorant of Leo's death, is waiting in his apartment for his return. The interaction between the two women is isolated from Leo's story because of that ignorance, and it is the only moment in the entire text which does not serve to clarify some point about the opening crime scene.

The neighbor, whose husband has just left for work, invites Gladys over to her apartment, and the two women sit on the couple's bed. They talk about Gladys's art and the other woman's family while the neighbor changes her baby boy's diaper. Finding comfort in the neighbor's company, Gladys, who has been drinking and taking sleeping pills, gradually falls asleep in the bed. The young mother is left to her thoughts of the baby, of her own dead mother, and of her husband and their lovemaking the night before:

> La joven volvió al niño, éste batió palmas y al sonreír mostró dos dientes diminutos. . . . La joven sintió los ojos llenárseles de lágrimas, su madre había muerto antes del nacimiento del niño, ni siquiera había conocido a su esposo. . . . Cerró los ojos y pensó en él. Experimentaba todavía una sensación agradable de calor en la vagina, y más arriba un leve ardor. Pensó si dentro de ella no estaría por brotar un nuevo ser, decidió que si era niña le pondría el nombre de su madre muerta. (222)

> [The young woman returned to the boy; he clapped his hands, and, smiling, revealed two tiny teeth. . . . She felt her eyes fill with tears—her mother had died before the baby was born, and she had not even met her husband. . . . She closed her eyes and

> thought of him. She still felt a pleasurable warmth in her vagina, and a slight heat higher up. She wondered if a new being might be sprouting inside of her; she decided that if it was a girl, she would name her after her dead mother.]

These final lines of *The Buenos Aires Affair* unexpectedly shift attention from the protagonists' sadomasochistic exchanges to this "girl next door." The scene abruptly thrusts Gladys and readers into the nonviolent world of a loving family. This world's difference from the rest of the novel is striking. In contrast to all other aspects of masculine and feminine subjectivity in *The Buenos Aires Affair*, the maternal element is not parodied here. This young mother not only satisfies the baby boy, but arouses the husband's attentive desire, soothes Gladys's nerves, and hopes for more children. In all of her nurturing capacities, this figure serves as an antidote to the model of domination/submission that governs interaction between Leo and Gladys. Of course, this idealized model of feminine subjectivity as quintessentially maternal is as much a projection of the male imaginary as is the image of the denigrated female body, but Puig's text does allow for the mother's sexual desire to be expressed. The connection between the young mother, her own dead mother, and her hope for a daughter establishes a loving and sentimental feminine realm that might sustain both men and women (the baby boy and the hoped-for baby girl). If we look to *The Buenos Aires Affair* for alternatives to Leo's story of inadequacy, fear, and self-destruction, we read the final scene as utopian. It shows that the most important task for readers is to resist the dominant fiction of the necessity of hierarchy and violence, and to continue trying to imagine masculine and feminine subjectivities differently.

Still, the strange separation of this scene from the rest of the novel hints at the tragic possibility that the destructiveness of the repudiation of femininity is likely to reappear in even the most idealized family romances. The loving nuclear family depicted here mirrors precisely the image of productive citizens promulgated by the *campañas moralizadoras* of the early 1960s, which create the cycle of sexual obsession and guilt evidenced in Leo's experience. This view of the family caters to the idea of reforming or taming sexualities that deviate from the pattern of benevolent patriarchal structures, structures that depend on women like the young housewife who actively desires her protected, private, procreative, and nurturing role in the social order. If we consider all the types of scripted gender roles and fantasies that appear in *The Buenos Aires Affair*, it becomes more difficult to accept the final scene as hopeful. Its realism and sanity in comparison to Leo's and Gladys's horrific experience of sexuality threatens to offer just another form of illusion, just another story of gender coercion couched as a reflection of individuals' natural and wholesome heterosexual desire.[7]

Puig's novel cites detective fiction, Germanic opera, Hellenic sculpture, folksongs, Freudian and Lacanian psychoanalysis, Argentine newspaper headlines, surrealist painting, Hollywood films and the *femme fatale*, methods of genital torture, child-care customs in the middle and upper classes of Buenos Aires, personal accounts of migration from Argentina to Europe to New York, one-sided telephone conversations, police surveillance tactics, and female as well as male masturbatory fantasies. Such proliferation of discourses, registers of language, and artistic genres, all espousing and performing contradictory masculinities in the private and public spheres, frees us from bondage to any one definition of manliness. The difficulty of assigning utopian or critical status to the final scene underscores the pedagogical function of the novel; if it argues anything, it argues for our enjoyment of the performances of gender *as a series of scenes* and for our suspicion of versions of masculinity and femininity that discipline us into compulsively acting out relations of dominance and submission in the real. Puig's condemnation of state-sponsored terror, violence, and censorship, combined with his celebration of fantasies of violence as well as fantasies of egalitarian harmony, never quite explains the difference between the political real and private fictions. He finds menacing fictions of masculinity everywhere, and *The Buenos Aires Affair* seems to offer as a solution to their destructiveness only the free choice of our fictions in full awareness that they are fictions. As the straight character Valentín puts it in the last line of the film version of *Kiss of the Spider Woman*, "This dream is short, but this dream is happy."

CHAPTER SIX

Revolutionary Matricide, Patricide, Suicide

Reinaldo Arenas's *El asalto*

Cuba será libre. Yo ya lo soy.
[Cuba will be free. I already am.]

Reinaldo Arenas, suicide note

Matricide is our vital necessity,
the *sine-qua-non* condition of our individuation.

Julia Kristeva, *Black Sun: Depression and Melancholia*

Cuban exile Reinaldo Arenas's posthumously published novel *El asalto* (1991a, *The Assault*) celebrates rape and murder in its paradoxical critique of the violence of Fidel Castro's military dictatorship. With a relatively simple plot rendered in relentlessly hateful and vulgar language, the first-person narration turns a prism through which the protagonist's desires become a series of allegorical hallucinations. His perspective is the fragmented result of the state's imposition of restrictive definitions of masculinity, citizenship, and revolution. In its final scenes *El asalto* crystallizes frustration, limitation, and barriers to the self-assertion of the individual into one striking figure: the male dictator, "El Reprimerísimo Reprimero" (which Andrew Hurley [Arenas 1994] translates into English as the "Represident"), who is also the narrator's own female, nameless mother. The narrator sexually assaults that dual male and female figure, and then kills him/her before the amassed citizenry of a dystopian, futuristic society. This single act of aggression, at once incestuous and public, kills the protagonist's own domineering mother and the state's dictatorial "father."

With that conclusion, Arenas takes literally the figurative equation of citizens and sons. *El asalto* treats violent, national revolution as if it were *the same thing* as violence against the mother to whom one owes one's very existence. Therefore, although ostensibly concerned with the liberation of the individual—specifically, the artist—from political oppression and the enforced conformity of Cuba's socialist project, this novel calls on readers to consider connections and tensions between two kinds of violence. First, it exposes in extraordinarily graphic terms the violence inherent in a cultural imperative for men to eschew identification with their mothers. Second, it advocates violence as a means to oppose illegitimate locations of political power. By displaying extreme violence perpetrated against citizens in an absurdly repressive police state, the novel critiques the effects of that repression on the protagonist's sense of masculinity. It suggests that monstrous acts of violence become the only available expression of masculine subjectivity in an abusive, dehumanizing political context. Ironically, though, Arenas writes a protagonist whose thorough indoctrination into the perverse logic of state-imposed self-repression leads him to attack the supreme leader *only because* the protagonist hallucinates that the leader is his own hated mother. With *El asalto,* Arenas explodes the values of revered motherhood and respect for authority. He portrays the rape and murder of the mother as the quintessential liberating gesture for a dehumanized island, for his protagonist, and for himself as author.

In an interview with Francisco Soto (1994, 137–54), Arenas explains his view of the connection between mature masculinity and independence from mothers. He associates mothers with political oppression, especially the oppression of gay men:

> F.S. In many of your texts mothers tyrannize or oppress their sons, they want to destroy them.
>
> R.A. It's a dual relationship. There's this type of relationship in all my novels. It's not completely a tyrannical relationship. The mother is destructive, but at the same

> time she is affectionate. She can destroy but also love. It's a relationship of power and control that she has with her son. She dominates him, but also cares for him; she destroys him, but also loves him. To a certain extent I see in this the tradition of the Cuban mother, a tradition that is the result of our Spanish heritage. The son loves his mother but also realizes that *he must get away from her* . . . .We don't dare *reveal our true selves* to our mothers, much less if we're homosexual. Mothers see that as absolutely taboo, completely immoral and prohibited; at least the majority of mothers see it that way. That love/hate, rejection and rapprochement of the mother is a contradictory relationship, but very real. *In* El Asalto *at the same time the protagonist destroys his mother he does it by possessing her. Therefore, there isn't total hate, but rather obsession and passion.* (143–44, emphasis added)

The author's comments on mothers and sons both illuminate and obscure the major issues at play in a reading of *El asalto* as a political allegory and a fantasy of omnipotence. Arenas posits a true self for the son, which he must hide from the mother in order to avoid her critical and controlling gaze. This notion of loving and yet needing to escape from the mother encapsulates the negative formation of masculine identity. The son's fantasy of independence blinds him to the fact that her gaze produces his individuality as reaction. Unaware of this even more profound dependence on her, the son guards his illusion of autonomous identity as if it were life itself. Yet its demand for absolute separation prevents his love *for* the mother, frustrating his desire for union with the other. That the identity he calls "true" must be hidden associates guilt and privacy with the very construct of self that he most wants others, and especially his mother, to recognize.

On the other hand, as *El asalto's* protagonist demonstrates, the son's "obsession and passion" regarding the mother lead him to rape and murder—the ultimate expressions of possessive knowledge (to know her in a sexual sense) and absolute control (over her very life). He inflicts *on* her precisely the invasion and abuse he expects to receive *from* her. By conflating this psychoanalytic representation of the phallic mother with a political caricature of the male dictator, this novel offers a complex commentary on tyranny. It appears as a relationship between the tyrant and the people predicated on unresolved vacillation between extremes of love and hate, identity and difference. *El asalto* processes that relationship through the portrayal of the mutually threatening intimacy of mothers and homosexual sons.

El asalto is the last installment in a five-part work which Arenas had planned for years.[1] He called it his *pentagonía,* a pentalogy of agonies, and the author himself suggests that it should be read as an extended autobiography whose fantastic elements express influences primarily of Borges, Kafka, and Lezama Lima. Its five novels relate the gay writer's conflicted relationship to the Cuban state as they follow the growth of the author-identified narrators. They trace the stages of boyhood, adolescence, and manhood, and they contextualize that initiation in the stages of Cuban history from the Batista regime through the Revolution and its betrayal.

Celestino antes del alba (1967), published in 1982 as *Cantando en el pozo*, treats the perceptions of an imaginative child-narrator in the poverty-stricken, prerevolutionary Cuban countryside. He invents an alter ego, his cousin Celestino, who escapes from family violence and misunderstanding through obsessive writing and poetic sensibilities. *El palacio de las blanquísimas mofetas* (1982b) coincides with the Batista era, highlighting the frustrated efforts of the adolescent Fortunato to understand and express his family's experiences. A cacophony of voices fills the text, each character fighting to find an audience for her/his personal tale of tragedy and hopelessness. *Otra vez el mar* (1982a) combines two monologues set in the period of institutionalized revolution. Hector and his wife (whose monologue, we learn in the end, was invented by Hector) express political and personal idealism, alienation, and self-doubt as they dream, hallucinate, and remember during a drive home to Havana. They are returning from a brief vacation, during which Hector flirted with having a homosexual encounter with a boy on the beach although his wife yearns for communication with her husband. *El color del verano* (1991b) is set in 1999, during the Cuban dictator's celebration of forty years in power (which he claims to be fifty years because that number attracts more publicity). This novel features a shared first-person narrative voice, in which Gabriel/Reinaldo/the Tétrica Mofeta write "the anecdotes, letters, tongue-twisters, stories, and so forth, that make up the novel and in turn give voice to Cuba's excluded and marginal homosexual subculture of the 1960s and 1970s" (Soto 1994, 69).

In each of the first four novels of the pentagonía, Cuban history circumscribes the writing subject. Although Arenas typically divides into different characters the alienated aspects of his *port-parole*, all of these texts deal with socioeconomic isolation of the gay male writer. They chart the changing dynamic of relative freedoms, from boyhood with *Celestino*'s child-narrator/Celestino, to adolescence with *El palacio*'s Fortunato and his family, to young adulthood with *Otra vez el mar*'s Hector, and to the gay culture of *El color del verano*. The central theme continues to be the frustrated drive to express individuality, or the true self, in prerevolutionary poverty and rural isolation, postrevolutionary conformist self-discipline, and contestatory sexual subculture. In every case, the main characters write as a form of escape and empowerment; they also always end up dead, only to reappear under a new name in the next novel.

The last installment in the series, *El asalto* projects a much more drastic reduction of individual freedoms into an unspecified future, imagining the extremes to which Castrista policies might lead. The narrative voice in this text maintains much more coherence of identity that any of the others, which split themselves off into different characters, and in this last novel of the *pentagonía,* the narrator-protagonist does not die. He kills in order to live, suggesting victory over the other characters' suffering throughout the series. However, in *El asalto* the narrator is more hostile, vindictive, and determined than the protagonists of the other novels. Dedicated to nothing other than hunting down his mother, he never considers himself a writer as they do. Soto argues that "[t]he nameless narrator of *El Asalto* is the only protagonist in the quintet that does not write, for in this futuristic world the individual, perceived only as a work dog that fuels the materialistic production of the state, has forgotten how to communicate, how to use language critically . . ."(120). This description is not entirely accurate, since *El Asalto*'s narrator does write as a form of self-identification in his control over others. He works in the surveillance forces for the state, and obsessively records his own identification number on walls, cages, and documents in order to receive recognition for his repressive zeal in arresting those who dare to break the law. Still, it is important to note that the only protagonist-narrator of the *pentagonía* who survives his own story is the one who does not pretend to be an artist, the one who assaults readers with his profanity and cruelty, and the one who finally strikes back against his mother physically rather than merely figuratively.

Accepting Arenas's own claim that the *pentagonía* constitutes a single tale concerning various creative responses to social marginalization, Soto (1994, 41) assesses *El asalto*'s contribution: "Ironically, the final novel of the pentalogy leaves the reader with a glimmer of hope. The decrepit tyrant el Reprimerísimo Reprimero . . . is destroyed, and the protagonist, who has suffered countless persecutions throughout the five-book cycle can finally stretch out on the beach and rest." This "glimmer of hope" confuses the liberation of the artist with the survival of his characters; it also confuses the liberation of an oppressed nation with the rape and murder of a woman. If we compare the first and last scenes of the pentagonía, we can begin to discern the complex relationship among gender identities, sexuality, and totalitarian power to which Arenas seems to have dedicated all of his writing. With this series of texts in particular, Arenas explores the most complicated, perverse, hopeful, and cruel elements in the production of the masculine subject who seeks personal and creative autonomy. His notion of personal and political revolution demands reconsideration of the violence of mothers and men, the transgression of genders and genres, and finally the legitimation of authority and authorship.

All of Arenas's novels feature the mother as one of the principal themes. The first scene of *Celestino antes del alba* narrates a young boy's confusion, terror, and guilt when he sees his mother run to throw herself into the well. The boy rushes to try to pull her out, but when he looks down into the well, he sees only his own reflection in the calm water. This fantasy involves multiple elements in Arenas's characteristic depiction of mother figures from the sons' viewpoints. The mother never dies in the realist plane of the novel, and her threat to commit suicide, at first horrifying for the son, comes to function as an unfulfilled promise to him. She teases him with the possibility of her death; yet by refusing to die, she creates his desire for the dreaded closure of the game. Her self-absorption, tendency toward despair, desire to be saved by the son, and indifference to his need for her presence betray him. Her threats of suicide expose his love/need for her while demonstrating no reciprocal love/need for him.

The most haunting feature in the mother-son relationship as it appears in all of Arenas's narratives is the mutual reflection. The mother mirrors the son back to himself as in the scene at the well in *Celestino*, when the son first associates his own image with the mother's threat to kill herself. He feels guilty for not finding and saving her, yet the victim he sees when he gazes into the water is himself. Ever after that, whenever the mothers appear to bear an excessive physical similarity to the male protagonists in the *pentagonía*, the sons are repulsed by the association between their own faces and feminine characteristics. This strong negative reaction corresponds to theories of masculinity as a reaction-formation in which the male child achieves masculine identity through repudiation of associations with the mother. At a more fundamental level of identity-formation for the male child, however, perfect correspondence between the mother and the son's self-image signifies symbiosis, the deeply desired yet vigorously denied wish for absolute union. Individuated selfhood requires suppression of that wish, and so the overwhelming desire for symbiosis with the mother, fulfillment of which would lead to erasure of self, causes a severe counter-reaction. As this mirror-mother threatens to absorb the son into her own image, he feels compelled to kill her so that he might live as a separate and identifiable being. The strength of the son's desire to return to an imagined, prenatal, absolute unity with the mother prior to his entry into socialization actually fuels his reactive behavior and fantasies *against* her. Ironically, the degree to which he acts out those fantasies measures his "success" in the social, because he conforms to misogynist logic and seems to defend masculinity against women's maternal power.

Arenas wrote *El asalto* in exile, and it was published almost a year after his suicide. The novel intricately combines those elements of political disenfranchisement and psychological crisis that apparently informed its author's final decision to carry out the same threat with which the mother opens *Celestino*. Offering multiple images of revolution as integral to the performance of masculine subjectivity for the narrator-protagonist, *El asalto* frames the political within the personal, ultimately rendering the two spheres indistinguishable. While structured like a grotesque-realist thriller which denounces dictatorship, the novel includes such a proliferation of fantastic, condensed, and displaced images that it also begs to be read as a dream text. My reading traces out the multiple layers of the novel, first analyzing its references to a variety of narrative forms, its use of highly charged vocabulary, and its modes of characterization. Then I focus on the convergence of these elements in the final scene to argue that, when understood as both political allegory and masculinist fantasy *at the same time*, this novel becomes a rich source for a psychoanalytic understanding of revolution, counterrevolution, and the violence they engender.

Most critics treat *El asalto* as an experiment in genre under the rubric of anti-totalitarianism. They read it against the norms of Cuban documentary fiction, as a parody of a thriller, or as a Kafkaesque critique of bureaucracy (Soto 1994). It is a thriller as Todorov (1977) defines the genre (versus the whodunit brand of detective fiction): the narration of events coincides with their occurrence in chronological fashion, and suspense, or excited expectation about what will happen next, maintains readers' interest. "Indeed it is around these constants that the thriller is constituted: violence, generally sordid crimes, the amorality of the characters" (48).

El asalto also cites elements of epic, picaresque, and twentieth-century futuristic narrative, or science fiction. The fifty-two chapters are very short, distinct episodes in the protagonist's search to find and kill his mother. Each chapter title consists of a quotation from the Western literary canon, especially from texts reflecting major social upheaval or geographical discovery, and functions as an epigraph to the section. However, the citations do not directly refer to the chapters' content. Rather, they suggest loose associations among vague intertextual memories of conquests, exiles, illusions, and landscapes. Readers are left to ponder the implications of the juxtapositions. For instance, the title of chapter 2 is a quote from Cervantes , "De lo que le avino a Don Quijote con una bella cazadora" [Of what occurred to Don Quixote with a beautiful huntress], yet the chapter offers no plot advancement at all; it consists of a satirical description of the *Polifamiliar* [Multi-Family], a communal living arrangement designed to save space and facilitate supervision of citizens in Arenas's imagined totalitarian state. As Soto (1994) has pointed out, such descriptions of modes of social control echo dystopian novels such as Huxley's *Brave New World* or Orwell's *Nineteen Eighty-Four. El asalto* is more a combination of those futuristic texts with the allegorical *Animal Farm* and with Cervantine parody of courtly love, however. The narrator's accounts of such phenomena as the *polifamiliar*, with its ridiculous distribution of space, or the *guaguas,* which are comic postmotorization versions of buses, bitingly mock the Cuban government's rhetoric of social planning and organization, along with its denial of a disintegrating infrastructure in the 1980s:

> Es obligatorio vivir en el Polifamiliar. . . . Allí tenía mi lugar exacto, como todo el mundo. Como yo soy solo me toca un metro y pico de suelo, es decir la extensión de mi cuerpo y el ancho del mismo con los brazos recogidos. Otros tienen más espacio, pues tienen mujer o hijos. Por la nonoche, cuando se reparten los espacios, hay siempre quien ocupa un poco de espacio más que el que le toca. Si se dan cuenta se le reduce su espacio a la mitad del que le toca, de manera que entonces tiene que dormir de lado. . . . Una familia quedó tan reducida que dormían todos sobre un viejo, el abuelo, quien a su vez tenía que dormir de costado. . . . (9)
>
> [The law states that "All citizens are required to live in the Multi-Family. . . ." Like everyone else, I was issued my own place there. Since it was just me and no one else, I was allotted a little over one square yard of floor space, which was the length of my body by the width of my body with my arms at my sides. Other people were assigned more space, because they had a wife or children. At not-night, when the spaces were assigned, there was always someone that tried to take more space than they were issued. If Multi-Family headquarters found out, the space would be cut down to one-half the original issue, so the person would have to sleep on their side. . . . One family lost so much space that they all had to sleep stacked on top of an old man, the grandfather, who in turn had to sleep on his side. . . . (3)[2]

> Enseguida me incorporo a la fila y hago la guagua, mis codos se ensartan al siguiente y así sucesivamente, cuando sumamos setenta y cinco, el encargado del transporte grita

> completo, suelta un fustazo, y la guagua, nosotros enganchados en fila india por los codos, partimos veloces. Marchamos. (17)

> [Then I immediately get into line to make a bus; I hook my elbows into the next person's, and the next person hooks his into the next person's, and so on, and when there are seventy-five of us, the man in charge of transport yells *Full up!* Cracks his whip once, and the bus, which is all of us hooked into an Indian file by our elbows, takes off. We march. (11)]

In spite of this satiric element of the novel, with its comic exaggeration of Cuba's failed social engineering, *El asalto* depicts multiple forms of serious assault on the people: psychological, physical, political, and systemic. The consistent cruelty of the narrator and government bureaucrats takes the wind out of readers' already uneasy laughter. The undefined future of Castro's state is imagined as a hellish place where human beings have been reduced to the status of rats and pigs, where any spontaneous speech—even whispering—is detected by the "contrasusurrador" forces [the counterwhisperers] and punishable by death. Citizens betray fellow citizens in order to curry government favor, and acts of ferocious violence fill the text.

Language in *El asalto* marks the cause-and-effect relationship between state tyranny and individual violent obsession. Whereas the government hypocritically (and again, hyperbolically) couches everything in the most positive terms in order to disguise its exploitation of citizens as workers, the narrator blindly projects his self-hatred onto all others. In each case, the level of exaggeration reaches ludicrous proportions and lends a dreamlike air to the novelistic world. As Soto (1994, 115) notes, Arenas's ironic inclusion of neologisms to refer to enforced productivity, satisfaction, and good humor in postrevolutionary Cuban society destroys any semblance of legitimate authority the totalitarian government might wield:

> La idea de nonoche (al igual que todas las ideas) es del Reprimerísimo. "Cómo—y aún recuerdo también este discurso—concebir que en nuestra sociedad exista la noche. No, no podemos admitirlo, la aboliremos." Y creó la nonoche, en la cual, y más aún durante el día, debemos mantener el trabajo y el optimismo. Aboliremos pues del idioma, de la memoria y de la realidad todos los conceptos decadentes y contravitales que el pasado reaccionario nos ha legado. Optimicemos el idioma así como la vida. (39)

> [The idea of the not-night (like all authentically brilliant ideas) was the Supreme Represident's. I can recall the speech introducing the concept as though it were

> yesterday: *How*, the Represident scolded, *can one imagine night existing in our society? No—we cannot accept that. We therefore abolish night.* And on that day he created the not-night, all during which, and even more so during the glorious day, we are exhorted to keep up our work and maintain our optimism. *We abolish from the language, from our memory, and from the world . . . all those decadent and anti-vital concepts that we have inherited from the reactionary past. We shall optimize the language as we have optimized life itself.* (37)]

Other terms such as *nonoche* [not-night] appear throughout the novel as part of the depiction of a society's loss of realism, creative thought, and human expressiveness. Citizen-workers respect the *noreposo* [not-rest] and the *nodescanso* [not-break]. They learn to avoid the nobancos del noparque [not-benches of the not-park] and strive at all times to be productive and loyal subjects of the Represident. By the end of the novel, the level of repression reaches such depths that citizens must parrot only officially approved scripts (102).

The narrator, believing himself an exception to the rules, maintains a degree of critical distance from the processes of thought and language control. However, as the story tension mounts, his diatribes become increasingly repetitive and predictable, just as his frustration level rises. Even he begins to lose vocabulary, lashing out at the readers:

> La corneta, la lata o cuero o silbato o pito, o váyase usted a la porra retumba, o suena o clama o llama, o váyase a la mierda. De modo que el traqueteo de las bestias que ansiosas y encorvadas trabajaban, cesa. (45)

> [The cornet, or tin can, or horn, or whistle, or conch shell, or whatever the hell it is—what do I care, anyway—echoes, or sounds, or cries out, or calls, or shit, you get the picture. At the sound, there is a sudden and complete cessation of the terrible racket that the beasts have been making as they feverishly worked. (44)]

This continual reference to other people as *bestias* [beasts] with *garfas* [claws], whose bodies reek with what the narrator finds to be a nauseating stench of sweat, urine, and sex, places him in the position of mindful (if cruel and distorting) observer of their inhumanity. He relies on an exaggerated mind/body split to differentiate himself from all others. While they suffer, bleed, twitch, ooze, copulate, scream, and cry, the narrator imagines himself to be a dry, silent, self-contained observer; all distanced eyes and thought, he replicates the panoptical logic of totalitarian power. Everyone whom the narrator describes receives the same deprecating treatment, but he aims the strongest and most explicit language at his mother:

> Las orejas de mi madre son largas, ásperas y anchas como las de un murciélago gigante, ratón, perro o elefante o qué coño de bicho, siempre alerta; sus ojos redondos, giratorios y saltones, como de rata o sapo, o qué carajo. Su nariz es como un pico de pájaro furioso, su hocico, su trompa, es alargada y a la vez redonda, con mucho de perro o de boa o de quién carajo podrá decirlo. (41)
>
> [My mother's ears are large, rough-skinned, and stick out from the side of her head as far as a giant bat's, or a rat's, or a dog's, or an elephant's, or any other fucking animal's you can think of, and they are always pricked up. Her eyes are round, revolving bug-eyes, like a rat's or a frog's, or whatever the fuck other kind of disgusting, nervous, twitching little animal you can think of. Her nose is like the beak of some furious bird; her snout, or trunk, is very, very long, but round at the same time. It reminds you of a dog's or a boa constrictor's, or—but let someone else try to describe the fucking thing, it makes me sick to think about it. (39)]

The novel opens with the narrator's attack against his mother in a chapter called "Vista de Mariel"; the act of looking, and the location from which one looks, establish from the beginning their battle to the death over subjectivity. For Sartre, people look in order to wield power over others, as in his example of peeping through the lock of a closed door; this voyeur, however, dreads being caught by another's spying look. When he raises his eyes from the peephole to exchange a look with the one who sees him seeing, both participants become subject and object of one visual moment. They share in the guilt of spying, even though the one who had looked through the closed door disallows that the original object of his observation looks back at him. Those who share a reciprocal look acknowledge the chain of subjectivity that uneven ocular exchanges confer. They recognize that there will always be an other to see them, to relegate them to object status (being seen) in the same look that registers their guiltily positive subject status (they are spies who wish to avoid being seen).

In *El asalto*, the first moment of mutual recognition between mother and adult son occurs at the Mariel port, famous for the exodus of Cuban dissidents and political prisoners in 1980, and the same port from which Arenas himself left the island that year (Santí 1980). The novel opens with a conflation of *vista* [view] and *mirada* [look], shifting "Vista del Mariel" away from a look out to sea. It turns the view back to the land, and to a surreptitious act. The narrator sees his mother from behind; she is stealing wood. When she turns around it is not to return his look, but in fear of being caught by the authorities:

> La última vez que vi a mi madre . . . estaba así, de espaldas, agachada. . . . No perdí tiempo y me le abalancé para matarla. La cabrona, parece que me miraba con el ojo del culo, pues antes de que yo pudiese reventarla se volvió asustada, no por mí, sino por las leyes del Reprimero y sus agentes, que si la cogen llevándose las sobras del aserrío Patrio, la ajustician. Es decir, la matan. (7)
>
> [The last time I saw my mother, . . . she was standing with her back to me, bent double. . . . This was my chance; I knew I could not waste a second. I ran straight for her, and I would have killed her, too, but the old bitch must have an eye where her asshole ought to be, because before I could get to her and knock her down and kill her, the old woman whirled around to meet me. She was terrified—oh, but not because of me. She was afraid of the represidential laws and the agents that enforce them, that's what she was afraid of. Because if she had been caught stealing scraps from the National Sawmill, she would have been arrested and tried and sentenced. Which means she would have been killed. (1)]

This uneven exchange of looks establishes from the first paragraph the dynamic of hunter and hunted that the narrator-protagonist will play out. He thinks he is the privileged observing subject, the one who understands government vigilance of citizens and does not fear it. He watches the people, who in turn watch out for the repressive forces of surveillance. From that position, he attacks the weak beasts, precisely because their servitude disgusts him. In attacking his mother in particular, however, he sees that she never sees him, never acknowledges him as a relevant object of her desire or gaze. He feels that she observes him from "el ojo del culo," combining an infantile notion of anal omnipotence (representing for himself the earliest sense of power over his own body) with one of anal birth (representing the omnipotence with which the mother grants life to the baby). In desiring to be noticed, but despising his dependency on the look of a person he cannot respect, the son projects that look onto what is for him the foulest of his mother's body parts. She sees him from the denigrated site of production, the asshole that produces only waste.

We immediately find this vision, however, to belong solely to the narrator. When he admits that the mother never saw him at all but rather sensed the presence of the government agents, he belatedly and indirectly explains his rage. His own mother looks to the military apparatus, not at her son. No maternal gaze confers objectivity, subjectivity, or guilt onto him, and his resentment over that sense of invisibility devolves into his identification with the forces to which his mother turns her attention—the forces that threaten them all with death if they ever exceed their subjectedness to become human subjects of their own emotions and actions. Paradoxically, the narrator seeks recognition from his mother by becoming that which prevented her from looking at him in the first place. In other words, he becomes, or takes the place of, the cause of his own annihilation as subject. Although the narrator vehemently denies any desire to be seen in or by his mother, he is convinced that only by killing her can he be free of her control. The strength of his denial confirms that he seeks to kill exactly that which he wants too strongly. He must kill the object of his desire—his mother's capacity to see him—first by asserting that he does not desire it, and then by making it unavailable to be desired.

At the level of consciousness, the narrator's greatest fear is that he is becoming exactly like his mother *physically*. He hallucinates his own metamorphosis into the object of his obsession, occupying through physical resemblance the site from which he both wishes and fears to be seen:

> Naturalmente, siempre he odiado a mi madre. Es decir, desde que la conozco. Al principio mi odio hacia ese animal era por rachas. Después se quedó fijo. Un día me miré en un espejo y vi que me daba un aire a ella. . . .Volví a mirarme, y al poco tiempo, al remirarme, vi que aún me parecía más a la maldita. Entonces, ya mi odio no fue fijo, sino creciente. Más adelante me seguí mirando. Hasta comprender, cada vez más claramente, que me iba pareciendo cada vez más a ella, que mis ojos, mi nariz, mis patas y mi jeta iban siendo cada vez más los de ella. Que iba yo dejando de ser yo para ser ella. (14)

> [I've always hated my mother, of course. As long as I've known her, that is. At first my hatred for the cow came in fits and starts. Then it was always there. One day I saw myself in a mirror and I noticed that there was something about me that reminded me of her. . . . I looked at myself again, and I had the same sensation, and then not long after that, when I examined myself a fourth time, I could clearly see that I was coming to look more and more like the damned woman. And after that, my hatred was no longer just *there* anymore—it began to grow. It was then that I began looking at myself all the time, and at last I could see, more clearly every day, that everything about me was beginning to look just like her—my eyes, my ears, my paws, and my snout were becoming virtually *hers*. I was slowly but surely changing away from myself and changing into her. (8)]

This fantasy of transformation is both a personal pathology and a negative reflection of the identification process necessary to maintain group cohesion under dictatorship. The narrator is aware of his resemblance to the mother, but remains unconscious that he condenses an image of the political dictator into that mirror image of himself (as his mother). Extreme love and hate permeate his self-contemplation, leading to murderous and objectifying (illegal, illegitimate) fantasies of omnipotence (the very form that legality takes under totalitarianism). He identifies with irreconcilable sites of power: with his own through narcissistic defensiveness, with his mother's through conscious hatred born of resentment, and with the represident's through unconscious hatred and admiration.

Brad Epps (1995) analyzes the relationship between identity, sexuality, and the iconic political leader (Castro) for the gay subject in Arenas's work, citing Žižek's attempt to account for group formation in modern totalitarianism. Žižek (1989, 105) analyzes the subject's relation to the Freudian ego ideal (*Ichideal*), the source of moral conscience and self-censorship, as "identification with the very place *from where* we are being observed, *from where* we look at ourselves so that we appear to ourselves likeable, worthy of love." In *El asalto*, however, the narrator confers that power onto his mother, and by identifying with the place from where he is observed, he appears to himself unlikable and unworthy of love. The most negative image he can reflect is the frightful ugliness he finds in that location of the gaze. His conviction that he must kill his mother in order to escape taking her place, then, has a certain psychological validity. Her death would disrupt that perverse identification, and he would be free, he thinks, of the imposition of her face between himself and his mirror.

The protagonist cannot locate his mother, though, unless he convinces the counterwhispering forces that he is a zealous patriot. He argues that he needs special clearance to enter restricted areas in order to further the state's project of controlling all individual desires and eliminating all unauthorized activities. He willingly enforces the very repression he despises in order to gain access to all the social sectors where he thinks he might find his mother. Unaware of his unconscious association of her with the state, he assumes that he will find her in the periphery, either in the secondary work camps outside of the "represidential capital" or in the prisons. He privileges his own tendencies toward rebellion in taking for granted that his mother would be shunned or marginalized by the hegemonic center. The narrator voluntarily begins to resemble the dictator more and more *in behavior* in order to avoid physical resemblance to his mother. In attempting to oppose his own ostensibly law-abiding identity to the overtly criminal one he imagines for his mother, he shifts his allegiance to the "group ideal as embodied in the [political] leader" (Freud 1921, 79).

The psychological, emotional, and ethical web of *El asalto* is caught on three poles: the mother's threatened usurpation of the son's identity, the narrator's obsessive attention to phallic imagery, and his progress toward identification with the Reprimerísimo reprimero (coded male) as he moves up through levels of bureaucracy in the futuristic totalitarian state. This state organizes citizens into work and prison (rehabilitation) cells, and the protagonist gains access to all of them in order to search for his mother. As a pleasure only apparently secondary to his obsessive search, he enjoys torturing those accused of whispering. That sadism thinly veils the character's own masochism, since he himself is a whisperer who exploits the laws to his own ends. Therefore, his active punishment of others is a secret system of reflected desire to be caught himself and rendered passive.

The protagonist sends memos to the central government office to propose ever more invasive, reactionary, and absurd prohibitions. For example, in a particularly cutting display of homophobic hysteria, he institutes a law against glancing at the crotch of any government officials (who are all male in the novel), then orders all of his subordinates to stuff their pants and wear bizarre decorations which call attention to their genitals, ostensibly to make recognizing perverted citizens more efficient. Of course, this prohibition very efficiently produces exactly that behavior which it condemns and quickly becomes more and more exaggerated. The narrator relishes executing people for any sign at all of desire, but especially of desire directed at the male body, whether by men, women, or children. He rails against the government-approved procreative sex as a disgusting, loud, messy, filthy act, but his most extreme reaction against any evidence of desire in relation to the penis is to strangle to death one woman for having tried to seduce him. The denial and repression attain such depths that he associates glances, gestures, or even the slightest indication of any communicative capacity at all with perverse, phallic desire; the narrator punishes everyone who dares express illegitimate subjectivity, which is to say, everyone who evidences any trace of humanity. Only workers who imitate blind drones escape execution.

The novel's violence increases in intensity, horror, and rhythm just as in a thriller. In the final scenes, the narrator mounts a platform during a huge public celebration for the anniversary of the revolution. He is to receive a commendation from the Reprimerísimo himself for outstanding service to the state. He climbs to the top of the stairs, scanning the amassed citizenry, as always, for signs of his mother. Furious because he has exhausted all methods of searching for her on the island, he finds everyone, especially the dictator, to be hideous and revolting. The narrator places himself in the position of the subject who surveys all, even the seat of absolute power, with contempt; he will accept recognition from the state for his services, but he guards the secret that his work has always been only self-interested. The dictator turns to face him, and there she is, in the center of the capital, raised high on the platform for all to see, disguised as the dictator all along:

> Allí, en la parte delantera de la plataforma está él, la ventruda, peluda, gigantesca figura, de espaldas a mí, como una tortuga erguida en su carapacho, extasiado ante su mar de esclavos. . . . Entonces, . . . el culo gigantesco gira, el vientre prominente se dirije hacia mí, enfrentándome todo su fofo andamiaje, sosteniendo entre sus garfas la lata centelleante que ha de incrustarme. . . . [A]lzo la vista hasta su jeta. Y entonces la veo, la veo, la veo a ella. Es ella, ese rostro que está ante mí es el odiado y espantoso rostro de mi madre. Y ése es también el rostro del Reprimerísimo. Los dos son una misma persona. Con razón me había sido tan difícil encontrarla. Mi sorpresa, mi furiosa alegría es tal que demoro unos segundos en recuperarme. (137)

> [And there, on the precipice of that high plateau, he stands—that big-bellied, hairy, gigantic figure—with his back to me, like some turtle in its shell standing erect and in ecstasy before a sea of slaves. . . . And then, the huge backside turns, the protruding belly swings around toward me, and I am facing that enormous doughlike mound of flesh that holds in its claws the sparkling medal which is to be bestowed upon me. . . . I raise my eyes to his face. And I see it, see that snout, see her snout—I see her. That face before me is the hated and horrible face of my mother. And it is also the face of the Represident. They are the same person. *That* is why it has been so hard to find her, I think, in fury. My surprise, my enraged joy, is so great that it takes me a second or two to recover. (142)]

By this point in the novel, the narrator's anxious quest for recognition has been reduced to pure rage through frustration. The mother looks straight at him, and he attacks her with his suddenly enormous erect penis, imagined as grossly out of proportion to the rest of his body. Wielding it as a huge weapon, he knocks layers of disguise, armor, and weaponry off of the assaulted figure until his mother stands naked before him:

> Y ahora la veo, está ahí, con sus millones de manchas y arrugas; la inmensa vaca encuera, con sus enormes nalgas y tetas descomunales, con su figura de sapo deforme, con su pelo cenizo y su hueco hediondo. . . . Entonces, la gran vaca, desnuda y deforme,

> blanca y hedionda, se juega su última carta de perra astuta, y cruzando por sobre sus inmensas tetas sus garfas desgarradas, me mira llorando y dice: hijo. (138–40)
>
> [And now I see her—she is there before me, covered with blotches and wrinkles. She is naked. Her huge buttocks and breasts, her body like some monstrous toad's, her ash-gray hair and her stinking hole are exposed for all to see. . . . And then the great cow, naked and horrible, white and stinking, plays her last card; the sly bitch, crossing her ragged claws over her monstrous breasts, looks at me with tears in her eyes and she says *Son.* (144)]

The narrator explicitly attributes the subsequent rape to his mother's having appealed to him as *son*:

> Todo el escarnio, la vejación, el miedo, la frustración el chantaje y la burla y la condena que contiene esa palabra llega hasta mí abofeteándome, humillándome. Mi erección se vuelve descomunal, y avanzo con mi falo proyectándose hacia su objetivo, hacia el hueco hediondo, y la clavo. (140)
>
> [All the derision, all the harassment, all the fear and frustration and blackmail and mockery and contempt that that word contains—it slaps me in the face, and I am stung. My erection swells to enormous proportions, and I begin to step toward her, my phallus aimed dead for its mark, that fetid stinking hole. And I thrust. (144–45)]

Being called *son* is the greatest insult, the most abject humiliation, for this character whose sole mission is to rid himself of traces of any origin beyond his own control. He penetrates her, and the mother/dictator howls, exploding into a shower of "tornillos, arandelas, latas, gasolina, semen, mierda y chorros de aceite" (140) [screws, washers, cans, gasoline, semen, shit, and streams of oil]. This dream-scene in which the penis performs as weapon harks back to *Otra vez el mar's* Rabelaisian fantasy of the Trojan War fought with penises rather than swords. In *El asalto*, a similar battle to the death for individual and collective identity turns the male warrior's penis simultaneously on the state and on the mother; they are both sources of his sense of inadequacy *as a man*. The mother in *El asalto* is completely annihilated, and when her remains—all that is left of the repressive machine—fall onto the platform, the assembled crowd erupts in riot, destroying everything in sight. This scene equates rape to murder, and murder of the mother to collective liberation. The fantasy gives birth to a new revolutionary hero.

If the narrator hates his mother because of his denied desire for union with her, *El asalto* treats violent, eroticized revolution with a similar ambivalence.

Though revolution is unambiguously condemned throughout the text as the cause of social horror in the repression which follows the dictator's coming to power, another revolution returns in the end as the source of new freedom. Even though he acknowledges the novel's unresolved relation to revolution as renewal, Soto (1994) tends to accept all transgression as the same; in a nation under illegitimate, totalitarian rule, any transgression constitutes a form of liberty: "Clearly, the copulation with the mother, a societal taboo, can be read as a transcoding or displacement of the narrator's reaffirmation of his own (homo)sexuality" (102). One need not equate male homosexuality, and its inherent transgression of heterosexist norms, with incest, however, and certainly not with rape. Although Soto is right to point out that the final scene of the novel looses the narrator's sexual aggression, he misses the complex implications of the difference between gender and sexuality in this final assault.

In "Proper Conduct: Reinaldo Arenas, Fidel Castro, and the Politics of Homosexuality," Epps (1995) brilliantly analyzes Arenas, the man and the author, in crisis over the play between desire for and identification with the powerful other. He traces the conflicting scripts through which Arenas tries to write his singularity in the face of a political regime intent on reading male homosexuality as a crime against both the state and masculinity itself. Arenas also writes in resistance to overdetermined scripts for gay aesthetics and political positions, which makes his work improper in Epps's view. It strains at the limits of directly oppositional contestation, often "reiterating . . . without ironic subversion, some of the most troubling stereotypes of women and gay men. It disturbs, in short, the properties and proprieties of virtually all comers" (246).

While male homosexuality is a central focus of much work on Arenas's prose, relatively few literary critics focus on gender itself or male-female relations in the *pentagonía*.[3] Epps's essay, although principally dealing with Castro's shadow over all of Arenas's work, successfully distinguishes between those issues. It focuses particularly on Arenas's bold exploration of desires that not only represent anti-totalitarianism, but that also trouble those who reject sexism on ethical grounds. Epps argues that in the context of Cuba's revolutionary ideology, masculinity must be coded heterosexual, stoic, military, and submissive only to Castro himself, who paradoxically must represent collective will through his extraordinary singularity and his iconic encoding of hypermasculinity (taking female lovers without marrying them, wearing military garb, displaying the proverbial cigar, and so on). Arenas as author and as gay Cuban exile exists in opposition to empty socialist rhetoric and militaristic coercion as well as the version of masculinity that Castro exudes. However, Arenas's oeuvre and authorial persona depend on that very opposition for their singularity. "Castro is thus the phantasmatic coauthor of Arenas's writing, the authority who by striving to disauthorize Arenas ultimately only authorizes him all the more. This, at any rate, is what Arenas makes of Castro" (Epps 1995, 246). "The Cuban leader is for Arenas what Butler calls a 'defining negativity,' a terrible touchstone by which the subject, though abjected and repudiated is, and by which the writer writes" (267, quoting Butler 1993, 190).

Epps (1995, 271) charts representations of homosexual desire in a variety of Arenas's texts to show the complexity of his opposition to Castro's heterosexist machismo, arguing that their relationship (from Arenas's point of view) is as productive as it is destructive, as full of attraction as of direct rejection: "For Arenas, himself no stranger to the poetic potential of paradox, the predicament of homosexual desire lies in the desire for a man, a real man, a man who is not also and at the same time a homosexual. If the real object of male homosexual desire is a man who is the opposite of the male homosexual, then the paradigmatic object of desire could well be, for Arenas, Fidel Castro himself." Epps's reading, attentive to the particularities of discourse on homosexual identities versus homosexual practices in Cuba,[4] finds that the rape of the mother in *El asalto* functions like an attack against homosexuality itself. Unlike Soto, Epps sees the episode not in transgression of the taboo against homosexuality, but rather in violation of Arenas's own homosexual desires. If the narrator of the novel has abandoned all semblance of political integrity in order to find his mother at all costs, "[h]omosexual desire is likewise abandoned; in fact, it is, along with the Mother, what the narrator-protagonist most mercilessly assaults . . . [But] even though both (apparent or assumed) homosexuals and the Mother are singled out for assault, that does not mean that Arenas is simply assaulting what he truly values, what he truly loves" (282). In other words, this is not a case of inversion, in which a direct reversal of terms might reveal to us the true motivations behind the protagonist's violence.

The confusion of the protagonist's assumed homosexuality with his more fundamental sense of gender as masculinity that repudiates femininity keeps both Epps and Soto focused on the mother as representative of *either* exaggerated phallic power (the essential dictator) *or* the "passive" homosexual's surrender of power. I want to argue that, while Epps has shown that the final rebellion in *El asalto* is not reducible to any simple opposition, neither is it reducible to the issue of Arenas's (or his character's) homosexuality. The death of the mother founds a masculine subjectivity that gives birth to itself in order to be experienced in all its "desperate beauty" (Epps 1995, 283). The misogynist ending vexes our appreciation of the protagonist's revolutionary toppling of the dictator. We applaud his new freedom and his inspiring example for the masses, and yet the production of this autonomous, self-born subject requires the violation and elimination of the mother. The rape must validate phallic power, and the murder must remove evidence of the male aggressor's ontological dependence on an Other. The horror of this scene's violence and irrationality, though, resists full reader identification with the protagonist's goals.

Just as the protagonist commits multiple assaults in this novel, he also presents multiple (re)births for himself. He first appears as a lone hunter, denying from the beginning that his mother has made any positive contribution to his existence. By opening the text with his hatred for her, he establishes the primacy of his own emotional reality over any biological relation to his mother. In fact, it is she, or the image we have of her, who is born of his disdainful look. His second textual birth is as a successful agent of the state. He produces and reproduces ever more restrictive laws, justifying his own passionate infiltration of every corner of the nation by enacting the principle of total surveillance upon which totalitarianism is based. The protagonist intentionally makes himself over into an image of phallically obsessed state power. The third moment of self-generation occurs with the overthrow of the dictator.

As we saw earlier, the protagonist makes himself a hero for the collective by hunting the mother, abusing the powerless on his way to the top, and finally sexually dominating both of the figures he had perceived to hold power over him. His annihilation of the mother represents a masculinist repudiation not only of her female body, but also of her procreative power. She has always been the barrier between the protagonist and his illusion of a true self that would escape her influence. The same holds for the male Reprimerísimo. He must be destroyed in order for the whisperers to revolt. The vestiges of communication and creativity spontaneously erupt in violence and noise as the id is freed in the protagonist's assault on his mother. Birth into liberty, then, must be motivated by violent masculine desire, not by nurturing maternal desire. This masculine desire, however, must express itself as unfettered sexuality, whether homo- or heterosexual, in order to be legitimate according to the dream-logic of *El asalto*. It must resist the productive, ordered, passionless discipline enforced by the illegitimate, hypermacho Reprimerísimo.

Amidst the rioting of the crowds after the murder, the protagonist walks away unnoticed. He peacefully removes himself from the tumult:

> Y cansado, abriéndome paso en medio del estruendo sin que nadie se percate de mí (tan entusiasmados están ellos en gritar *al fin acabamos con el asesino reprimero, al fin la bestia cayó*) puedo llegar hasta el extremo de la ciudad. Camino hasta la arena. Y me tiendo. (141)

> [Weary, I make my way unnoticed trough the noise and the riot (the crowd in a frenzy of destruction, like children, crying *The Represident is dead, the beast at last is dead!*), and I come to the wall of the city. I walk down to the shore. And I lie down in the sand. (145)]

If we accept Arenas's own claims that the *pentagonía* is fantastic autobiography, we must note that the final resting place of the protagonist, after all the travails from *Celestino* to *El asalto*, is the same word as the author's name. He walks toward "la arena" [the sand], announcing that the entire textual and historical journey leads to his patronymic.

Andrew Bush (1988, 393) has established that Arenas's short story "El hijo y la madre" (1967), published seven months after the UNEAC edition of *Celestino antes del alba*, effects the burial of his matronym. Before that story, all of his publications were signed "Reinaldo Arenas Fuentes." Bush's cryptonymic reading finds that "El hijo y la madre," a story of a son's enclosure and reduction to silence in the maternal home, exemplifies Lacanian forclusion, "a rejection of reality so radical as to be anterior to the advent of symbolization: the riddled text is one which, having failed to learn the *nom du père*, will not be led out of the mirror stage" (375). *El asalto,* the author's final work in the pentalogy, revels in the mirror stage, the conclusion literally staging its continued effects in the protagonist's phantasmic relation to power. Reasserting the patronymic in the last line of his novel as affirmation of independent subjectivity introduces the father's invasion (here, associated with the reprimero's national nom du père) into the suffocating relationship with the mother. The real author, Reinaldo Arenas, dies in suicide with this invasion. The protagonist who survives him, after successfully committing parricide, rests on the sand of the author's unstable, intangible, and yet forcefully narrated identity-in-difference, with and against both parental figures.

Masculinity for the narrator of *El asalto* is attainable only through the simultaneous overthrow of two types of power. The island dictator's illegitimate power over the people in general competes for primacy with the mother's physical and psychological power over the protagonist in particular. He is a hero for others insofar as he assaults illegitimacy, and he is a phallocentric, homophobic, misogynist monster insofar as he attacks the mother. This culmination of suffering in the *pentagonía* constitutes strong evidence that the dream of individual freedom is the same dream as that of masculinity itself, when understood as self-produced, self-contained, carefully managed identity in ambiguous, mirrored relations of desire and rejection. The last scenes of the novel celebrate the violent achievement of male individuation and resist readers' desires to privilege either the psychoanalytic or the political implications of the mother/dictator's demise. This text depicts horrific and personalized violence as a requirement for successful revolution. The narrator-protagonist believes that his own psychological, emotional, and creative freedom depends on his ability to overcome his mother's power over him. The story is carefully designed to keep her ever present in the protagonist's imagination, and yet always just out of reach in the real.

The protagonist pursues political autonomy first through duplicity. He appears to obey and even add to the tyrannical government's absurd rules of social discipline at the same time that he despises the system, which, according to the novel's hyperbolic descriptions, reduces the citizenry to animal dumbness. By the end of the novel, however, that role as double agent coalesces into the moment when the protagonist is to be rewarded for his service to the dictator by finally meeting him face to face. Such direct access to power in the person of the dictator precipitates the protagonist's murderous impulse. Killing the dictator initiates revolution against what Arenas imagines to be the most extreme results of the betrayed socialist revolution in Castro's Cuba. More importantly for the protagonist, however, it resolves the split produced in the citizens of any totalitarian system. Forced to speak, work, and even rest according to government dictates, individuals strive to conform while inwardly seething. The stress of such internal conflict produces exaggerated forms of sadomasochism, or schizophrenic self-discipline. Not surprisingly, the protagonist's personal pathology results from the political system under which he must display those elements in himself that he hates, and hide those that he most values. Necessary political revolution is paradoxically perverted and made possible by sexual attack. The protagonist overthrows the dictator's system of regimentation by raping his own mother, onto whom he had projected the power to silence individual creativity on the part of citizens/sons.

El asalto stands out among contemporary Latin American narratives on masculinity for its disturbing presentation of the protagonist's liberation. By combining the threats to his autonomy (understanding autonomy here in the two senses of independent selfhood and freedom from political coercion) into the single image of the male dictator who is also the narrator's mother, this novel explores the dynamics of Lacanian forclusion (the son's mirror reflects back to him the mother's face) as well as the violence inherent in male differentiation from the mother. This stunningly graphic text displays a fundamental contradiction in liberal notions of political liberty and self-determination which unconsciously base themselves on the ideal of autonomous masculine subjectivity while consciously touting nonviolence. The text displays the contours of a primary aggression generated by a presymbolic split within the self. It also engages in a political project of presenting totalitarianism as a groundless complex of adult neuroses. Finally, it seems to defend literary authorship as a greater freedom than life itself.

Although this combination appears to achieve resolution through the assertion of the writer's patronymic in the last lines of the novel, the fact that Arenas's assault on coercive government policies both requires and is the rape of the mother distinguishes this text for its refusal to deny contradictory desires. The rape/murder ultimately affirms a pre-oedipal narrative structure: conflation of father/mother into one figure with whom the son identifies and yet whom he kills through sexual assault. The only available freedom for subjects caught in the logic of reactionary masculinity (for the protagonist, for the author Arenas, or for Cuba) is that double form of suicide[5] effected through killing the objects/subjects with which one identifies. According to the tensions at play in *El asalto*, no matter how much this type of freedom is lauded as subversive or creative, its requirement of radical individuality is self-destructive for those who seek it in the real.

Juxtaposing his protagonist's terrible success to the author's suicide demonstrates the inseparability of individual psychology, group psychology, and political power relations in the constitution of masculinities. *El asalto* depicts successful masculinity as a goal (whether conceived as a psychological formation, a social role, or a discursive subject position) which is impossible to achieve without killing (in the real or figuratively) all figures with whom one might identify. For Arenas, its triumph is destructive, lonely, fraught with ethical contradictions, and yet also the essential enabling factor in free artistic production. The novel's aesthetic power bursts forth in its ethical ambivalence over the two most problematic terms in the construction of masculinity: the mother and the law. Arenas boldly attacks them both at once, directly confronting, and yet ironically celebrating, the principle of violent revolution necessary to the category of masculinity itself.

CHAPTER SEVEN

Murder and Masculinity

An Other Look

Reinaldo Arenas's *El asalto* differs dramatically from the other narratives in this study. It homes in most directly on the relationship between masculinity, political activism, fantasy, and fiction. Its conclusion portrays the entanglement of individual psychology, mass consciousness, and revolutionary violence in a quest for a variety of forms of legitimation. Through murder, the male narrator seeks legitimation of a private, differentiated ego and of his public role as active citizen. The exiled author seeks legitimation of his creativity through suicide in defiance of physical illness, Cuban censorship, and the state's disciplining of all forms of improper desire. In both cases, violence turned toward a feminized other or toward the feminized self claims an ethical goal. On the level of plot, *El asalto* ends in peace and male wholeness achieved through the sexualized sacrifice of a woman. In that sense, it is the only text analyzed here that perpetuates the tradition that Bronfen outlines in *Over Her Dead Body: Death, Femininity and the Aesthetic* (1992). It is also the only text in this book that reflects the Boom tendency to celebrate the birth of the male author as the ground of a continuously recreated regional or national identity.

El asalto delves into the depths of the contradictions of these attempts to legitimate masculinity. For Arenas sacrifice and suicide are almost always indistinguishable, whether he deals with the sacrifice of women (or Woman) to maintain the illusion of male invulnerability to death and/or split subjectivity, or with the sacrifice of women to create metaphors of the land, the people, and wild urges that need to be tamed (illegitimate rulers). The chain of resemblance established in *El asalto* between the narrator, his mother, and the Reprimerísimo actually negates any advantage to the protagonist when he kills. The radical point of this novel is that there are no others; there are only illusions of separation and opposition. That explains why the final act in the novel, the flight to the beach in escape from the rioting crowd, seems more filled with exhaustion caused by split subjectivity than with the peace that might follow a genuine revolutionary victory. Readers attentive to Cuban history are well aware of the costs of such peace. When they reach the end of the novel and read his suicide letter, readers are faced with the evidence of Reinaldo Arenas's personal choice to seek death at his own hand. Through suicide, the authoring self overtly and concretely rejects the no of the father insofar as it represents Castro's patriarchal totalitarianism and prohibitions against the son's desire for the mother or for other men. With his narrator taking refuge on the sand, *en la arena*, however, the author ends the *pentagonía* in identification with the father through patronymic assertion. The pseudo-autobiographical *pentagonía* opens with the threat of the mother's watery suicide in a well (*Celestino antes del alba*), but ends with the dry name *Arenas* rather than the author's fluid maternal name *Fuentes*. Given the protagonist's pathological aversion to all forms of bodily fluid throughout *El asalto*, this association in the end cannot remain a purely positive declaration of male self-containment. The power of perversion in the novel has tainted any real possibility for reader identification with the protagonist's supposed victory through assault against the mother/father/dictator. We are left with the unresolvable contradictions between equally strong drives toward absolute differentiation from that figure and toward complete identification with it. Those contradictions produce the violence that the reading experience simultaneously celebrates (the pleasures of the id unbound) and condemns (the dangers of the id unbound).

Borges's "La intrusa" also seems to represent the success for men that killing women can offer. But unlike *El asalto*'s implicit anti-Castro appeal, which partially seduces readers into rooting for the murderer/revolutionary, Borges's account of illegitimate versus legitimate masculinities impedes readers' identification with the Nilsen brothers' goals in a much more direct way. The plot of "La intrusa" leaves us with a purportedly inevitable ending that validates the connection between men and misogynist violence. However, the narrator's interventions and the biblical references unsettle any resignation to that inevitability.

Although the plot (and Borges himself, in the Burgin interview) might seem to expect us to accept the story as a straightforward portrait of ignorant hoodlums, the complexity of the text calls upon us to exercise our powers of detection. It invites us to look far beyond plot and to investigate the age-old, violent fictions of reactive masculinity that subtend so many of our supposedly simple stories.

All of the narratives I have discussed represent the false promise of the penis/phallus equation in different ways, and they all attend to impasses that block masculinity's potential escape from ties to violence. As in *Crime and Punishment*, the murders they portray are the culmination of projections onto women of all of the feminine characteristics which the male protagonists wish to eliminate from their own identities. Whether they be physical, social, psychological, or only symbolic of men's power and/or weakness, many of those characteristics persist within the protagonists even after the murder of the women seen to embody them. Dostoevsky found for Raskolnikov an ultimately satisfying relationship with the master signifier of masculinity, the Christian God. The Latin American texts that I have analyzed, however, begin with a Raskolnikovian situation only to demonstrate that killing the person who has been made into the repository of everything "devalued, mauled, battered, violated" (Paz 1950, 72) does nothing to remove those adjectives from the killing subject's self-description. As in *Crime and Punishment*, the murder of women emphasizes the imaginary quality of their being such repositories in the first place. But whereas *Crime and Punishment* resolves the crisis by resorting to the transcendent legitimation of Raskolnikov's Christian, heterosexual masculinity, these Latin American narratives resist legitimation itself. Whether through strategic intertextuality, the mixing of crime fiction and detective fiction, the marvelous real *(lo real maravilloso)*, or the strong presence of feminine characters who resist masculine domination, they attempt to establish subjectivities free of the violence that available fictions of masculine legitimacy require. Because of the ambivalent desires inherent in the narratives, however, none of them fully succeeds.

Somers's "El despojo" examines the root causes of masculine subjectivity's alliance with hierarchy and violence. It also points to the existence of an unexamined feminine reality, the recognition of which alone might provide a different way to conceptualize subjectivity. Lispector's *A maçã no escuro* shows Martim's altered relationship to law and women after he discovers that his wife, whom he thought he had murdered, did not in fact die. In killing her, he had tried to escape the world of social and linguistic imitation, but through the extended existential experiment on Vitória's farm, he realizes that imitation is the ground of human self-knowledge, and that its erasure would not result in the establishment of a transcendent self, as he had hoped; rather, it results in an all too real death of the murderous subject. Martim is able to explore his alienated subjectivity in his wife's absence only because he thinks she is dead. Ironically, however, in the end he is glad that the murder attempt did not succeed, because by that time he has learned (through relationships with the mulata, Ermelinda, and Vitória) that his desire for absolute independence was illusory. Martim is ready to participate in a non-idealized world of social and linguistic imitation by choice now, paradoxically affirming his faith in human beings through his disbelief in independent, autonomous subjectivity. The novel ends in a tentative and fragile gesture toward a masculinity self-consciously open to otherness. Tellingly, however, in concluding with Martim's antireligious epiphany, Lispector stops short of attempting to represent his life *after* he has learned this lesson.

The Buenos Aires Affair repeats the tragedy of "El despojo" with the suicidal death of its male protagonist, Leo. Like Somers's character, Leo is trapped within the parameters of masculinity envisioned as control and power over others. Upon discovering that his own desire is dependent on the desire of the other, Leo assumes that he lacks masculinity. This situation arises, as in "El despojo," from the culturally reinforced assumption that masculine subjectivity must be exclusive of femininity. Therefore, Leo loses desire as his "masculine" behavior reaches its peak (for example, the rapes of the other young man and the female prostitute, and the simulated crime scene with Gladys) because that behavior denies the other's desire, overcomes it, and leaves Leo with nothing against which to measure his own strength except for himself. That is an intolerable state of affairs, and his only way out is to die. But *The Buenos Aires Affair* also moves beyond Leo's impasse to privilege the nonphilosophical, highly intersubjective perspective of an idealized mother figure in the last chapter. This shift away from the supermacho stance prescribed for Leo, both by his failed oedipal stage and by the militaristic state in which he lives, introduces a glimmer of hope. The birth of a new child into a loving nuclear family might be the realization of a subjectivity freed from obsession with domination. We have already seen, however, how the cynical combination of often incompatible discourses such as psychoanalysis, detective fiction, realist police documents, or Hollywood films featuring femmes fatales destabilizes any such ideal resolutions to the problems posed by violent masculinities.

Thus, not only on the level of plot, but also in their citation of multiple discourses of masculinity as well through their transgression of the rules of literary genre, all these narratives enjoy associating masculinity with violence. Whether it be through homosocial bonding (Borges), feminist revenge (Somers), the pleasures of atonement (Lispector), the spectacle of death (Puig), or the recovery of political agency (Arenas), each of the authors reveals contradictory impulses to celebrate and to punish male violence against women. Their ambivalence leads me to complicate the discussion I began in the introduction. Is it possible to resignify masculinity such that it loses its association with real or imagined violence against women? What is the role of literature and feminist literary criticism in such a process?

All of the theorists of masculinity that I cited in the introduction, whether they approach the topic through psychoanalysis, sociology, or cultural and literary studies, call for change in the dominant fictions of masculinity. They attribute the danger of such fictions to their being predicated on the objectification, subordination, or repudiation of femininity and women. They assume, of course, that individual men never live up to those fictions anyway, but that the discursive power of prevailing notions of gender identity limits options for behavior, the possibilities for self-knowledge, and the avenues for reducing levels of personal frustration. While arguments for gender-role theory advocate the reorganization of mothering and family structures (Chodorow 1978), arguments based on Lacanian psychoanalysis hope that "typical male subject[s] might learn to live with lack" rather than destructively deny it (Silverman 1992, 65). In his exploration of masculinities, Connell (1995) combines the influence of individual psychology, parenting and family practices, dominant discourses of gender identity, and socioeconomic history in his exploration of masculinities; he suggests that any real change in prevalent definitions of manliness will require collective consideration of "the structural sources of emotional contradiction for men" as they try to measure up to impossible norms, whether those norms are modeled by a few elite men or imagined by all.

Bracher (1997) offers a menu of elements necessary to combat the harmful effects of projection. If projection is an inevitable ego defense mechanism, then cultures, he suggests, should provide subjects the means to channel it into nonviolent avenues. He argues that cultural critics and social analysts have an obligation to resist and correct popular distortions of groups of people that facilitate their serving as the objects of projection by other groups. An example would be the integration movements in many countries, where women and members of racial, ethnic, or sexual minority groups enter formerly exclusive work sites, neighborhoods, or educational institutions and dispel myths about their differences.

Bracher prefers increasing the viability of alternatives to projecting denigrated characteristics of the self onto other people, such as the sublimation or displacement of self-critique in art and sport. Finally, Bracher posits that by increasing a population's general awareness of the mechanism of projection, the effort required for individuals to maintain an unconscious relation to their prejudice will become too costly and result in a loss of potential gratification to the id for violent expressions of sexism or racism.

Such programs for the reform of misogynist masculinities certainly sound promising. The nagging problem with reform, however, has two faces. It either modernizes and makes more palatable a fundamental social inequality by further hiding it in more successful sublimations and displacements,[1] or it pretends that inevitable psychological mechanisms can be tamed by conscious discovery and critical analysis. It risks leaving such discovery to the culturally privileged social sectors—psychologists, artists, writers, professors—who would then presumably impart their awareness to the masses. That scenario, of course, seems to ignore the fact that disenfranchised men are most typically the ones who engage in physical violence as a form of participation in the rhetoric of violence that supports patriarchy; in Bracher's own argument, they do so because they do not partake of the benefits of hegemonic masculinity. Therefore, identifying pedagogical methods by which mass-scale consciousness raising regarding masculinity might be achieved remains problematic.

Connell is more pessimistic and also more historical in his analysis of the possibilities of individual and collective therapy for destructive versions of masculinity. He recognizes that masculinity is consistently deployed as the exemplary trait or group of traits that leaders must exhibit and to which followers must be loyal—either through identification (implying a perpetual striving to "live up to it" for typical men) or through love (implying either admiration or envy of it for women). In citing major genres of commercial popular culture in the developed European-American countries, such as "the pulp western, the thriller, the sports broadcast . . . and the Hollywood movie," he finds that they compensate in repetition and dissemination for a general decline of religious legitimations for patriarchy over the past two centuries. Even though women's movements, gay movements, and various other forms of contestatory identity politics are proliferating, he provocatively claims that

> the "change" of which there is so much awareness is not the crumbling of the material and institutional structures of patriarchy. What has crumbled, in the industrial countries, is the *legitimation* of patriarchy. (226)

If the perceived increase in overt and physical male violence against women depends on a crisis of legitimacy rather than a crisis of masculinity itself, then Bracher may be right that resignification of what constitutes *legitimate masculinity* could compensate individual men for their loss of faith in the commensurability of penis and phallus. Connell points to popular electronic media as the contemporary replacement for a loss of religious legitimation in Western industrial countries, and there he finds evolving or reformed modes of instituting hegemonic masculinity.

I have sought out a different kind of text than the legitimating ones in Connell's study. With an eye toward reconsidering specifically Latin American cultural history (rather than a more broadly painted "Western" history) through the relationships among masculinity, regional identity, and literary production, I find narratives that refuse to compensate for the crumbling of the region's institutional structures of patriarchy. In fact, they facilitate the loss of legitimacy by graphically displaying the logic of hegemonic masculinity taken to its self-destructive extremes. "La intrusa" and "El despojo" serve as cautionary tales against faith in masculine domination. *A maçã no escuro* proposes a wryly self-conscious faith in social interaction as a "good enough" solution to beleaguered masculinity. *The Buenos Aires Affair* presents a variety of scripts from which to choose, suggesting that flexibility saves. *El asalto* clamors as loudly for reactionary misogyny as it does for a just revolution; caught in a death grip between those two ideals, Arenas's text both relishes and decries the suffering caused by masculinity's desire for union and its demand for liberty.

Admitting to the knotty problem of carving out ethical or socially relevant positions through or in the practice of feminist literary criticism, Debra Castillo has wisely acknowledged that it "is far, far easier to describe undesirable stances than to propose a positive program" (311). Writing specifically about the possibility of renegotiating our relation to the penis/phallus equation, Silverman (1992, 51) implies that men's confrontation with and acceptance of lack can be encouraged through psychoanalysis, through literary and film criticism, and through the social criticism inherent in certain primary works of art: "Renegotiating our relation to the Law of Language would thus seem to hinge first and foremost upon the confrontation of the male subject with the defining conditions of all subjectivity, conditions which the female subject is obliged compulsively to reenact, but upon the denial of which traditional masculinity is predicated: lack, specularity, and alterity. It would seem to necessitate, in other words, dismantling the images and undoing the projections and disavowals through which phallic identification is enabled."

All of the Latin American narratives in this study foreground lack, specularity, and alterity perhaps more explicitly than any other texts from the region. Through the trope of murder, they confront their male characters with the fundamental conditions of subjectivity. They dare to examine the incompatible identifications and desires that bolster rigid gender divisions. Do these texts thereby accomplish a resignification of masculinity? Yes and no. The best one can do, these narratives suggest, is to play between the two poles of social determinism and imaginative liberation. On the one hand, individual psychology and hierarchical power relations operate in each of these texts as, in key ways, inescapable scripts for their characters. On the other hand, all of the works engage the ambiguous and multiple identifications that experimental crime fiction offers to readers. They paradoxically resist violence against women by reen*acting* it, providing staged enjoyment of radical transgression at the same time that they force readers to criticize static and destructive dominant fictions. Such literary experimentation opens a potentially therapeutic and fluid space for the collective imagination to engender new, or at least hybrid, scripts of masculinity. Through character and plot, these texts show that masculinity is dangerous and shifting (sandy?) ground on which to base collective identity. By pushing at the boundaries of literary genre, they force readers to recognize *as fictions* the competing modes of masculinity that motivate misogynist violence in the real. Finally, they model the risks, the pleasures, and the ethical necessity of continually challenging and refashioning those fictions in the service of the myriad ongoing struggles for political and cultural legitimacy in Latin America.

NOTES

Chapter I: Murder and Masculinity

1. There is certainly no shortage of reductive claims that Latin America boasts a more developed and pervasive form of "machismo" than other regions in the world. Even in otherwise excellent studies of gender relations in social structure and literature such as Sharon Magnarelli's *The Lost Rib: Female Characters in the Spanish-American Novel* (1985), one finds relatively unexamined statements on the issue: "Because our language tends to offer only antithetical extremes, one inevitably views oneself as either the conqueror or the conquered, the winner or the loser. The Hispanic emphasis on *machismo* merely intensifies this polarity. Similarly, once the entire issue of winners and losers is articulated by means of a sexual metaphor (as it is in most Western cultures but perhaps more so in Hispanic countries) then the male/female interrelationship, by linguistic implication if nothing else, becomes a question of power, of winners and losers. Unquestionably, the Hispanic's view of the history of his culture magnifies such polarities. *More than any other Western group, the Hispanic views his beginnings as a conquest.* From what he understands as the origins of his civilization, he was the conquered and perhaps must eternally strive to compensate for that initial loss, that metaphoric "original sin" (191–92, my emphasis). Such comparative statements that measure the relative polarities of gender in broadly defined cultures do not contribute to what Magnarelli's book aims for, "debunking mythic antitheses and recognizing other possibilities." As I argue in this study, it is the generalization of characteristics supposed to adhere to certain social groups—"Hispanics," "men," "women," etc.—that leads to the polarization of which Magnarelli speaks, and not the other way around.

2. "[A] variety of novel national ideals are all ostensibly grounded in "natural" heterosexual love and in the marriages that provided a figure for apparently nonviolent consolidation during internecine conflicts at mid-century. Romantic passion . . . gave a rhetoric for the hegemonic projects in Gramsci's sense of conquering the antagonist through mutual interest, or "love," rather than coercion. And the amorous overtones of "conquest" are quite appropriate, because it was civil society that had to be wooed and domesticated after the creoles had won their independence." (Sommer, 6)

3. Octavio Paz argues in "La tradición de la ruptura" (*Los hijos del Limo*, 1974) that this anxiety marks Latin American modernity.

4. Derived from Gramsci's theory of class relations, this concept of hegemonic masculinity refers to the complex of institutions and languages that legitimates patriarchy in a particular time and place because it "guarantees (or is taken to guarantee) the dominant position of men and the subordination of women" (Connell 1995, 77).

5. Titles in men's studies—Ray Gonzalez's *Muy Macho,* David Gilmore's *Manhood in the Making,* Robert Bly's *Iron John,* Joseph Pleck's *The Myth of Masculinity*—focus on individual men's struggles to conform to rigid social roles.

6. Middleton (1992) divides these perspectives into two groups—affective theory and poststructuralist theory—roughly distinguishing between a sociological, role-based analysis that draws from clinical psychology and a semiotic, language-based analysis that draws from Lacanian psychoanalysis.

7. "Most men do not attack or harass women; but those who do are unlikely to think themselves deviant. On the contrary they usually feel they are entirely justified, that they are exercising a right. They are authorized by an ideology of supremacy" (Connell 1995, 83).

8. Althusser argues in "Freud and Lacan" (1971) that the symbolic order is structured around the Law of Language and the Law of Kinship Structures. The Law of Language is, in Lacanian terms, the castration that every subject experiences with entry into signification. The subject's subordination to a discursive order—one that pre-exists it and positions it—guarantees its lack and dependency. The Law of Language produces lack in everyone, but the Law of Kinship Structure positions the father as the ground of social law, thus compensating men for the lack produced in the order of language with the promise of mastery in the social order (although this mastery is always in part withheld from individuals). See Lacan's *The Four Fundamental Concepts of Psycho-analysis* (1978, 203–29) for a discussion of the subject's initiation into lack upon its entry into the order of signification, an initiation that founds the incompatibility of being (as wholeness) and meaning.

9. Curiously, this quote from Mark Bracher's essay on psychoanalysis and racial prejudice takes gender identity, "You're the man!," as its clearest example of the embodiment of signifiers. While not a study of gender identity per se, Bracher's article is peppered with such asides on sexual division and clearly illustrates, as Freud and Lacan would both agree, that the primary other in the symbolic order is "woman," making the self in their discourse "man."

10. For a detailed description of projection, see Freud's "The Unconscious" (1915, 184).

11. "The discourse of the sciences of man constructs the object as female and the female as object. That, I suggest is its rhetoric of violence, even when the discourse presents itself as humanistic, benevolent, or well-intentioned" (De Lauretis 1987, 47).

12. Freud, Sigmund, "On Transience," 14, pp. 303–7 (1916).

13. Deborah Cameron and Elizabeth Frazer (1987, 143), for example, draw connections between the gender system and murder in *The Lust to Kill: A Feminist Investigation of Sexual Murder:* "Representations help construct and shape people's desires by offering them certain objects, certain channels, certain meanings. What aspirations and pleasures are available, what practices, identities and dreams are even thinkable is determined to a very large extent by the culture. Our culture has violent, pornographic dreams; it has aspirations to (male) freedom and transcendence. Not coincidentally, it has sadistic sexual murder."

14. Michel Foucault, ed., *I, Pierre Rivière, Having Slaughtered My Mother, My Sister and My Brother. . . : A Case of Parricide in the Nineteenth Century,* trans. Frank Jellinek (1975): "When all is said and done, battles simply stamp the mark of history on nameless slaughters, while narrative makes the stuff of history from mere street brawls. The frontier between the two is perpetually crossed. It is crossed in the case of an event of prime interest—murder. Murder is where history and crime intersect. Murder it is that makes for the warrior's immortality (they kill, they order killings, they themselves accept the risk of death); murder it is that ensures criminals their dark renown (by shedding blood, they have accepted the risk of the scaffold). Murder establishes the ambiguity of the lawful and the unlawful" (205–6).

15. It is no accident, then, that Connell's history of masculinities in the West (1995, 187) looks to Latin America and the conquistadors, who simultaneously embodied the goals of empire and resisted being controlled by their own rulers, for the first group of ambiguous models of manliness in the modern era: "The conquistador was a figure displaced from customary social relationships, often extremely violent in the search for land, gold and converts, and difficult for the imperial state to control. (The hostility between the royal authorities and Hernan Cortés, the Spanish conqueror of Mexico, was notorious.) Loss of control at the frontier is a recurring theme in the history of empires, and is closely connected with the making of masculine exemplars." Bartolomé de Las Casas's denunciation of the Spanish conquerors' violence, *Brevísima relación de la destrucción de las Indias* (1552), exemplifies the clash over ethics and viable models of masculinity in relation to state-sponsored domination, a clash that has continued throughout colonial history into the present.

16. "La Chingada es la Madre abierta, violada o burlada por la fuerza. El 'hijo de la Chingada' es el engendro de la violación, del rapto o de la burla. . . . En efecto, toda mujer,

aun la que se da voluntariamente, es desgarrada, chingada por el hombre. En cierto sentido todos somos, por el solo hecho de nacer de mujer, hijos de la chingada, hijos de Eva. Mas lo característico del mexicano reside, a mi juicio, en la violenta, sarcástica humillación de la Madre y en la no menos violenta afirmación del Padre" (Paz 1950, 72). [La Chingada is the Mother who is open, raped, or humiliated by force. The "son of la Chingada" is the "bad fruit" of rape, abduction or ridicule. . . . In effect, every woman, even she who gives herself voluntarily, is ripped apart, fucked by the man. In a certain sense, all of us, by the single fact of having been born of woman, are sons of la Chingada, sons of Eve. But the most characteristic aspect of the Mexican resides, in my opinion, in the violent, sarcastic humiliation of the Mother and in the no less violent affirmation of the Father.]

17. "Si la Chingada es una representación de la Madre violada, no me parece forzado asociarla a la Conquista, que fue también una violación, no solamente en el sentido histórico, sino en la carne misma de las indias" (Paz 1950, 72). [If la Chingada is a representation of the violated Mother, it does not seem forced to me to associate her with the Conquest, which was also a rape, not only in the historical sense, but also in the very bodies of the Indian women.]

18. "The need to sever the identification with the mother in order to be confirmed both as a separate person and as a male person—and for the boy these are hard to distinguish—often prevents the boy from recognizing his mother. She is not seen as an independent person (another subject), but as something other—as nature, as an instrument or object, as less than human. . . . The repudiated maternal body persists as the object to be done to and violated, to be separated from, to have power over, to denigrate . . ." (Benjamin 76–77).

19. International criticism on canonical twentieth-century works such as *Cien años de soledad* (García Márquez 1967), *La vida breve* (Onetti 1950), *Los pasos perdidos* (Carpentier 1953), *Pedro Páramo* (Rulfo 1955), or *La invención de Morel* (Bioy Casares 1953) demonstrates the widespread acceptance of this role for Latin American narrative.

20. See Nina Pelikan Strauss (1993) for a thorough and lucid discussion of *Crime and Punishment*'s focus on masculinity: "Dostoevsky renames men's experience in response to "the feminine" and points to the possibility of Raskolnikov's becoming a representative "life poised on the threshold" [Bakhtin] of reinvented forms of the "masculine" (54).

21. "There was not a moment to lose. He pulled the axe out, swung it up with both hands, hardly conscious of what he was doing, and almost mechanically, without putting any force behind it, let the buttend fall on her head. *His strength seemed to have deserted him, but as soon as the axe descended it all returned to him.* The old woman was, as usual, bareheaded. Her thin fair hair, just turning grey, and thick with grease, was plaited into a rat's tail and fastened into a knot above her nape with a fragment of horn comb. Because she was so short the axe struck her full on the crown of the head. She cried out, but very feebly, and sank in

a heap to the floor, still with enough strength left to raise both hands to her head. One of them still held the 'pledge.' Then he struck her again and yet again, with all his strength, always with the blunt side of the axe, and always on the crown of the head. Blood poured out as if from an overturned glass and the body toppled over on its back. He stepped away as it fell, and then stooped to see the face: she was dead." (Dostoevsky, 1964, my emphasis)

This famous murder scene occurs early in *Dostoevsky's Crime and Punishment,* and the graphic portrayal of Raskolnikov's attack on an old pawnbroker introduces fundamental changes in the protagonist's experience of his subjectivity. At first "hardly conscious," he "lets" the axe fall onto the woman's head. Immediately, his strength—and will—are restored. Gary Cox explains in *Crime and Punishment: a Mind to Murder* (1990) that both the Garnett and Coulson translations of the novel report that as soon as the axe came down, Raskolnikov's strength "returned to him," but that the Russian text states specifically that his strength "was born" (*rodilas*). The young man's strength ("[H]e struck her again and yet again, with all his strength") and consciousness (he "stooped to see the face") are "born" precisely as the pawnbroker's blood "pour[s] out as if from an overturned glass." An emptying vessel, the woman is sacrificed for the man's "birth" as a newly powerful subject.

The planned murder of the pawnbroker (and the subsequent murder of her half-sister Lizaveta, who stumbles onto the scene before the criminal can escape) has occupied Raskolnikov's thoughts for days; it channels into one avenue of action his contradictory feelings of love and hate toward the people around him. The old woman's murder partially centers him and stabilizes his haphazard impulses, but in the midst of the violent moment, the dependent nature of Raskolnikov's masculine subjectivity is exposed. His strength is reborn, but it is born of the very woman he has killed. Therefore, the centered subjectivity which the murder had—at least in part—promised to provide to the protagonist is made utterly contingent upon the hated woman's own recognition that he is an acting subject with a will of his own. In that sense, even though her death serves as proof of his power to act, his need to kill her in the first place actually establishes the woman as the ultimate ground of Raskolnikov's new subjectivity. He quickly discovers that he cannot maintain the strength which the murder produces for him, and his search for a stable subjectivity after the crime is the primary theme of the rest of *Crime and Punishment.*

Chapter Two: Telling Secrets of Brotherly Love

1. For a detailed history of Borges's efforts to promote detective and crime fiction in the Americas, see "La narrativa policial en la Argentina" (Lafforgue and Rivera 1981) and Amelia Simpson's *Detective Fiction from Latin America* (1990).

2. Sedgwick (1985) argues that the regulation of male homosocial bonds structures *all* culture. In relation to Borges's characters, though, her explanation of the origins of

homophobic panic in male bonds hysterically defined as *not homosexual* is the most relevant: "[T]he historically shifting, and precisely the arbitrary and self-contradictory, nature of the way *homosexuality* (along with its predecessor terms) has been defined in relation to the rest of the male homosocial spectrum has been an exceedingly potent and embattled locus of power over the entire range of male bonds, and perhaps especially over those that define themselves, not *as* homosexual, but *as against* the homosexual" (Sedgwick 1989, 245).

3. Translation by Alastair Reid (Borges 1981). The rest of the translations, unless otherwise marked, are mine.

4. For insightful analyses of Borges's play on the production and reception of the short story form as it appears throughout his work, see Molloy 1994 and Shaw 1992.

5. Borges comments, "And if you read the story, there's a fact I would like you to notice. There are three characters and there is only one character who speaks. The others, well, the others say things and we're told about them. But only one of the characters speaks directly, and he's the one who's the leader of the story" (Burgin 1968, 48).

Chapter Three: Fantasies of Erotic Domination

1. First published in Armonía Somers, *El derrumbamiento* (1953) and later in *Todos los cuentos (1953–1967)* (1967).

2. Evelyn Picon Garfield (Somers 1988) renders "El enjuiciado" as "The Accused" in her translation of "El despojo." "The Accused" does not adequately convey the ambiguity of the last section of the text, however, so I prefer to use "The Judged One," a phrase that, I hope, avoids an unquestioned assignment of guilt. Throughout this chapter I will, however, be relying on Picon Garfield's translation of the story, except for the alterations I find it necessary to make, which I will signal in the text.

3. Angel Rama, "Raros y malditos en la literatura Uruguaya" (1966): "No sólo se presencia una intensa subjetivación de la creación artística, sino que, heredando las aportaciones extranjeras, se busca expresar la complejidad y la interna contradicción de la situación hombre-mundo en que se encuentran los jóvenes escritores . . . la prosa se plegará muy pronto al impulso experimental del que, al principio, saldrá una que más que literatura fantástica, habría que llamar 'invención fantasmagórica,' como muestran los escritos de Mario Arregui, José Pedro Díaz, Armonía Somers, María Inés Silva Vila, y parcialmente las páginas de infancia de Martinez Moreno." (31) [Not only is there an intense subjectivization of the artistic creation, but also, inheriting foreign contributions, there is the search to express the complexity and internal contradiction of the man-world situation in which the young writers find themselves . . . the prose yields very early to an experimental impulse from which, at first, will come a literature that, more than fantastic

literature, would have to be called "fantasmagoric invention," as shown by the writing of Mario Arregui, José Pedro Díaz, Armonía Somers, María Inés Silva Vila, and partly the childhood pages of Martinez Moreno (my translation)].

4. For Somers's own assessment of her relationship to her Southern Cone contemporaries, see the 1978 interview in *Women's voices from Latin America* (Picon 1985, 38). Rama (1966) claims Somers was the most faithful to the original aesthetic espoused by the *Sur* group: "Sobre todos ellos es muy visible la influencia de los argentinos agrupados en *Sur,* para algunos la influencia omnímoda de Borges, pero muy pocos han seguido fieles a esos comienzos. Quizás quien más tesoneramente representa el espíritu experimental, inconformista, subjetivo, de entonces, sea Armonía Somers" (31). [The influence on them of the Argentines gathered in *Sur* is very evident. For some it was the all-encompassing influence of Borges, but very few have remained faithful to those beginnings. Perhaps the one who most tenaciously represents the experimental, noncomformist, subjective spirit, from that period, would be Armonía Somers. (my translation)]

5. This argument about rape is the same one used by Sartre to discuss sadism in *Being and Nothingness* (1956, 379–413).

6. Picon Garfield translates "y a dejarla clavada con su sexo sobre los sacos" as "and pin her womb to the sacks." The words "con su sexo" are ambivalent, capable of referring to either male or female anatomy, and I have chosen to translate the phrase "by his sex" to highlight the verb "dejarla clavada," which would imply that the girl's body has been pinned by something which has already passed through her womb and to her vertebrae. The penis is used as sexual tool, but also as the sword by which the girl's entire body is immobilized.

7. "The repudiation of the mother, to whom the boy is denied access by the father—and by the outside world, the larger culture that demands that he behave like a little man—engenders a fear of loss, whether the mother is idealized or held in contempt" (Benjamin 1988, 163).

Chapter Four: Crime and Punishment Reconsidered

1. References throughout are from Clarice Lispector, *A maçã no escuro,* 6th ed. (1981). The English version of citations is based on Gregory Rabassa's 1967 translation, published as *The Apple in the Dark* (Lispector 1986). Where necessary, and as indicated in my text, I have altered Rabassa's translation. Citations from *Crime and Punishment* are from the Jessie Coulson 1953 translation, as published in 1964 (Dostoevsky 1964).

2. When asked once about her reading habits and early literary influences, Lispector explained that in her youth she had lived near a pay library, saying, "I would read alphabetically by author, so I got to *Crime and Punishment* rather quickly" (Lowe 1980, 37).

3. See Benedito Nunes's (1989, 114) discussion of the abstraction of geographical location as a technique to focus on the interiorized journey: "Martim é o *Homem,* termo genérico

pelo qual tantas vezes a narradora o nomeia. É o ser humano em trajetória, apenas localizado no espaço das coisas e dos seres, que recama outro espaço, geográfico e nacional, vagamente referido: 'O Homem estava no coração do Brasil' (ME, 16). Efetivamente, o centro de o País, aqui aludido, encerra mais uma acepção de *lonjura*, de *internamento*." [Martim is the Man, the generic term with which the narrative names him so many times. He is a human being in trajectory, barely located in the space of things and beings who claims another space, geographically and national, vaguely mentioned: "The Man was in the heart of Brazil." Effectively, the center of the Country, alluded to here, encloses more of an acceptence of length, of internment.]

4. See especially *Fyodor Dostoevsky's "Crime and Punishment"* (Bloom 1988), which contains a collection of essays that reach varied and often contradictory conclusions about the merits and importance of Dostoevsky's epilogue to the novel. Also, see Philip Rahv's critique (1962) of the epilogue. He argues that Raskolnikov's radical personality change would be more appropriate in a sequel to *Crime and Punishment*, and that its undeveloped inclusion at the end of the novel should be omitted: "About his regeneration we are told only in the epilogue, when at long last the pale sickly faces of the murderer and the saintly prostitute become 'bright with the dawn of a new future.' But this happy siberian aftermath is the beginning of something altogether new and different" (22). Rahv does not believe that Raskolnikov has really changed at all. The brevity and shift of tone in the epilogue seem to confuse critics. In striking contrast to the obsessive display of the character's psychological makeup, the conclusion of the novel denies reader access to the inner workings of Raskolnikov's transformation; it simply asserts that there has been definite change.

5. In "Raskolnikov's Motives: Love and Murder," Edward Wasiolek (1988) offers a clear discussion of Raskolnikov's projections and displacements. Wasiolek traces the connections made between Raskolnikov's negative image of his mother (and sister) and his hatred of the pawnbroker. The essay argues that Raskolnikov's relationship to his mother and sister—who sacrifice their personal honor to support him—makes him increasingly vulnerable to seeing their love for him as emotional control, or accusation. To avoid this control, Raskolnikov commits murder, at least in part to "pursue the punishment of society so that he can feel victimized, and thus justified and on a deeper level, so that by the punishment he may be . . . forced back into the fold of humanity" (15).

6. Wasiolek (1988) reads this husband/wife relationship, which I understand as an erasure of the relevance of the murders, as a healthy resolution of psychological problems.

Chapter Five: Genre, Violence, and the Mystery of Masculinity

1. "After the fall of Perón begins the long struggle to overcome the economic situation which had arisen during the decade of the 40's. From 1955 to 1966 there is a series

of failed efforts to destroy Peronism and to create a civilian alternative with majority support. Military governments, as well as anti-peronist civilian ones, came to power but were not able to keep it. The country does not recuperate its prosperity; on the contrary, there is a continuation of inflation-and-recession cycles that hinder "progress" toward industrialization. Argentina loses importance in Latin America, isolated from the global community. Military power is imposed ever more frequently, and by the end of 1970 Argentina is famous for politically motivated violence and repression" (Beckford-Jessen 1989, 50, my translation).

2. See Méndez Rodenas 1983 for a discussion of Sarduy's contact with French writers and critics involved with *Tel Quel.* The essay also analyzes the development of Sarduy's theory and production of Latin American "neobaroque" writing in relation to structuralist theories of Saussure, Levi-Strauss, and Jacques Lacan, and to Roland Barthes's work on semiology and the "ambiguity of writing." See also González Echevarría 1972.

3. See Epple 1976, which compares Puig's novel to the traditional detective story or mystery thriller.

4. See Kerr 1987, 131–35, for an excellent detailed discussion of the narrative structure of *The Buenos Aires Affair* and its relation to Todorov's treatment of the detective form's fundamental narrative and temporal duality.

5. See Merrim's reading (1984, 147) of the novel's relation to Freudian theories of sexual repression.

6. "[T]he scene that is set up to look like a prelude to death turns out to be an introduction to sex. This scene moves in the opposite direction from the one in Leo's youth (the latter moves from sex to apparent death, the former from apparent death to sex) and thereby seems to undo or rewrite it. However, the scene in 1969 goes beyond the bounds of its criminal predecessor in other ways as well, for the seduction scene into which it is transformed involves a seduction of those who are presumably beyond as well as within its borders. María Esther, originally cast as the witness to crime, is seduced not only by the fiction set up for her but also by the actors engaged in its provocative activity. When she enters the scene, it is as an accomplice in sexual activity: although Leo begins by pretending that he will kill Gladys with the revolver he holds in his hand, he ends by having intercourse with her and, at the same time, caressing María Esther, who all the while also watches everything that goes on" (Kerr 1987, 157–58).

7. See Butler 1993, 12–16, on performativity of sex and sexual identity as citationality.

Chapter Six: Revolutionary Matricide, Patricide, Suicide

1. Soto 1994 traces the series's subversive relationship to the Cuban documentary novel. Soto focuses on narrative voice, chronology, documentation, and the destabiliza-

tion of literary forms in each of the five novels to offer a comparative and evolutionary reading of the texts Arenas intentionally grouped together.

2. Unless otherwise noted in the text, all English versions are from Andrew Hurley's translation (Arenas 1994).

3. Kessel Schwartz (1990) and Andrew Bush (1988) are notable exceptions.

4. Epps cites Ian Lumsden (1991) and Roger Lancaster (1992) in his explication of the importance, in designating the male homosexual in Latin American contexts, placed on performance, appearance, and adopting the so-called passive sexual position. These signs outweigh the fact of having sex with another man; many men—"the active, insertive, masculine-acting *bugarrón*"—are "not necessarily labeled . . . homosexual" (Epps 1995, 232).

5. By committing suicide in 1990, Reinaldo Arenas sealed his position as political and artistic martyr to the struggle for individual freedoms in Castro's postrevolutionary Cuba. Suffering from the physical ravages of advanced AIDS, the writer penned a public declaration of independence before he killed himself. The open letter confirmed Arenas's own notion of the import of his fantastic, baroque narrative style for a country controlled by an ideology of conformity, imposed "normalcy," and censorship: "Mi mensaje no es un mensaje de derrota, sino de lucha y esperanza." [My message is not a message of failure, but rather one of struggle and hope.] The letter is reprinted in the 1991 Ediciones Universal edition of *El Asalto* (Arenas 1991a, 152). For notes on suicide as personal assertion of political autonomy, especially among postrevolutionary Cubans, see Cabrera Infante 1983a and 1983b.

Chapter Seven: Murder and Masculinity

1. Some of most "successful" of these sublimations are found in the aesthetic works that Bronfen's project addresses. From a feminist perspective, she discloses the hidden function and social consequences of such sublimations: "Because they are so familiar, so evident, we are culturally blind to the ubiquity of representations of feminine death. Though in a plethora of representations feminine death is perfectly visible we only see it with some difficulty" (Bronfen 1992, 3).

BIBLIOGRAPHY

Althusser, Louis. 1971. *Lenin and philosophy and other essays.* Translated by Ben Brewster. London: New Left Books.

Arenas, Reinaldo. 1967. *Celestino antes del alba.* Havana: Ediciones Unión.

———. 1967. El hijo y la madre. *Unión* 6.4:222–26.

———. 1982a. *Otra vez el mar.* Barcelona: Editorial Argos Vergara.

———. 1982b. *El palacio de las blanquísimas mofetas.* Barcelona: Editorial Argos Vergara.

———. 1991a. *El Asalto.* Miami: Ediciones Universal.

———. 1991b. *El color del verano.* Miami: Ediciones Universal.

———. 1994. *The assault.* Translated by Andrew Hurley. New York: Viking.

Armstrong, Nancy, and Leonard Tennenhouse, eds. 1989. *The violence of representation: Literature and the history of violence.* London and New York: Routledge.

Auerbach, Erich. 1953. *Mimesis: The representation of reality in Western literature.* Princeton: Princeton University Press.

Bacarisse, Pamela. 1986. The projection of peronism in the novels of Manuel Puig. *The historical novel in Latin America.* Edited by Daniel Balderston. Gaithersburg, Md.: Hispamérica.

———. 1993. *Impossible choices: The implications of the cultural references in the novels of Manuel Puig.* Calgary and Cardiff: University of Calgary Press and University of Wales Press.

Badinter, Elizabeth. 1995. *XY: On masculine identity.* New York: Columbia University Press.

Bakhtin, Mikhail. 1984. *Problems in Dostoyevsky's Poetics.* Translated by Carol Emerson. Minneapolis: Minnesota University Press.

Barquet, Jesus J. 1993. El socialismo en cuestión: Anti-utopía en *Otra vez el mar* y *El asalto* de Reinaldo Arenas. *La palabra y el hombre* 85:119–34.

Barrett, Michele. 1988. *Women's oppression today: The marxist/feminist encounter.* London, New York: Verso.

Barzun, Jacques. 1961. Introduction to *The delights of detection.* New York: Criterion.

———. 1971. Introduction to *A catalogue of crime.* New York: Harper & Row.

Bataille, George. 1962. *Death and sensuality.* New York: Walker.

———. 1993. *Literature and evil.* Translated by Alastair Hamilton. London and New York: Marion Boyars Publishers.

Baudrillard, Jean. 1984. The precession of simulacra. *Art after modernism: Rethinking representation.* Edited by Brian Willis. New York: New Museum of Contemporary Art; Boston: Godine.

Beauvoir, Simone de. 1952. *The second sex.* New York: Knopf.

Beckford-Jessen, Patricia. 1989. The social/political construction of reality in the narrative of Manuel Puig. Ph.D. diss., Rutgers University.

Beechey, Veronica and James Donald . 1985. *Subjectivity and social relations.* Philadelphia: Open University Press.

Belsey, Catherine. 1980. *Critical practice.* London and New York: Methuen.

Benjamin, Jessica. 1983. Master and slave: The fantasy of erotic domination. *Powers of desire.* Edited by Ann Snitow, Christine Stansell and Sharon Thompson. New York: Modern Review Press.

———. 1988. *The bonds of love: Psychoanalysis, feminism, and the problem of domination.* New York: Pantheon Books.

Binyon, T. J. 1989. *Murder will out: The detective in fiction.* Oxford and New York: Oxford University Press.

Black, Joel. 1991. *The aesthetics of murder: A study in romantic literature and contemporary culture.* Baltimore and London: Johns Hopkins University Press.

Bloom, Clive, ed. 1990. *Twentieth-century suspense: The thriller comes of age.* New York: St. Martin's Press.

Bloom, Harold, ed. 1988. *Fyodor Dostoevsky's Crime and Punishment.* New York: Chelsea House Publishers.

Bly, Robert. 1990. *Iron John: A Book about Men.* Reading: Addison, Wesley, Longman.

Borges, Jorge Luis, and Adolfo Bioy Casares , eds. 1940. *Antología de la literatura fantástica.* Argentina: Editorial Sudamericana.

Borges, Jorge Luis. 1964. El arte narrativo y la magia. *Discusión.* Buenos Aires: Emecé Editores: 81–92.

———. 1982. El cuento policial. *Borges, oral lectures, Universidad de Belgrado.* Buenos Aires: Emecé.

———. 1986. *Ficciones—El Aleph—El informe de Brodie.* Caracas, Venezuela: Biblioteca Ayacucho.

Bourdieu, Pierre. 1984. *Distinction: A social critique of the judgement of taste.* Translated by Richard Nice. Cambridge, Mass.: Harvard University Press.

———. 1990. *In other words: Essays toward a reflexive sociology.* Translated by Matthew Adamson. Stanford, Calif.: Stanford University Press.

———. 1993. *The field of cultural production.* Edited by Randall Johnson. New York: Columbia University Press.

Bracher, Mark. 1997. Psychoanalysis and racism. *JPCS: Journal for the Psychoanalysis of Culture and Society* 2 (Fall):1–11.

Brod, Harry, ed. 1987. *The making of masculinities: The new men's studies.* London: Allen and Unwin.

Bronfen, Elisabeth. 1992. *Over her dead body: Death, femininity and the aesthetic.* Manchester: Routledge.

Burgin, Richard. 1968. *Conversations with Jorge Luis Borges.* New York: Avon.

Bush, Andrew. 1988. The riddled text: Borges and Arenas. *Modern Language Notes* 103.2:374–97.

Butler, Judith. 1990. *Gender trouble.* New York: Routledge.

———. 1993. *Bodies that matter: On the discursive limits of "sex."* New York: Routledge.

Butler, Judith, and Joan W. Scott, eds. 1992. *Feminists theorize the political.* New York: Routledge.

Cabrera Infante, Guillermo. 1994 (1992). *Mea Cuba*. Translated by Kenneth Hall. New York: Farrar Straus and Giroux.

Cameron, Deborah, and Elizabeth Frazer. 1987. *The lust to kill: A feminist investigation of sexual murder*. Cambridge: Polity Press.

Cascardi, Anthony J. 1992. *The subject of modernity*. Cambridge: Cambridge University Press.

Cawelti, John G. 1976. *Adventure, mystery and romance*. Chicago: University of Chicago Press.

Chapman, Rowena, and Jonathan Rutherford, eds. 1988. *Male order: Unwrapping masculinity*. New York: Routledge.

Chodorow, Nancy J. 1978. *The reproduction of mothering*. Berkeley: University of California Press.

———. 1994. *Femininities, masculinities, sexualities: Freud and beyond*. Lexington: University Press of Kentucky.

Chow, Rey. 1993. Ethics after idealism. *Diacritics* 23 (Spring):3–23.

Cixous, Hélène. 1990. *Reading with Clarice Lispector*. Translated by Verena Conley. Minneapolis: University of Minnesota Press.

Colás, Santiago. 1994. *Postmodernity in Latin America: The Argentine paradigm*. Durham and London: Duke University Press.

Colmeiro, José F. 1988. Lenguajes propios y lenguajes apropiados *The Buenos Aires Affair* de Manuel Puig. *Hispanic Review* 57 (Spring):165–88.

Connell, R. W. 1995. *Masculinities*. Berkeley: University of California Press.

Corbatta, Jorgelina. 1988. *Mito personal y mitos colectivos en las novelas de Manuel Puig*. Madrid: Editorial Orígenes.

Coward, Rosalind, and John Ellis. 1977. *Language and materialism: Developments in semiology and the theory of the subject*. London, Henley and Boston: Routledge & Kegan Paul.

Cox, Gary. 1990. *Crime and Punishment: A mind to murder*. Boston: Twayne.

De Lauretis, Teresa. 1987. *The technologies of gender*. Bloomington: Indiana University Press.

Deforge, Regine. 1979. *Confessions of O: Conversations with Pauline Réage*. Translated by Sabine D'Estree. New York: Viking.

Deleuze, Gilles, and Felix Guattari. 1983. *Anti-Oedipus: Capitalism and schizophrenia.* Translated by Robert Hurley, Mark Seem, and Helen R. Lane. Minneapolis: University of Minnesota Press.

Delgado, Celeste Fraser. 1994. Private eyes in Argentina: The novel and the police state. *Latin American Literary Review* 22.44:48–73.

Derrida, Jacques. 1979. *Spurs: Nietzsche's styles.* Translated by Barbara Harlow. Chicago: University of Chicago Press.

Di Stefano, Christine. 1991. *Configurations of masculinity: A feminist perspective on modern political theory.* Ithaca: Cornell University Press.

Dostoevsky, Fyodor. 1964. *Crime and punishment.* Translated by Jessie Coulson. Edited by George Gibian. New York: Norton.

Dworkin, Andrea. 1974. Woman as victim: Story of O. *Feminist Studies* 2.1:107–11.

Echevarren, Roberto. 1986. La superficia de lectura en *The Buenos Aires Affair. Manuel Puig: Montaje y alteridad del sujeto.* Edited by Roberto Echavarren and Enrique Giordano. Santiago: Instituto Profesional del Pacífico.

Edley, Nigel, and Margaret Wetherell. 1995. *Men in perspective: Practice, power and identity.* London and New York: Prentice Hall/Harvester Wheatsheaf.

Eisenstein, Hester, and Alice Jardine, eds. 1980. *The future of difference.* Boston: G. K. Hall.

Epple, Juan Armando. 1976. *The Buenos Aires Affair* y la estructura de la novela policíaca. *La palabra y el hombre* 18 (April–June):43–59.

Epps, Brad. 1995. Proper conduct: Reinaldo Arenas, Fidel Castro, and the politics of homosexuality. *Journal of the History of Sexuality* 6.2:231–83.

Fast, Irene. 1984. *Gender identity: A differentiation model.* Hillsdale, N.J.: Analytic Press.

Felman, Shoshana. 1981. Rereading femininity. *Yale French Studies* 62:19–44.

Fiedler, Leslie. 1960. *Love and death in the American novel.* New York: Stein and Day.

Fitz, Earl. 1985. *Clarice Lispector.* Boston: Twayne Publishers.

Foster, David William. 1984. Latin American documentary narrative. *Publication of the Modern Language Association* 99.1:44–55.

Foucault, Michel. 1965. *Madness and Civilization*. Translated by Richard Howard. New York: Random House.

———, ed. 1975. *I, Pierre Rivière, having slaughtered my mother, my sister and my brother . . .: A case of parricide in the Nineteenth Century*. Translated by Frank Jellinek. New York: Pantheon.

———. 1977. *Discipline and punish: The birth of the prison*. Translated by Alan Sheridan. New York: Pantheon.

———. 1978. *The history of sexuality, volume I: An introduction*. Translated by Robert Hurley. New York: Random House.

Franco, Jean. 1969. *An introduction to Spanish American literature*. Cambridge: Cambridge University Press.

———. 1989. *Plotting women: Gender and representation in Mexico*. New York: Columbia University Press.

Frank, Manfred. 1989 (1984). *What is neostructuralism?* Translated by Sabine Wilke and Richard Gray. Minneapolis: University of Minnesota Press.

Fraser, Nancy. 1989. *Unruly practices: Power, discourse and gender in contemporary social theory*. Minneapolis: University of Minnesota Press.

Freud, Sigmund. 1905. Three essays on the theory of sexuality. *Standard Edition* 7:123–245.

———. 1914. On narcissism: An introduction. *Standard Edition* 14:67–104.

———. 1915. The Unconcious. *Standard Edition* 14:161–215

———. 1916. On Transience. *Standard Edition* 14:303–07.

———. 1921. Group psychology and the analysis of the ego. *Standard Edition* 18:67–143.

Friedman, Susan Stanford. 1995. Making history: Reflections on feminism, narrative, and desire. *Feminism Beside Itself*. New York: Routledge.

Gallop, Jane. 1982. *The daughter's seduction: Feminism and psychoanalysis*. Ithaca: Cornell University Press.

———. 1988. *Thinking through the body*. New York: Columbia University Press.

Gambaro, Griselda. 1985. Algunas consideraciones sobre la mujer y la literatura. *Revista Iberoamericana* 51 (July–Dec.):471–73.

Gilbert, Sandra M., and Susan Gubar. 1985. Sexual linguistics: Gender, language, sexuality. *New Literary History: A Journal of Theory and Interpretation* 16 (Spring):515–43.

Gilman, Sander. 1985. *Difference and pathology: Stereotypes of sexuality, race, and madness*. Ithaca and London: Cornell University Press.

Gilmore, David D. 1990. *Manhood in the making: Cultural concepts of masculinity*. New Haven: Yale University Press.

Girard, René. 1978. *"To double business bound": Essays on literature, mimesis, and anthropology*. Baltimore and London: Johns Hopkins University Press.

González Echevarría, Roberto. 1972. In search of the lost center. *Review* (Fall):28–31.

———. 1977. *Alejo Carpentier: The pilgrim at home*. Ithaca: Cornell University Press.

———. 1987. Sarduy, the Boom, and the Post-Boom. *Latin American Literary Review* 15 (Jan.–June):57–72.

———. 1990. *Myth and archive: A theory of Latin American narrative*. New York: Cambridge University Press.

González , Ray. 1996. *Muy Macho: Latino men confront their manhood*. New York: Doubleday.

Guerra-Cunningham, Lucia. 1979. La mujer latinoamericana y la tradición literaria feminina. *Fem* 3 (June–Oct.):14–18.

Habermas, Jürgen. 1974. The Public Sphere. *New German Critique* 1.3:49–55.

Harper, Ralph. 1969. *The world of the thriller*. Cleveland: Case Western Reserve University Press.

Hegel, Friedrich. 1977. *Phenomenology of spirit*. Translated by A. V. Miller. New York: Oxford University Press.

Hekman, Susan. 1990. *Gender and knowledge: Elements of a postmodern feminism*. Boston: Northeastern University Press.

Henriques, Julian, et. al. 1984. *Changing the subject: Psychology, social regulation and subjectivity*. New York: Methuen.

Herbold, Sarah. 1995. Well-Placed Reflections: (Post)modern Woman as Symptom of (Post)modern Man. *Signs* 21 (Autumn):83–115.

Hernández-Miyares, Julio, and Perla Rozencvaig, eds. 1990. *Reinaldo Arenas: Alucinaciones, fantasías y realidad*. Glenview, Ill.: Scott, Foresman and Company.

Higgins, Lynn, and Brenda Silver, eds. 1991. *Rape and representation*. New York: Columbia University Press.

Hilfer, Tony. 1990. *The crime novel: A deviant genre*. Austin: University of Texas Press.

Hirsch, Marianne. 1989. *The mother/daughter plot: Narrative, psychoanalysis, feminism*. Bloomington: Indiana University Press.

Holquist, Michael. 1988. Puzzle and mystery, the narrative poles of knowing: Crime and punishment. *Fyodor Dostoevsky's Crime and Punishment*. Edited by Harold Bloom. New York: Chelsea House Publishers.

Holzapfel, Tamara. 1978. Crime and detection in a defective world: the detective fictions of Borges and Durrenmatt. *Studies in Twentieth Century Literature*. 3:53–71.

Horney, Karen. 1932. The dread of women: Observation on a specific difference in the dread felt by men and by women respectively for the opposite sex. *International Journal of Psycho-Analysis*, 18:348–60.

Hubben, William. 1952. *Dostoevsky, Kierkegaard, Nietzsche and Kafka*. New York: Collier Books.

Hutcheon, Linda. 1988. *A poetics of postmodernism: History, theory, fiction*. New York and London: Routledge.

Irigaray, Luce. 1985. *Speculum of the other woman*. Translated by Gillian C. Gill. Ithaca: Cornell University Press.

Iser, Wolfgang. 1978. *The act of reading: A theory of aesthetic response*. Baltimore and London: Johns Hopkins University Press.

Jameson, Frederic. 1981. *The political unconscious: Narrative as a socially symbolic act*. Ithaca: Cornell University Press.

Katz, J. 1988. *The seductions of crime: Moral and sensual attractions of doing evil*. New York: Basic Books.

Keller, Gary D., and Karen S. Van Hooft. 1976. Jorge Luis Borges's "La intrusa": The awakening of love and consciousness/The sacrifice of love and consciousness.

The Analysis of Hispanic Texts: Current Trends in Methodology. Edited by Lisa E. Davis and Isabel C. Tarán. New York: Bilingual Press.

Kerr, Lucille. 1987. *Suspended fictions: Reading novels by Manuel Puig.* Urbana and Chicago: University of Illinois Press.

Klein, Kathleen Gregory. 1995. *Women times three: Writers, detectives, readers.* Bowling Green: Bowling Green State University Popular Press.

Knight, Stephen. 1980. *Form and ideology in crime fiction.* Bloomington: Indiana University Press.

Kristeva, Julia. 1980. *Desire in language: A semiotic approach to literature and art.* Translated by Thomas Gora, Alice Jardine and Leon S. Roudiez. Edited by Leon S. Roudiez. Oxford: Basil Blackwell.

———. 1982. *The powers of horror: An essay on abjection.* Translated by Leon S. Roudiez. New York: Columbia University Press.

———. 1987. *In the beginning was love: Psychoanalysis and faith.* Translated by Arthur Goldhammer. New York: Columbia University Press.

Lacan, Jacques. 1978. *Four fundamental concepts of psycho-analysis.* Translated by Alan Sheridan. New York: Norton.

———. 1988. *The seminars of Jacques Lacan, Book II: The ego in Freud's theory and the technique of psychoanalysis, 1954–1955.* Translated by Sylvana Tomaselli. Cambridge: Cambridge University Press.

Lafforgue, Jorge and Jorge Rivera. 1981. Narrativa policial en la Argentina. *Capitulo 104: La historia de la literatura argentina.* Buenos Aires: Centro Editor de America Latina.

Lancaster, Roger N. 1992. *Life is hard: Machismo, danger, and the intimacy of power in Nicaragua.* Berkeley: University of California Press.

Lavers, Norman. 1988. *Pop culture into art: the novels of Manuel Puig.* Columbia: University of Missouri Press.

Leiner, Marvin. 1994. *Sexual politics in Cuba: Machismo, homosexuality, and AIDS.* Boulder: University of Colorado Press.

Leps, Marie-Christine. 1992. *Apprehending the criminal: The production of deviance in nineteenth-century discourse.* Durham, N.C.: Duke University Press.

Lispector, Clarice. 1981 (1961). *A maçã no escuro.* 6th ed. Rio de Janeiro: Editora Nova Fronteira.

———. 1986. *The apple in the dark.* Translated by Gregory Rabassa. Austin: University of Texas Press.

Lowe, Elizabeth. 1980. The passion according to Clarice Lispector. *Review.* 24:34–37

Lyotard, François. 1984. *The postmodern condition: A report on knowledge.* Translated by Geoff Bennington and Brian Massumi. Minneapolis: University of Minnesota Press.

MacCannell, Juliet Flower, and Laura Zakarin, eds. 1994. *Thinking Bodies.* Stanford, Calif.: Stanford University Press.

Macherey, Pierre. 1978. *A theory of literary production.* London: Routledge & Kegan Paul.

Mackinnon, Catherine. 1987. *Feminism unmodified: Discourses on life and law.* Cambridge: Harvard University Press.

Mandel, Ernest. 1984. *Delightful murders: A social history of the crime story.* London: Pluto.

Manguel, Alberto, ed. 1986. *Other fires: Short fiction by Latin American women.* New York: Clarkson N. Potter, Inc.

Martin, Gerald. 1989. *Journeys through the labyrinth: Latin American fiction in the twentieth century.* London and New York: Verso.

Marx, Karl. 1973. *Grundrisse.* Translated by Martin Nicolaus. Harmondsworth: Pelican.

———. 1975. Economic and philosophical manuscripts. *Karl Marx: Early writings.* Harmondsworth: Pelican.

McGowan, John. 1994. Thinking about violence: feminism, cultural politics, and norms. *Centennial Review* 27 (Fall):445–69.

Méndez Rodenas, Adriana. 1983. *Severo Sarduy: El neobarroco de la transgresión.* Mexico: Universidad Nacional Autónoma de México.

———. 1990. La economía de lo simbólico en la narrativa de Reinaldo Arenas. *Reinaldo Arenas: Alucinaciones, fantasías y realidad.* Edited by Hernández-Miyares and Perla Rozencvaig. Illinois: Scott, Foresman and Company.

Merrim, Stephanie. 1984. For a new (psychological) novel in the works of Manuel Puig. *Novel: A Forum on Fiction* 17 (Winter):141–57.

Middleton, Peter. 1992. *The inward gaze: Masculinity and subjectivity in modern culture.* London and New York: Routledge.

Miller, Alice. 1983. *For your own good: Hidden cruelty in child-rearing and the roots of violence.* Translated by Hildegarde and Hunter Hannum. New York: Farrar, Straus, Giroux.

Moi, Toril. 1991. Appropriating Bourdieu: Feminist theory and Pierre Bourdieu's sociology of culture. *New Literary History* 22:1017–49.

Molloy, Sylvia. 1994. *Signs of Borges.* Translated by Oscar Montero. Durham and London: Duke University Press.

Montenegro, Nivia. 1990. El espejismo del texto: Reflexiones sobre *Cantando en el pozo. Reinaldo Arenas: Alucinaciones, fantasías y realidad.* Edited by Hernández-Miyares and Perla Rozencvaig. Illinois: Scott, Foresman and Company.

Morretti, Franco. 1983. *Signs taken for wonders: Essays in the sociology of literary form.* Translated by Susan Fischer, David Forgacs, and David Miller. London: Verso.

Mortimer, Ruth. 1956. Dostoevsky and the Dream. *Modern Philology* 54 (November):106–16.

Most, Glenn W., and William W. Stowe, eds. 1983. *The poetics of murder.* New York: Harcourt, Brace, Jovanovich.

Muñoz, Miguel Elds. 1987. *El discurso utópico de la sexualidad en Manuel Puig.* Madrid: Pliegos.

Munt, Sally. 1994. *Murder by the book?: Feminism and the crime novel.* London and New York: Routledge.

Murch, Alma. 1968. *The Development of the detective novel,* rev. ed. London: Owen.

Murphy, Cornelius F., Jr. 1995. *Beyond feminism: Toward a dialogue on difference.* Washington, D.C.: The Catholic University of America Press.

Murphy, Peter F. 1994. *Fictions of masculinity: Crossing cultures, crossing sexualities.* New York and London: New York University Press.

Nietzsche, Friedrich. 1979 (1888). *Ecce Homo.* Translated by R. J. Hollingdale. Middlesex, England: Penguin Books.

Nunes, Benedito. 1989. *O Drama da Linguagem*. Sao Paulo: Editora Atica, S.A.

Nuttall, A. D. 1978. *Crime and punishment: Murder as philosophic experiment.* Edinburgh: Sussex University Press.

Offord, Derek. 1988. The causes of crime and the meaning of law: *Crime and Punishment* and contemporary radical thought. *Fyodor Dostoevsky's Crime and punishment.* Edited by Harold Bloom. New York: Chelsea House Publishers,Paz, Octavio. 1950. *El laberinto de la soledad.* México: Fondo de Cultura Económica.

Peixoto, Marta. 1994. *Passionate fictions: Gender, narrative, and violence in Clarice Lispector*. Minneapolis and London: University of Minnesota Press.

Pelikan Straus, Nina. 1993. Why did I say "women!"?: Raskolnikov reimagined. *Diacritics* 23 (Spring):54–65.

Pleck, Joseph. 1981. *The myth of masculinity*. Massacusetts: MIT Press.

Polk, Kenneth. 1994. *When men kill: Scenarios of masculine violence*. New York: Cambridge University Press.

Porter, Dennis. 1981. *The pursuit of crime: Art and ideology in detective fiction.* New Haven: Yale University Press.

Puig, Manuel. 1973. *The Buenos Aires affair*. Barcelona: Seix Barral.

———. *The Buenos Aires Affair: A detective novel.* Translated by Suzanne Jill Levine. New York: E. P. Dutton.

———. 1976. *El beso de la mujer araña*. Barcelona: Seix Barral.

Rahv, Philip. 1962. Dostoevsky in Crime and Punishment. *Dostoevsky: Critical Essays. Edited by Rene Wellek*. Englewood Cliffs, NJ: Prentice Hall, Inc.

Rama, Angel. 1963. La fascinacion del horror: la insolita literatura de Armonia Somers. *Marcha* 1188 (27 December):30.

———. 1966. Raros y malditos en la literatura Uruguaya. *Marcha* 1319 (2 September): 30–31.

Reid, Alastair, and Emir Rodríguez Monegal, eds. 1981. *Borges: A reader*. New York: E. P. Dutton.

Reilly, John M., ed. 1985. *Twentieth-century crime and mystery writers*. New York: St. Martin's Press.

Reilly, Patrick. 1988. *The literature of guilt: From Gulliver to Golding.* Iowa City: University of Iowa Press.

Reynaud, Emmanuel. 1983. *Holy virility: The social construction of masculinity.* London: Pluto Press.

Rezzori, Gregor von. 1985. *The death of my brother Abel.* Translated by Joachim Neugroschel. New York: Viking Penguin.

Ricoeur, Paul. 1970 (1961). *Freud and philosophy.* New Haven: Yale University Press.

Rodríguez-Monegal, Emir. 1980. The labyrinthine world of Reinaldo Arenas. *Latin American Literary Review* 7 (Spring-Summer):126–31.

Rutherford, Jonathan. 1992. *Men's silences: Predicaments in masculinity.* New York: Routledge.

Rycroft, Charles. 1957. A detective story: Psychoanalytic observations. *Psychoanalytic Quarterly* XXVI: 229–45.

Santí, Enrico Mario. 1980. Entrevista con Reinaldo Arenas. *Vuelta* no. 47: (October)18–25.

Sarduy, Severo. 1980 (1972). The Baroque and the Neobaroque. Translated by Mary G. Berg. *Latin America in its literature.* Edited by César Fernández Moreno. New York and London: Holmes & Meire Publishers, Inc.

Sartre, Jean-Paul. 1956. *Being and Nothingness.* New York: New Philosophical Library.

Sayers, Janet. 1995. *The man who never was: Freudian tales of women and their men.* New York: Basic Books.

Scarry, Elaine. 1985. *The body in pain: The making and unmaking of the world.* New York: Oxford University Press.

Schwartz, Kessel. 1990. Maternidad e incesto: Fantasías en la narrativa de Reinaldo Arenas. *Reinaldo Arenas: Alucinaciones, fantasías y realidad.* Edited by Hernández-Miyares and Perla Rozencvaig. Glenview, Ill.: Scott, Foresman and Company.

Schwenger, Peter. 1984. *Phallic critiques: Masculinity and twentieth century literature.* New York: Routledge and Kegan Paul.

Scott, Sutherland. 1953. *Blood in their ink: The march of the modern mystery novel.* London and New York: S. Paul.

Sedgwick, Eve Kosofsky. 1985. *Between men: English literature and male homosical desire*. New York: Columbia University Press.

———. 1989. The beast in the closet. *Speaking of gender*. Edited by Elaine Showalter. New York: Routledge.

Segal, Lynne. 1990. *Slow motion: Changing masculinities, changing men*. New Jersey: Rutgers University Press.

Shaw, Donald L. 1992. *Borges' narrative strategy*. Leeds: Redwood Press, Ltd.

Silverman, Kaja. 1992. *Male subjectivity at the margins*. New York: Routledge.

Simon, Robert I. 1996. *Bad men do what good men dream: A forensic psychiatrist illuminates the darker side of human behavior*. Washington, D.C.: American Psychiatric Press, Inc.

Simpson, Amelia S. 1990. *Detective fiction from Latin America*. Rutherford: Farleigh Dickinson University Press; London: Associated University Presses.

Smith, Paul. 1988. *Discerning the subject*. Minneapolis: University of Minnesota Press.

Somers, Armonía. 1967. *Todos los cuentos (1953–1967)*. Montevideo: Arca.

———. 1988. Plunder. *Women's fiction from Latin America*. Edited and translated by Evelyn Picon Garfield. Detroit: Wayne State University Press.

Sommer, Doris. 1991. *Foundational fictions: The national romances of Latin America*. Berkeley: University of California Press.

Soto, Francisco. 1994. *Reinaldo Arenas: The Pentagonía*. Gainesville: University Press of Florida.

Spivak, Gayatri. 1987. *In other worlds*. New York: Methuen.

Symons, Julian. 1974. *Bloody Murder*, revised edition. Harmondsworth: Penguin.

Taussig, Michael. 1992. *The nervous system*. New York: Routledge.

Tittler, Jonathan. 1984. *Narrative irony in the contemporary Spanish American novel*. Ithaca: Cornell University Press.

———. 1993. *Manuel Puig*. New York: Twayne Publishers.

Todorov, Tzvetan. 1977. *The poetics of prose*. Translated by Richard Howard. Ithaca: Cornell University Press.

Torres, Vicente Francisco, ed. 1982. *El cuento policial méxicano*. México: Diógenes.

Wasiolek, Edward. 1988. Raskolnikov's motives: Love and murder. *Fyodor Dostoevsky's Crime and Punishment*. Edited by Harold Bloom. New York: Chelsea House Publishers.

Wellek, René, ed. 1962. *Dostoevsky: Critical essays*. Englewood Cliffs, N.J.: Prentice-Hall, Inc.

Winks, Robin, ed. 1980. *Detective fiction: a collection of critical essays*. Englewood Cliffs: Prentice Hall.

Winnicott, D. W. 1974. The use of an object and relation through identifications. *Playing and reality*. Middlesex: Penguin.

Yates, Donald A., ed. 1964. *El cuento policial latinoamericano*. México: Andrea.

——— 1981. Argentine detective story. *Narrativa policial en la Argentina*. Buenos Aires: Centro Editor de América Latina.

Young-Bruehl, Elisabeth. 1996. *The anatomy of prejudices*. Cambridge, Mass.: Harvard University Press.

Žižek, Slavoj. 1989. *The sublime object of ideology*. London: Verso.

———. 1992. *Enjoy your symptom! Jacques Lacan in Hollywood and out*. New York and London: Routledge.

———. 1992. *Everything you always wanted to know about Jacques Lacan but were afraid to ask Hitchcock*. London and New York: Verso.

———. 1992. *Looking awry: An introduction to Jacques Lacan through popular culture*. Cambridge, Mass. and London: MIT Press.

———. 1993. *Tarrying with the negative: Kant, Hegel, and the critique of ideology*. Durham, N.C.: Duke University Press.

INDEX

Rebecca E. Biron is assistant professor of Spanish at the University of Miami. She teaches and publishes on contemporary Latin American narrative, culture, and gender.